16 Jan. 1996.

Inside the ANC:

The Evolution of a Terrorist Organization

Inside the ANC:
The Evolution of a Terrorist Organization

by
Morgan Norval

Selous Foundation Press
Washington, D.C.

Selous Foundation Press
Publishers since 1987
Washington, DC

Designed by William R. Wright
Manufactured in the United States of America

Photos by Morgan Norval, Reuters, World Wide Photos, Inc., African Museum, Afrikaanse Pers. Publikasies, Voortrekerpers, Beeld, Rapport, Al J. Venter, and the Durban Daily News.

Second Printing

Library of Congress Cataloging-in-Publication Data

Norval, Morgan.
Inside the ANC: the evolution of a terrorist organization/Morgan Norval.
p. cm.

Includes bibliographical references and index.
1. African National Congress--History. 2. South Africa--Politics and government --20th century. 3. Terrorism--South Africa--History. 4. Blacks--South Africa--Politics and government. I. Title
JQ1998.A4N67 1991
324.268'083—dc20 90-63074
CIP

ISBN: 0-944273-07-6 (v.1)

utcumque placuerit Deo

ACKNOWLEDGEMENTS

This book was made possible by the generosity and support of the Selous Foundation, Inc., the F.M. Kirby Foundation, Inc., the G.A. Buder, Jr. Patriotic Trust, the Herbert T. and Olive S. Randall Foundation, the John Oster Family Foundation, Inc., the Adams Fund, and the following individuals: Mr. George E. Atkinson, Jr., Miss Helen B. Buckland, Mr. Brian D. Curry, Mr. Barron K. Grier, Mr. Ellice McDonald, Jr., Mrs. George Roberts, Mr. Elmer R. Noyer, Miss Julie Lauer-Leonardi, Mr. Dean B. Smith, Miss Elizabeth C. Smith, Mr. Edgar J. Uihlein, and Mr. Clifton Ward.

Table of Contents

1

THE BIRTH OF THE ANC

In 1909, seven years after the end of the Anglo-Boer War in South Africa, the victorious British government was ready to return self-government to its vanquished former foe. The House of Commons, in that year, passed the South African Act of Union establishing the Union of South Africa as a British dominion. It was accepted by ratification of the South African Parliament on May 31, 1910, the eighth anniversary of the ending of the Boer War—the signing of the Treaty of Vereeniging. However, the peace treaty contained the seed that would germinate and grow to plague South Africa to this day. Article 8 (Clause 9) stated there was to be "no franchise for the natives until after the introduction of self-government."[1] That attitude was incorporated in the British grant of independence to the new Union of South Africa.

The Act of Union passed by the British government contained a clause that also affected a large portion of the people of South Africa. It precluded blacks from becoming members of the South African Parliament, even though at the time one in every seven voters in the Cape Province of the new Union was either black or coloured.[2]

In 1908-09 delegates had assembled in a National Convention in Durban to draft the South Africa Act, subsequently passed by both the British and South African Parliaments, which created the new Union of South Africa.

The most vexing issue facing the National Convention was the question of the political franchise. Delegates from the former Boer republics of the

[1] Harrison, D., *The White Tribe of Africa*, McMillian S.A., Johannesburg, 1983, p. 45.

[2] Radu, M., 'The African National Congress: Cadres and Credo", *Problems of Communism*, USIA, Washington, D.C., July-August 1987, p. 4.

Orange Free State and the Transvaal, as well as Natal Province, wanted voting rights restricted to the whites. Only the Cape Province favored including the blacks and coloureds. The delegates reached a compromise whereby the former Boer republics excluded blacks while the Cape allowed multi-racial voting.

Groups representing black interests, among them the precursors of the African National Congress (ANC) such as The Natal Native Congress, The Native Vigilance Association of the Orange River Colony and The Transvaal Native Union, not getting any satisfaction from the Convention over their inclusion in the franchise, sent a delegation to London to protest the South Africa Bill to Parliament. Although sympathetic to their complaints the British government did nothing.

The British government had fought a costly and highly unpopular war against the Boers only a few short years before and were only too happy to find a solution allowing South Africa to become a self-governing British dominion. So the British sacrificed black political rights to the expediency of establishing the new Union, thus stemming the drain on the British treasury caused by their presence in South Africa.

It was obvious to many blacks that their interests had been ignored during the formation of the Union. Many well educated blacks realized that what blacks lacked, but sorely needed, was an organization of their own which could speak on behalf of their grievances in South Africa. Many of these black intellectuals had been educated in Europe and the United States. They, along with other groups of blacks who had met throughout the country passing resolutions against discriminatory legislation, were all working, in their separate ways, to provide a voice for the blacks in the new South Africa.

While these groups were going their separate ways, two black intellectuals were striving for unity among the groups so that black Africans could speak with one voice. They were Pixley ka Isaka Seme, educated at Columbia University and Oxford, and Solomon T. Plaatje, a well-known black South African journalist.

These intellectuals set about organizing meetings among the different groups in order to unite blacks in South Africa. The avowed purpose was to look out for black political and economic rights.

In 1908, prior to the British government passing the Act of Union, blacks held a South African Native Convention in Bloemfontein from March 24 thru 26th. The Convention selected a delegation of blacks including Rev. W. Rubusana, T.M. Mapikela, D. Divanya, Tengo Jabuva, Alfred Mangena and Pixley Seme to go to England and express black concerns over black exclusionary provisions in the proposed South Africa Act which established the new government in South Africa. The gathering further resolved that a permanent national black organization should be established.[3]

In 1911 Seme, Plaatje and other blacks met in Johannesburg to plan for setting-up a nationwide united black political organization. They decided to hold a nationwide meeting of black representatives early the next year to formally organize a united black group.

On January 8, 1912, blacks from all over South Africa and Bechuanaland (present day Botswana) met once again at Bloemfontein to discuss the formation of the new organization. Seme set the theme in his opening address: "Chiefs of royal blood and gentlemen of our race, we have gathered here to consider and discuss a theme which my colleagues and I have decided to place before you. We have discovered that in the land of their birth, Africans are treated as hewers of wood and drawers of water. The white people of this country have formed what is known as the Union of South Africa—a union which we have no voice in the making of the laws and no part in their administration. We have called you therefore to this Conference so that we can together devise ways and means of forming our national union for the purpose of creating unity and defending our rights and privileges."[4]

Shortly after his opening speech Seme formally requested the gathering that they establish the South African Native National Congress. According to Francis Meli, the editor of the ANC's monthly magazine *Sechaba*, Seme's motion ". . . passed unanimously with loud cheers, . . ."[5]

The South African Native National Congress, the fore-runner of the African National Congress, was essentially concerned with the economic and political well being of blacks during its early formative years. In 1925, the name of the organization was changed to the South African National Congress, which has since been shortened to the African National Congress (ANC).

The activities of Seme and his colleagues were taking place at the same time that inter-white relationships were severely strained in South Africa. There was much bitterness and hard feelings between the Afrikaans- and English-speaking South Africans. The Boer War memories were still fresh in the minds of many and feelings ran high between the vanquished—the Afrikaner—and his conqueror, the British. The Afrikaner viewed English-

[3] Willan, B., *Sol Plaatje:South African Nationalist 1872-1932*, London, 1984, p. 139.

[4] Walshe, P. *The Rise of African Nationalism in South Africa: The African National Congress 1912-1952*, Berkeley, 1971, p. 14.

[5] Meli, F., *South Africa Belongs to Us: The History of the African National Congress*, Zimbabwe Publishing House, Harare, 1989, p. 38.

speaking South Africans as collaborators of the conquering enemy who had inflicted so much suffering upon him and his family. It was a period of bitterness similar to that after our own Civil War. The new white government in power in the early days of the Union was greatly concerned and preoccupied with working out inter-white relations. The government often carried out policies to reconcile these differences explicitly at the expense of the non-whites—such as the Native Land Act of 1913.

It is well to remember that South Africa had been seized by a severe economic depression lasting from 1904 to 1909 which exacerbated the growing problem of the poor whites.

South Africa's biggest industry at the time was the mining industry. Its development was causing rapid economic changes—from a subsistence agriculture to a more complex one centered on mining. Rinderpest infestation of their cattle had wiped out many white farmers financially and sent them to towns seeking work opportunities. Adding more misery to the agricultural sector were the lingering effects of the Boer War. The British scorched-earth policy during that conflict had destroyed farm homes, buildings, and stock. It had left many whites landless and destitute.

Thus much of the policy of the early Union government was to alleviate the problems of the whites—at the expense of the blacks and coloureds.

During the same period of time, militant trade unionism was rearing its head. Also underlining this activity were racial concerns. The object of this trade union effort was to protect the interests of the white workers, especially those in the mining industry.

A series of violent strikes occurred as whites attempted to prevent mine owners from hiring cheaper black labor. During one of the strikes in 1911, the labor leader William "Bill" Andrews, a founding father of the South African Communist Party, sought help from the new Union government "to protect against the encroachment of coloured labour in the skilled trades of South Africa", stating further, that "the Government was guilty of a crime not only against the white people, but against the 'nigger' himself in forcing him to go to the mines and work for the benefit of the capitalist class."[6]

The government passed the Native Land Act of 1913 to accomplish several goals. First, it set aside certain areas of South Africa as exclusive native reserves; second, it tried to preserve the status quo in the remaining areas of South Africa; and, third, it provided for a source of cheap labor by displacing black tenant farmers in white areas and forcing them into the labor pool.

[6] Roux, E., *Time Longer than Rope: A History of the Black Man's Struggle for Freedom in South Africa*, University of Wisconsin Press, Madison, WI, 1964, p. 124.

Although opposed to such measures as the Native Land Act, the South African Native National Congress opposition took the form of voicing their concerns and petitioning the South African Parliament in Cape Town.

When that approach failed they again turned their appeals to the British government. Once again they sent a delegation to London to plead their case. Officials in London turned a deaf ear to their arguments.

In 1914, some 19,000 white miners, led by the communist Bill Andrews, went out on strike. By the time the strike was put down, twenty-one civilians and six police and military personnel had been killed. The strike also caused widespread destruction of property.

The fledgling Native Congress did not take part in the 1914 labor unrest caused by the white striking mine workers. In fact one of three resolutions passed by the organization at its third conference and sent to the government disassociated the Congress entirely from the armed clashes between the white workers and the government on the Witswatersrand. Instead, the Congress preferred to seek redress for their grievances through constitutional means. They did not want to be caught in the middle of the turbulent situation between the striking miners and the government. The government had proclaimed martial law and mobilized 70,000 armed men to crush the strike. Hundreds of strikers and trade union leaders were arrested. Some of the trade union leaders were deported to Britain under the hurriedly introduced, and passed, Indemnity and Undesirables Special Deportation Bill.[7]

The blacks had trod a very cautious path while the unrest had flared and been stamped out.

During the First World War, the South African Native National Congress, as a demonstration of their "loyalty to the King and Empire"[8], refrained from criticizing the Union government. Instead, the organization embarked "itself at once into a patriotic demonstration, decided to hang up native grievances against the South African Parliament till a better time and to tender the authorities every assistance."[9]

After the war had ended, labor unrest returned to South Africa and a wave of strikes shook the land. The Native Congress's action during this period took the form of protest demonstrations against the pass laws and in

[7] Walker, I.L., & Weinbren, B., *2,000 Casualties: A History of the Trade Unions and the Labour Movement in the Union of South Africa*, Johannesburg, 1961, pp. 32-58.

[8] Meli, p. 48.

[9] Plaatje, Sol. T. *Native Life in South Africa before and since the European War and the Boer Rebellion*, Cape Town, 1982, p. 301.

support of striking black African mineworkers. One consequence of this activity was to increase the membership of the organization.

Once again, in 1919, the Native Congress sent a delegation to London, made up of H. R. Nycayiya, Selope Thema, L. T. Muvabaza, J. T. Gumede and Sol Plaatje, to appeal to the British government for assistance to redress their grievances in South Africa. Instead of being ignored or palmed-off on minor governmental functionaries, the delegation, to its surprise, met with the Prime Minister Lloyd George. They presented him with their complaints about discriminatory legislation in South Africa and their general concerns over the situation in their country. The Prime Minister told the delegation: "You have said enough to convince me that it is certainly a case which ought to be taken into the consideration of the South African Government and I shall certainly take the earliest opportunity of presenting the whole of the facts to General Smuts."[10]

Lloyd George did broach the subject to the Smuts government in South Africa, but there the matter rested and no action was taken.

However, the London travels were not a total failure for the delegation. They were given a warm reception by the socialist movement in England. The delegates wrote on their problems in South Africa; they went on speaking tours under the sponsorship of the Independent Labour Party in Great Britain. Interviews with them appeared regularly during this period of time in left-wing newspapers throughout England.[11]

This was the organization's first brush with the socialist movement outside South Africa. It was not to be their last.

[10] Willan, p. 124.

[11] Meli, p. 54.

2

BIRTH OF THE SOUTH AFRICAN COMMUNIST PARTY

Two events in the history of South Africa in the late nineteenth century hastened the appearance of communism in that troubled land. They were the discovery of rich deposits of diamonds and gold and the Boer War. There was also a cause and effect relationship between the two.

The discovery of the mineral riches brought swarms of fortune seekers, most of whom came from the British empire, to the barren veld.

The discovery of gold on the Witswatersrand ridge right in the middle of the Transvaal, one of the independent Boer republics, started a wild gold rush. To make matters worse, the gold field, the richest in the world, was only forty-odd miles from the republic's capital, Pretoria.

Thousands of foreigners suddenly descended, en masse, and a boom-town, Johannesburg, sprang up with all the problems and troubles accompanying such creations.

Although appreciating the riches in their midst, the Afrikaners in the Transvaal were horrified at the mass of humanity that had descended upon them like a plague of locusts. Most of the gold seekers were British, the same people they had trekked into the wilderness to get away from less than fifty years previously. Now, the uitlanders (foreigners) threatened to overrun them.

To add to the fears of the already suspicious Transvaalers, the new riches in their midst were stoking the lusts of the imperialists seeking to expand the British Empire. One in particular who cast his covetous eye upon the new riches of the Transvaal was that premier imperial pirate Cecil John Rhodes.

Rhodes had long pursued the dream of the British Empire in Africa stretching from the Cape of Good Hope north all the way to Cairo in Egypt. Standing squarely in his way were the two independent Boer republics—the Orange Free State and the Transvaal. The newly discovered riches on the Rand in the Transvaal only whetted his appetite to incorporate them into the Empire. He got his wish, although at the cost of much suffering and bloodshed, as the Boer War extinguished the two republics and placed them under British imperial rule.

It took over 400,000 British imperial troops from the far-flung corners of the Empire, a scorched-earth campaign and concentration camps for the women and children, to crush the independent Boers. Some of the British troops either stayed on in South Africa after the war or returned a few years later as civilians to seek their fortunes. Many returned in the manner of the carpetbaggers from the victorious Union North who descended upon the ruined Confederacy after our Civil War. Some of these rascals brought with them the infectious germ of socialism and wasted no time and effort in trying to turn this new piece of the Empire into a socialist paradise.

As mentioned earlier, the discovery of rich deposits of diamonds and gold had drawn thousands to South Africa. Among them were people from every walk of life—the good as well as the evil. The doctor, butcher, baker, blacksmith, tailor and carpenter, as well as the loafer, gambler, thief, murderer and prostitute all showed up in South Africa, lured by the prospect of riches.

Since many were experienced artisans and workers from the industrial areas of England and Europe, they brought with them the idea of trade unions. Militant trade union activists were also part of the crowd rushing to South Africa. Where the trade union treads, the socialist and Marxist aren't far behind. "Trade unionism was another innovation brought to South Africa through the diamond fields. Though small craft unions, including those of printers, were previously in existence, a new type of socially conscious workman had come not only from Britain, but also from the continent and the United States."[1]

The newly arrived trade unionists soon got busy and started forming various labor groups similar to those in their native countries, with the first being formed in 1881.[2]

The labor groups fell into two basic categories: those formed to protect

[1] Rosenthal, E., *Gold! Gold! Gold!*, McMillan Co., Johannesburg, 1970, p. 42.

[2] du Toit, M.A., *South African Trade Unions: History, Legislation, Policy*, McGraw Hill, Johannesburg, 1976, p. 11.

and advance the interests of a group of workers possessing a special skill; and, those who viewed the labor organization as a vehicle for carrying out the socialist's fundamental mission of the class struggle against the hated capitalists. The latter group viewed the union as a fighting movement, not a workers betterment society.

Violence wasn't far behind the creation of the unions. Three years after formation of the first union, bloody rioting broke out in the Kimberly diamond mines over the issue of strip-searching white miners to prevent theft of the precious stones. The militant Knights of Labor organization had stirred up the miners. Among the Knights' appeals to the strikers were calls to create socialism. By the time the strikes ended, five men had been killed and forty injured. Thus, the first workers' strike in South Africa not only resulted in death, bloodshed and destruction, but was led by a radical organization, preaching violence and Marxist socialism.[3]

Trade unionism soon spread to the gold fields in the Transvaal. The first trade union founded there was the Witswatersrand Mine Workers Employees and Mechanics Union, established in August 1892. W. Tyler, J.T. Bains and E.B. Rose were its founders. The union was clearly a political body reflecting the Marxist views of its organizers. It had a questionable and short history, collapsing in a wave of corruption with various union officials stealing large sums of money from its treasury.

In 1894, one of the founding fathers of the Communist Party of South Africa set up a branch of the British Amalgamated Society of Engineers in Johannesburg. He was William Henry ("Bill") Andrews, who would become the leading member of the early South African Communist Party. Another member was the infamous J.T. Bains of the soon to be defunct Witswatersrand Mine Employees and Mechanics Union. Andrews admiringly described Bains: "I have never known a man to hate capitalism more than J.T. Bains."[4]

In 1897 the Transvaal mineworkers struck over the issue of wage reductions. The strike leaders were none other than Bill Andrews and J.T. Bains.

The advent of the Boer War caused a drastic drop in labor disputes in South Africa. With the end of the war, however, the mining industry quickly returned to full-scale production, attracting scores of workers to South Africa

[3] Roberts, B., *Kimberly-Turbulent City*, David Phillips Publishers, Cape Town, 1976, pp. 269-270; McNish, J.T., *Graves and Guineas*, C. Struik Co., Cape Town, 1969, pp. 117-122; Andrews, W.H., *Class Struggles in South Africa*, Stewart Printing Co., Cape Town, 1940, pp. 59-60.

[4] Cope, R.K., *Comrade Bill*, Stewart Printing Co., Cape Town, n.d., p. 45.

from all over the world. Labor strife, which had been somewhat dormant during the war, reappeared with a new vigor. Most prominent in the reappearance of strikes and labor troubles were the socialists. They were the ring-leaders in the strikes, fights, rabble-rousing agitation, and other activities associated with the labor problems.[5]

In 1902, the British Social Democratic Federation was formed in Cape Town along with a branch in Johannesburg. They pursued Marxist socialist ideals and in 1905 held a solidarity meeting in support of the 1905 Russian Revolution. The Federation later split and became considerably weakened over the question of South Africa's entry into the First World War.

In 1902, the ubiquitous Bill Andrews returned to the South African labor scene. (He had earlier decided that discretion was better than valor and fighting the Boers was not his cup of tea. He had collected his family and speedily caught a ship for England, thus sitting out the bulk of the war.) He and the militant Australian carpetbagging socialist, Peter Whiteside, founded the Witswatersrand Trade and Labour Council. It was a political pressure group that was formed to advance the socialist agenda of Andrews and Whiteside in the South African gold fields.

The first general miners strike took place in May 1907 at the Knights Deep mine and spread rapidly across the gold fields on the Rand, eventually involving close to 6,400 men. The strike was organized by Tom Matthews, general-secretary of the Transvaal Miners Association. He was a noted socialist who had come to South Africa, in true carpetbagger fashion, less than a year before. He had quickly thrown himself into the socialist activity and the labor unrest in the gold fields. He played a key role in the general strike which was put down by police and troops called in to protect the mining machinery and property.

The general strike was followed by others and the foreign socialist element played key roles in each:

- The De Beers lock-out of 1908, when strikers led by Bill Andrews were locked out of the De Beers Mine in Kimberly.
- The Natal Railway Workers Strike of 1909, lasting several months, with strikers taking part in the Marxist labor movement's May Day Parade while singing the "Red Flag"—the movement's official anthem.
- The Rand Tramwaymen's Strike of 1911, organized by the Marxist-oriented International Workers of the World movement.

[5] Pike, H.R., *A History of Communism in South Africa*, Christian Mission International of South Africa, Germiston, 1985, pp. 38-43.

- The Kleinfontein Strike of 1913, involving 63 mines and 18,000 workers. One of the strike leaders was the rabid socialist associate of Andrews, J.T. Bains.

The labor unrest was not taking place in a political vacuum as the socialists were also organizing politically. The most important of these various efforts was the formation in 1908 of the South African Labor Party. This group paved the way for the future South African Communist Party. Its genesis was the Labor Representation Committee, a group comprising six small organizations, founded in 1907 and headed by Bill Andrews.

The following year, activists held a conference in Durban to consolidate all the various groups into one united party. From this conference evolved the Labor Party and the familiar figure of Bill Andrews appeared again as a founding member of the Labor Party. Its members were extremely active in the trade union field and constantly clashed with the authorities, especially during the 1913 Kleinfontein Strike. Incited by fiery speeches of Bains and other socialist agitators, the striking miners went on a rampage looting and burning shops and stores in Johannesburg. The Botha government imposed martial law and deployed thousands of troops to break the strike. Twenty-one civilians and six policemen died before the strikes ended. Shortly after the strike ended the government deported nine of the strike leaders to England, among them J.T. Bains. However, they all returned to South Africa a few months later and resumed their agitation activities.[6]

The First World War in 1914 split the Labor Party over the question of South Africa's entry into the war. Some were in favor of the South African decision to enter the war against Germany. Others, including Bill Andrews, were vehemently opposed to the war.

Matters came to a head in 1915. The Labor Party held its conference that year in Selbourne Hall in Johannesburg. The pro-war faction had packed the meeting and their view carried the day. Andrews and his supporters walked out, taking with them ". . . three leading officials of the Labour Party and seven of the executive."[7] That group, six years later, became the nucleus of the South African Communist Party.

Shortly after the walkout, the radical breakaway group formed the International Socialist League (ISL) and elected Bill Andrews as chairman, David Ivor Jones as secretary and Gabriel Weinstock as treasurer.[8]

[6] Pike, pp. 52-53.

[7] Pike, p. 81.

[8] *Ibid.*

The communist proclivities of the ISL soon became evident in the pages of its newspaper, *The International.* An early issue carried a major article by David Ivor Jones which opened by proclaiming: "Here we plant the flag of the New International in South Africa. What the Labor movement requires is a return to the Communist Manifesto of Karl Marx."[9]

The ISL immediately sought alliances with similar thinking groups and organizations. Hearing of an overseas group that was trying to establish an international league of socialists, they wrote them expressing interest and sought affiliation. This group was led by Lenin and was called the Zimmerwald group. It quickly granted the ISL's request and thus the "ISL was drawn into the Leninist sphere of influence."[10]

The ISL enthusiastically proclaimed its support for the 1917 Russian Revolution by issuing a pamphlet in English, Zulu and Sotho entitled "We are South African Bolsheviks".

In 1917, the ISL shared a platform, for the first time, with the African National Congress (ANC), to jointly protest against the Native Administration Bill of the South African government.

Late in the summer of 1917, socialist organizations planned a Stockholm Socialist Peace Conference to rally worldwide support for the Russian Revolution. The organizers sent appeals to socialist groups throughout the world to send delegates to the conference. The South African ISL chose Bill Andrews to be their delegate. Allied government pressure prevented this meeting of world communist leaders. By controlling ship movements to the Swedish capital because of the on-going war, the allied governments were able to prevent the delegates from getting there. Andrews, for example, managed to get as far as England where he spent his time traveling and meeting with elements of the British communist movement.[11]

Shortly after Andrews returned to South Africa, the ISL's mouthpiece, *The International,* began churning out reams of articles proclaiming the Bolshevik revolution in Russia to be the answer to South Africa's problems. Lenin's coup was "enthusiastically hailed as the greatest event in the human history for the working class."[12]

The end of the First World War saw the ISL become more arrogant and militant. They brusquely rejected overtures by the Labor Party to rejoin their former comrades and in 1920, they began to issue threats to the government.

[9] *The International,* December 10, 1915.

[10] Katze, D.J., *Communism & South Africa,* Tafelburg, Cape Town, 1982, p. 199.

[11] Pike, p. 88.

[12] Roux, E., *S.P. Bunting,* The African Bookman, Cape Town, 1943, p. 37.

Andrews became so bold as to say in *The International*: "The ISL will continue its work of agitation and organization of the masses, irrespective of race, colour or creed, or class line, to fight and destroy the system (meaning capitalism) responsible for the present world misery—peacefully if possible, by force if need be."[13]

In 1919, Lenin established the Comintern (Communist International). Its purpose was to unite the world communist movement under Lenin's leadership. He intended to make the numerous communist movements in the world into the mirror image of his Bolsheviks. In short, world communism was to become the same thing as Russian communism.[14]

Andrews was determined that his ISL would become part of the Comintern. One of the rules for Comintern membership precluded the affiliation of more than one party from the same country. Thus, if the ISL were to be the one it had to head off rival groups. One way of doing this was to unite them under the ISL banner.

Andrews plunged into the task with vigor. He persuaded other interested socialist and Marxist groups in South Africa to join the ISL. In this way, he told them, they could unite with Lenin's Comintern through the ISL.

He proposed a meeting with the groups to set up a single unified communist movement in South Africa. On March 27, 1920, a unity conference was held in Johannesburg where they all voted to unite with the ISL.

The ISL then applied for affiliation with Lenin's Comintern and sent two delegates, David Ivor Jones and Sam Borlin, to the July-August second congress of the Comintern. This congress was important in that it was there that Lenin laid out his twenty-one points, or conditions, that had to be strictly followed by all groups seeking to unite with the Comintern. The gist of these points was that foreign communist parties were expected to follow faithfully all instructions issued by their Soviet leaders in Moscow without question. The twenty-one points require complete subordination to Moscow. The second Comintern Congress officially adopted these points.

A year later, organizers held a congress in Cape Town from July 21, 1921 to August 1, 1921 to formally establish a Communist Party in South Africa. The group officially adopted the constitution and manifesto of the Comintern. It elected its executive body and voted to place the headquarters of the new Party in Johannesburg.

[13] Pike, p. 92.

[14] Jacobs, D.M., *The Masks of Communism*, Harper & Row, New York, 1963, p. 58.

The officials were: C.B. Tyler, chairman, Bill Andrews, secretary and S.P. Bunting, treasurer. Africa's first communist party was born to the resounding cheers of the delegates. One exuberant delegate remarked to the press: " The moves in South Africa to stop the communist organization are doomed to failure and the doom of the capitalist class is sealed."[15]

Shortly after the Party's founding, Bill Andrews, in his official capacity, wrote to the Third International or Comintern of the Communist Party in Russia, applying for affiliation. In his letter Andrews stressed that the new communist party in South Africa ". . . accepted the 'twenty-one points' condition of affiliation to the Third International. . . ."[16]

Within six months of the founding of the communist party in South Africa, a series of strikes erupted across the Witswatersrand culminating in January 1922 in the Wits Miner's Strike, or the "Red Strike" as it is sometimes called. The strike, involving 22,000 white workers, started in the gold fields but soon spread across the country, forcing the South African government of Jan Smuts to declare martial law.

The unrest broke out when the Chamber of Mines in the gold fields made an ill-advised decision to reduce the wages of the white mineworkers, or even replace them with cheaper black laborers, as one of a series of economy moves.

Bill Andrews urged the striking white mineworkers "to regard the strikes as a phase of the global class struggle and to accept the natives as potential allies."[17] Led by the communists and socialists, the white miners took to the streets committing robbery and arson.[18]

The Smuts government ordered out the troops and open warfare broke out between the troops and the striking miners. There were battles at Benoni, Boksburg, Brakpan, Bruxton and Langlaagte which left 230 dead, including 50 policemen. Nearly 5,000 people were arrested, and 864 were convicted on charges of high treason. Eighteen strikers were sentenced to death but fourteen of them were granted reprieves.[19]

In April 1922, the government appointed a commission, the Martial Law Inquiry Commission, to investigate the strike and the Council of Action

[15] Roux, E., p. 58.

[16] Pike, p. 112.

[17] Shorten, J.R., *The Johannesburg Saga*, Shorten (Pty) Ltd., Johannesburg, 1970, p. 314.

[18] Louw, L., & Kendall, F., *South Africa: The Solution*, Amagi Publications, Bisho, Ciskei, 1986, p. 37.

[19] *Sunday Times*, March 19, 1972.

which had publicly supported the strike. After eight months of investigation and taking testimony of over 300 witnesses, it issued its findings. The commission reported: "It is established upon the clearest evidence that upon the 10th March the industrial dispute upon the Rand had developed into a Revolution". . . . "Also, it is clear to the Commission . . . that the Council of Action was closely connected with the Communist Party of South Africa. Indeed it is highly probable that the name was merely a blind, in order to attract recruits who might not wish to belong to a body of avowed communists. If the European workers on the Rand had realized that the real object of the communists was to bring about an armed uprising to establish a system which would lead to a complete abolition of the Colour Bar *[black restrictive labor law—ed.]*, and was merely a step in the direction of a Workers' Revolution to establish a Soviet Republic, it is probable that Andrews and his satellites, Fisher and Spendiff, would have had little or no support."[20]

The Communist Party of South Africa's initial baptism of fire involved violence. Such violence would not be its last.

[20] *Report of the Martial Law Inquiry*, Judicial Commission, Pretoria, 1922, p. 5.

3

THE REPUBLIC OF SOUTH AFRICA— A MULTI-ETHNIC SOCIETY

Before proceeding any further it would do well to pause and briefly examine the complex nature of South African society, the policy of apartheid and how both affect any understanding of the revolutionary situation underway in South Africa.

South Africa, the target of the African National Congress' revolutionary campaign, has always been considered a nation with cultural, as well as economic, political and strategic ties to the West. It fought on the Allied side in both World Wars and contributed to U.S.-led forces in the Korean War. Of late, however, it has been the target of a "get-South Africa campaign" because of its official governmental policy of apartheid. But few who have spent so much time riding the hate-South Africa bandwagon understand what apartheid is, its theoretical foundations, or why, in fact, they should be against it, although almost everyone is.

In Afrikaans, the lingua-franca of South Africa, *apartheid* literally means "apartness or separate." It is a race-related policy inaugurated in 1948 that outlawed intermingling of the races, institutionalized racial discrimination, based political participation or exclusion on racial criteria,[1] and segregated

[1] Geldenhuys, D.J., "The International Isolation of South Africa", *Strategic Review for Southern*

segregated the black population. The government achieved segregation by confining blacks to tribal areas, or homelands, and controlling the movement of black workers into cities and towns.

Although the ANC equates capitalism with apartheid, it is an incorrect analogy. Apartheid actually has more in common with the socialist agenda of the ANC than it does with capitalism. As the eminent black American economist Walter Williams points out: "Apartheid is the result of anticapitalist or socialistic efforts to subvert the operation of market (capitalistic) forces —with no intervention by political forces—that has always been seen as the enemy of white privilege and that apartheid ideology has always sought to defeat.

"South Africa's history is riddled with white contempt for market forces, from the highest levels of government on down. Prime Minister Jan Christian Smuts—in a *Century of Wrongs* (London: Review of Reviews, 1900) said, 'It is ordained that we (Afrikaners), insignificant as we are, should be amongst the first people to begin the struggle against the new world tyranny of capitalism.'

"Similar anticapitalist sentiment was echoed by Daniel F. Malan, who was later to lead the Afrikaner National Party to victory at the polls in 1948, Malan said, 'If war should come, it will mean, in my opinion, the end of the capitalist system . . . but whether this happens or not with or without war, by revolution or evolution, the capitalist system which is based on self-interest and the right of the strongest is in any case doomed. For us to work together until the correct adjustment has been made will also be South Africa's task in the future.'

"Later, *Volkshandel* (September 1941)—an Afrikaner business publication—carried more of the same: 'Every sober-minded, thinking Afrikaner is fed up to the top of his throat with so-called *laissez faire*—let-it-be-capitalism, with its soul destroying materialism and the spirit of "every man for himself and the devil for us all". We are sick of it because of its legacy of Afrikaner poor whiteism and the condition which makes the Afrikaner a spectator in the business of his own country.' "[2]

As we will see, these words could have been written, with slight modification to signify blacks instead of whites, by any number of African National Congress (ANC) spokesmen.

Africa, Vol. XI, No. 2, Institute for Strategic Studies, University of Pretoria, Pretoria, November 1989, p. 40.

[2] Williams, W., *South Africa's War Against Capitalism* A Cato Institute Book, Praeger, New York, 1989, p. 126.

To Americans, just recently finished with the process of emancipation of fellow black citizens, the policy of apartheid is abhorrent. Our attitude toward South Africa is influenced by our attitude toward blacks that evolved from the American civil rights movement of the 1960s. South Africa is, however, neither an American nor European society. Nor is South Africa unique—in many ways, it is a typical African country that responds to endemic problems in a typical African manner.

The single most dominant characteristic of the African continent is its lack of racial, cultural and linguistic unity. No other continent is so fragmented by so many different ethnic groups. Hundreds of years of colonialism on the African continent brought together and transformed many tribal societies into fifty superficially modern states, which since the end of the Second World War, have gained independence from their colonial overlords. When these states formed the Organization of African Unity (OAU) in 1961, they decided that all former boundaries would remain the same. Not one country is truly homogeneous. Even the smallest, like Rwanda, are split by tribal or racial fissures. The world has witnessed appalling violent, bloody civil wars in Nigeria, the Sudan, Chad, Zaire, Uganda, Angola, Mozambique and elsewhere.

South Africa is no exception. Her ethnic divisions are large and more complex than a simple black versus white situation, although the Boer-bashers of the world would have us believe otherwise. South African blacks are not an homogeneous group—they have no ethnic unity. They are part of the Southern Bantu ethnic group.

Hundreds of Negro tribes that inhabit Central and Southern Africa are classified ethnically as the Bantu. The Bantu form three major groups: Western, Eastern, and Southern Bantu. The Western and Eastern Bantu live in the area bordered on the north by a line running roughly from the Gulf of Guinea, in the west, to the east coast of the continent; to the south, by the two great rivers—the Zambezi and the Cunene. The Southern Bantu, the third major group, are spread over the rest of Southern Africa from the Mozambique Channel in the Indian Ocean to the Kalahari Desert, and south to the tip of Africa. The Southern Bantu of South Africa are subdivided into four main cultural-linguistic groups.

They are the *Nguni* (Zulus and Xhosa, for example), *South-Tswana* (live in Botswana and Bophuthatswana), *Venda* (live in the Northern Transvaal and are closely related to the neighboring Bantu tribes of Southern Zimbabwe) and *Shangaan-Tsonga* (live in the Northern Transvaal). The subdivisions can be further subdivided into nine separate ethnic groups, each with its own language, legal system, life-style, values and socio-political structures.

Of the nine ethnic groups, three belong to the *Nguni*, three to the *Sotho*. Ninety percent of the black population in South Africa is either *Nguni* or *Sotho*.

Of the remaining three the Lemba, though culturally distinct, are politically united with the Vhavenda, while the *Shangaan-Tsonga* are the product of more recent contact between different black cultures, initially with some *Nguni* from Natal and later with neighboring Northern Sotho and Vhavenda.

The *North Nguni* include the Swazi and Zulu. The Swazi are located mostly in their own independent kingdom of Swaziland. The Zulu are located in Natal.

The *South Nguni* are located in the Transkei and Ciskei. The best known subdivisions are the Pondo, Thembu, Xhosa, Bhaca and Ngqika.

The Ndebele in the Transvaal are also *Nguni* and are subdivided into northern and southern groups. The northern have lost almost all of their *Nguni* identity by virtue of being largely assimilated by the *Sotho* whose language they speak. The southern group includes the Manala and Ndzundza subdivisions.

The Northern Sotho live in the self-governing state of Lebowa in the Northern Transvaal. The best known subgroup of the Northern Sotho is the Pedi.

The Southern Sotho live in the independent nation of Lesotho or, a small number, in the self-governing state of QwaQwa. Two of their best known subgroups are the Fokong and Tlokwa.

The Tswana live mostly in either Botswana or Bophuthswana. The most important subgroups are the Thlaping, Kwena and Koni.

The Vhavenda are culturally homogeneous but include the Lemba and live mainly in the Venda homeland. The Lemba are regarded as a separate ethnic group because of their independent customs and tendency to avoid inter-marriage with other groups.

The *Shangaan-Tsonga* are a combination of *Tsonga* and *Nguni* who live mainly in the self-governing state of Gazankulu in the Northern Transvaal. They are neighbors of the Vhavenda and Northern Sotho.

Talk about cultural diversity, South Africa has it with a vengeance. Commenting on this diversity, the noted English historian, Paul Johnson, said: "The largest racial group is the Zulu, with 5,412,000 people. . . . The next largest are the whites, with. 4,454,000, but these too are composed of diverse ethnic groups—Dutch, French, English, and German—and have two distinct cultures and languages, Dutch-Afrikaans and English. The figure also includes other important subgroups, such as the large Jewish community,

Portuguese, Greeks, Italians, and 'Rhodesian Whites'. Third in size are the Xhosa, with 2,685,000, followed by the mixed-race group officially called Coloureds (2,556,000), the North Sotho (2,265,000), South Sotho (1,793,000), and Tswana (1,216,000).

"In addition to all these, there are seven other main groups, ranging from the Shangaan, with nearly 890,000 and the Asians with 780,000, to the Venda, with 185,000. This last is the most homogeneous group, but even it has 27 distinct tribes. The Asians are divided into Hindus (65 percent), Muslims (21 percent), Christians, Buddhists, and other cultures. As for language, there are four major and 23 minor African ones."[3]

"Ethnicity plays or has played an important role in African revolutionary politics from Algeria to Mozambique."[4] In South Africa it was common knowledge that the PAC *[Pan African Congress-ed]* (of the Sixties) had a predominantly Sotho support base as against the Xhosa-based support of the ANC. . . ."[5]

This is especially true in the top echelons of the ANC (see chart of the members of the ANC's National Executive Committee). Both Nelson Mandela and Oliver Tambo are Xhosas. Three of the pretenders to the throne in the ANC—Alfred Nzo, Thabo Mbeki and Chris Hani—are also from the same tribal group.[6]

This ethnic dominance has caused a lot of dissension within the ANC involving allegations of "Xhosa conspiracy" in personnel postings and promotions.[7] The strife caused by Xhosa domination refuses to fade away.[8] Such suspicions and internal tensions within the ANC over ethnicity cast grave doubts over their claim to be exclusive spokesmen for blacks in South Africa.

America has little to compare with this diversity, although American Indians are an apt analogy.

Another analogy that can give a reader an insight into the problem of tribalism throughout Africa is that of ethnic neighborhoods in large American cities. In such neighborhoods, the language and customs of the old country are preserved. Residents generally keep to themselves. Italian, Irish, Chinese and Polish-Americans often live in areas completely dominated by

[3] Johnson, P. "The Race for South Africa", *Commentary*, September 1985, pp. 27-28.

[4] See: Breytenbach, W., "The African Revolutionary", in *Challenge: The Southern African Revolutionary Context*, Al J. Venter, ed., Ashanti Publishing Pty (Ltd), Gibraltar, 1989, pp. 74-75.

[5] Breytenbach, *op. cit.*, p. 75.

[6] *Africa Confidential*, Vol. 30., No. 19, September 22, 1989, p. 2.

one ethnic group. Rarely do these groups cross lines out of their respective neighborhoods.

In Africa, a similar, but more intense, situation exists. Instead of ignoring or, in the worst case, chasing a stranger out of the neighborhood, the African may resort to more serious forms of expressing disapproval of strangers, as recent tribal clashes there indicate.

Another way of visualizing the nature of tribalism in South Africa is to compare the tribal animosities to the deadly squabbles that were common among the clans of Scotland.

Most of the tribes in South Africa base their economy on cattle. The number of cows a person owns is still a measure of his wealth among the rural, traditional blacks. Most, especially the Zulu, place great store in their tribal social hierarchy and history and the warrior tradition. Historically, one of the highest forms of prestige in this type of society was the ability to raid and steal cattle from a different tribe. Success in this venture was a mark of honor within one's tribe. Such activity, however, invited retaliation and numerous vendettas and intertribal wars were its inevitable result. All of these characteristics also describe the activity of the Scottish clans.

In the case of Scotland, however, the clans were hammered into a unified state by the results of the battle of Culloden, fought on April 26, 1743. In this battle the assembled clans of Scotland—mostly highland, or mountain dwellers—under the leadership of the incompetent Charles Edward Stuart (Bonnie Prince Charles) were crushed by the English and lowland Scots under the command of the Duke of Cumberland. After this disastrous defeat the clans were suppressed and forced to become one state, under the rule of the English Crown. The suppression, for example, forbade the wearing of the clan's tartan, a unique Scottish badge of recognition among the diverse clans as each clan had its own tartan. Only during the reign of Queen Victoria, when the rambunctious Scots were finally accepted as good subjects of the realm, were the Scots permitted to publicly wear their tartans.

In Africa, especially South Africa, although the various tribes had warred with each other, there was no unitary state that sent its Duke of Cumberland to subdue the unruly tribes and incorporate them into the unitary state. The closest example was the Zulu warrior Shaka, who hammered out a black Zulu nation in the early 1800s.[9] To this day, the Zulus consider themselves a nation

[7] *Africa Confidential*, Vol. 31, No. 4, February 23, 1990, p. 4.

[8] Williamson, C., "ANC Clandestine Operations", *Challenge*, p. 291.

[9] For the best history of the Zulu nation see: Morris, D.R., *The Washing of the Spears*, Simon & Shuster, N.Y. , 1965.

and not just a tribe. In South Africa there were numerous clashes between different black tribes and white settlers, but there was no effort made by the whites to exterminate the black tribes. On the contrary, the settlers allowed and encouraged the tribes to maintain their separate ethnic and cultural identities.

In this manner they could, in today's world, be looked on as analogous to Europe in this manner: A Frenchman is different from a Spaniard, Italian, German, Dane or Englishman, to name just a few. He differs ethnically, culturally, linguistically and socio-politically. Yet, in broad racial characteristic, all are considered white. But they all can readily tell a "foreigner" from one of their fellow countrymen. It is the same in Africa with its tribal composition and, more to the point, it is that way in South Africa.

Like the Frenchman, the Zulu can recognize another black as either a fellow Zulu or a non-Zulu. Like the Frenchman, who would be highly insulted if mistaken by one to be a Spaniard or Italian, the Zulu would be fit to be tied if he were mistaken by one to be a Xhosa, or Sotho or any other but a Zulu.

Since all cultures view others through their own cultural blinders, it is natural for Americans to view black Africans as they do American blacks. America's experience as a cultural melting pot makes it hard to understand events out of that context. Yet Africa, especially South Africa, is not a cultural melting pot. It is a land where the myriad cultures exist side by side and react with one another with all the tensions one would expect from the dealings of strangers who are constantly casting suspicious eyes at one another.

This is not to imply that Americans should not be concerned with the policy of racial discrimination but to point out that there are other factors involved than merely the color of one's skin. These must also be taken into account before an equitable and workable solution can be found to the problems not only in South Africa, but throughout the African continent.

Yet South Africa mirrors the rest of the continent. It is rich in cultural and ethnic diversity. African governments cope with this diversity by means of social engineering in which they sacrifice individual rights to so-called group rights, which usually means the fancy of the tribe in power. These governments often treat people not as individuals, but as sheep to be pushed around in herds.

They conduct this social engineering on a tribal basis since the continent is so lacking in homogeneity; one tribe can lord it over the rest. South Africa is no different from the rest of the continent in this respect.

There is not a single African country where tribal or racial origins, skin color or religious affiliation are not of prime importance in securing political or economic rights. The western concept of one man, one vote is understood, in general, by African politicians not as a means of peaceably transferring power over a period of time, but as a tool for seizing and holding power indefinitely.

The American philosopher Richard Weaver once said: "Ideas have consequences." The African experience bears out Weaver's observation. Most African socio-political theories are variants of socialism or despotic dictatorships. In this context, all African states are, in differing degrees, racist. Almost without exception, all practice discrimination against some group: Jews, whites, Asians, non-Muslim religious groups or disfavored tribes. Thus numerous states have codified a wide variety of discriminatory practices into their legal systems throughout the continent. Many have taken the form of a strange brand of socialism.

In Tanzania, for example, the government employs a particularly sinister doctrine called Ujauma; Ghana has its Consciencism; there is the Zambian doctrine of Humanism, and Senegal practices Negritude. Zaire is more honest, and calls its ruling doctrine Mobutuism, after the dictator of the same name. Academics in the political science or sociology departments of local universities cooked up most of these doctrines. All reflect the desires or whims of the ruling racial group.

Apartheid is no different. It is a philosophy developed in the social-psychology department under Dr. H.F. Verwoerd at Stellenbosh University, the elite Afrikaner university in South Africa. Apartheid, as do many of the other doctrines mentioned above, represents and protects the interests of the ruling group—in this instance Dutch-Afrikaners—just as Ujauma represents the interests of the regime founded in Tanzania by Julius Nyerere.

Apartheid exploits blacks economically, denies them political rights, segregates them and is enforced by a heavy-handed state bureaucracy. On the other hand, tribal or Marxist governments in black Africa run their economies into ruin, though occasionally giving people a vote—either a choice of a dictated one-party slate or coerced in a particular direction as in Zimbabwe. These black tyrants humiliate and oppress their tribal opponents, torture political prisoners, use police and troops to inflict genocidal policies of mass murder, and give their elites privileges that are abused in ways never dreamed of by the most recalcitrant racist Afrikaner politician.

The butchery of blacks by their fellow blacks has been the unfortunate history of post-colonial Africa. As the Ghanaian writer, George Ayittey said, "Political repression and the denial of basic civil liberties are rampant across Africa. Where is the freedom Africans fought for when they threw off the yoke of colonial rule? . . ."[10] It has been supplanted by military dictators or

[10] Ayittey, G.B.N., "In Africa, Independence Is Far Cry From Freedom", *The Wall Street Journal*, March 29, 1990.

one-party state rule. "Out of the 45 black African nations four—Botswana, The Gambia, Mauritania and Senegal—allow their people to vote and choose their leaders and express themselves freely. Twenty-three countries are military dictatorships where no political parties are permitted. The rest are one-party states ruled by dictators-for-life. . . ."[11]

One of the worst offenders is one of the premier critics of South Africa. He is Kenneth Kaunda, the only president Zambia has ever had. Ayittey describes the situation in Zambia: "Since independence in 1964, Zambia has labored under a 'state of emergency'. It is a one-party state and talk of lifting the ban on other political parties is a crime. Freedom of expression and assembly remains a fantasy in a country whose leader is one of the most vociferous critics of oppression in South Africa.

"The rest of the states bordering South Africa, except Botswana, are the same: one-party rule, life-presidents, an abuse of political freedom, and vicious violation of human rights."[12]

The chance for reform is greater in South Africa than in the rest of the continent to the north. "The great winds carrying democracy that have triumphed in the countries of Eastern Europe will not shake the coconut trees in Africa", wrote the daily *Nation* Gabonese newspaper in a recent editorial.[13]

But the winds of change are shaking the coconut trees in South Africa, as recent events have demonstrated.

All this goes on, yet there is not a single peep of protest by those who daily condemn the crumbling South African policy of apartheid. "Oh, but you see," our hate South Africa spokeman will say, "apartheid is worse because a man can't change the color of his skin, and that is the sole criterion of judgment under apartheid." But in black Africa where murder, torture, mayhem and other human rights violations are the order of the day, a man cannot change his tribal birth, either. In the vast majority of the continent he is trapped by this as surely as by skin color in South Africa, with less hope of relief through reforms and progress than is offered by the current South African government.

For over the past five years the South African government has begun the laborious process of dismantling apartheid, which requires a huge, clumsy bureaucracy to enforce it. The fact that over 10 million blacks live and work in areas that had been designated "white only" shows that the physical core, "apartness", has been crumbling. South Africa has done away with laws

[11] *Ibid.*

[12] *Ibid.*

[13] *Ibid.*

banning interracial marriage. It has abolished the hated "pass laws", which required blacks to carry identification cards when they traveled and has instituted other reforms leading to the removal of apartheid in South Africa.

It is quite clear, the Western liberal media notwithstanding, that, starting with former State President P.W. Botha, and current South African leader, F.W. de Klerk, South Africa's political leadership, with the exception of the opposition in Afrikaner right wing circles, is convinced that apartheid must go. Botha started slowly making reforms so as to avoid panic in the ruling National Party. de Klerk has accelerated the process by unbanning the ANC, the South African Communist Party and other proscribed political entities. He also freed Nelson Mandela and other Rivonia Treason Trial prisoners.

de Klerk has indicated a willingness to sit down and negotiate a future political settlement within South Africa with all political entities. So far-reaching have de Klerk's actions been that even harsh critics of South Africa in the U.S. Congress are impressed: "We are very encouraged that a real process of change has begun which holds enormous possibilities for negotiating a peaceful transition to a genuine democracy," said a group of anti-South African Congressmen.[14]

Unlike other African leaders, Botha and de Klerk have an electorate to which they must answer. They are not dictators like most fellow leaders on the African continent. The question remains: Will the change be peaceable and evolutionary, or violent—in the words of the proponents of violence, "revolutionary"? That is the dilemma facing South Africa. If it is not evolutionary, the white groups may well turn into terrorists themselves—and very sophisticated terrorists indeed.

Gatsha Buthelezi, head of the Zulu nation, argues for peaceful change: "If change is ever achieved in South Africa through violence, we will find that the foundations of the future will have been destroyed in the course of liberating the country. . . . I believe ways and means can be found to build up the black bargaining power to force whites to the negotiating table. . . . For the vast majority of blacks, the struggle has always been for inclusion in the existing South Africa; it has always been a struggle to transform the state rather than destroy and rebuild it."[15]

On the other hand, the proponents of violent revolutionary change

[14] Ottaway, D.B., "U.S. Panel Hails S. African 'Dynamic' ", *The Washington Post*, March 5, 1990.

[15] "The Only Road to Liberation", *The Washington Post*, October 28, 1984.

reject Buthelezi's method. Indeed, groups like the Marxist-dominated African National Congress are doing everything in their power to murder or terrorize their way into power in South Africa (see the chart on page 220).

Harmony and peace among all groups in South Africa is possible if, as Buthelezi said, the groups negotiate to change South African society and rebuild it, not destroy it. For it is out of the chaos of revolutionary change, with the willing connivance of Western liberals, that the Soviet-imperialists hope to establish their strategic hegemony over southern Africa, using the South African Communist Party/African National Congress (SACP/ANC) alliance as their tool to unleash revolutionary violence and establish a progressive client regime.

4

THE SACP TAKEOVER OF THE ANC

While Andrews and his cohorts were scurrying about South Africa trying to communize the workers they paid little, if any attention to the black workers. They were left on their own.

Before 1900 a few blacks had tried to organize themselves into political pressure groups. The first of these was formed by a few clergymen and teachers in the Eastern Cape in 1882. It called itself *Imbumba Yama Africa* —molding of Africa. It was small and ineffective, as were most of the black groups that sprang up from time to time in various parts of the country. They all suffered from the fact they were small local groups with meager resources and support.

In 1912, as mentioned earlier, Dr. Pixley Seme, and other black lawyers, organized the African National Congress (ANC) in Bloemfontein, capital of the Orange Free State.[1] In 1916, two ANC members, Saul Masane and A. Mbelle, addressed the first national conference of Bill Andrews' International Socialist League (ISL). At this meeting Sidney Bunting introduced a petition of rights for the black native workers. Bunting's petition was a championing of the rights of the black worker within the context of the Marxist worldview. It called for equal rights for the blacks and the abolition of the early pass laws.

With this new approach to the black social standing, the ISL began to direct its energy towards devising ways to spread the gospel of socialism among the black and other non-white workers.

Bunting worked hard to bring blacks into the ISL. He was assisted by David Ivor Jones, who had written an editorial in the ISL newspaper, *The*

[1] Because of its central geographical location, other political parties, like the National Party, were also founded in Bloemfontein.

International, titled: "The Parting of the Ways". It said: "An internationalism which does not concede the fullest rights which the native working class is capable of claiming will be a sham. One of the justifications for our withdrawal from the labour party is that it gives us untrammelled freedom to deal, regardless of political fortunes, with the great and fascinating problem of the natives. If the League deals resolutely in consonance with the socialist principles with the native question, it will succeed in shaking South African capitalism to its foundations. Then and not till then, shall we be able to talk about the South African proletariat in our international relations. Not till we free the native can we hope to free the whites."[2]

These initiatives of the ISL, to treat blacks as part of the working class, were unprecedented in South Africa at that time. Whites looked on black workers as dangerous competitors—workers who would work at a much cheaper rate.

Bunting and some of his colleagues in the ISL formed special study classes to educate blacks in Marxist theory. The classes started on July 19, 1917, and the effort continued for a little over a year. Central to the teaching was the standard communist message of the "class war and the need to overthrow and destroy the capitalist system." From these study groups came the short-lived black workers' movement called the Industrial Workers of Africa (IWA), started with the encouragement of both the ISL and the ANC. The IWA's slogan was "*Sifune zonke*" (We want everything).[3] That must have rattled a few cages of the old-guard white leadership of the ISL.

The group didn't prosper, however, as it had only attracted sixty-nine members by January 1918. Undeterred, white ISL members kept encouraging the blacks to rise up and emulate the recent Bolshevik revolution in Russia by means of revolution in South Africa.

One of the brightest stars in the IWA was a black schoolteacher, William Thibedi, who would become one of the first black members of the South African Communist Party (SACP).

Although the IWA finally collapsed in the early 1920s, it was important as it opened the doors for the blacks to the beguiling lure of communism. The ISL used the IWA, during its short existence, to stir up trouble by inciting the blacks to revolt against the capitalist system. The IWA incited and directed black workers into a series of wildcat strikes, for which they had to pay the price of going to jail while their white communist instigators went free. The

[2] Meli, F., *South Africa Belongs to Us—A History of the ANC*, University of Indiana Press, Bloomington, 1989, p. 58.

[3] Meli, p. 59.

blacks involved in these strikes were " 'lawfully prosecuted' and sent to prison and instructed that 'while in prison they would have to do the same work as they had been doing. . . . If they attempted to escape and if it were necessary, they would be shot down.' "[4] Many members of the ANC were also involved in these strikes.

The demise of the IWA did not end white interest in spreading the gospel of Marx among the blacks. In 1921, under the guiding hand of Edward Roux, militant communist youths formed the Young Communist League (YCL). Under the influence of Bunting and Roux, the YCL took up the cause of spreading communism to the blacks. Roux and other members of the YCL tried to recruit blacks into both the YCL and the SACP. Roux tried to convince doubting comrades in the YCL that its mission should be to spread communism among the blacks. Many of their comrades remained unconvinced and refused to support their efforts.

Undaunted, Roux and his allies pressed on. In January 1924, at the annual meeting of the YCL, Roux tried to get the delegates to adopt several of his "Bantu-conscious" proposals. The delegates soundly rebuffed Roux and his supporters who then appealed to the headquarters of the Young Communist International. They backed Roux and his proposals and directed the YCL to adopt Roux's viewpoint, which, being good communists and following orders, they did. Henceforth, the YCL in South Africa officially accepted the pro-black policy of Roux.

The next step was to persuade the SACP to adopt the YCL policy at its annual conference later in the year.

The question of whether or not to focus party attention on the blacks was the most important issue of the third conference of the SACP. The issue generated a lot of controversy at the meeting. "The Pro-Bantu group was led by S.P. Bunting who was zealously supported by the YCL and by the Cape delegation. S. Buirski, one of the leaders of the Cape group, enthusiastically related how the communists were drawing large Bantu audiences in Cape Town. The opposition 'conservative' group, however, was led by W.H. (Bill) Andrews, C.F. Glass and other members of the 'old guard'. They felt that the European workers still represented the most revolutionary force and as such should receive the most attention. The Bunting group, however, triumphed and a few days later Glass 'temporarily' resigned his membership of the party. Early in 1925, Andrews resigned in his capacity as secretary of the communist party, but retained his ordinary membership."[5]

[4] *Cape Argus*, June 11, 1918.

[5] Pike, p. 141.

The decisions taken at this conference were a decisive turning point in the history of communist and black relations in South Africa. Prior to the third conference the party had focused its attentions chiefly on the white workers; in the future the liberation of the black man would be regarded as the most important task of the SACP.

In 1924, a coalition of the National Party and Labor Party defeated the Smuts government at the polls and came to power. On the theory that the new government was an enemy of Britain (based on the anti-British rhetoric of the National Party politicians during the 1924 election campaign), the Comintern ordered the SACP to support the new government. That support didn't last long.

The communists soon fell out with the new government over its labor policy which was designed to protect white workers from the competition of non-white workers.

Emergency conferences were held by the SACP and other groups dissatisfied with the new government's policies. Among those groups meeting with the SACP were the ANC and, for the first time, the South African Indian Congress (SAIC). This was important because the Indian faction was destined, and still continues, to play a role, resented by many blacks,[6] within black politics in South Africa. The Indian faction wields great influence within the ANC and UDF, especially in Natal.

Although there were increasing contacts between the ANC and the communists in South Africa, there were still no formal links between the two groups. That would change in 1927.

In 1927 the two groups forged the first link when Eddie J. Khaile, a member of the SACP Central Committee who had also kept the Party's books, was elected as general secretary of the ANC. Later in the year J.T. Gumede, president of the ANC, traveled to Moscow. Going with him was James LaGuma, a coloured member of the SACP Central Committee.

During this period of time, the Soviets considered Great Britain to be the bastion of capitalism. As such it was the main capitalist enemy. One way to strike a blow against this enemy, Moscow reasoned, was to cripple parts of the British Empire. One way to do this was to use Lenin's concept of national liberation movements to chop off parts of the hated capitalist's Empire. Moscow thought that organizing liberation movements in the various British colonies, including South Africa, would greatly hasten the demise of capitalism. The ANC fitted perfectly into this scheme.

Moscow decided to court the ANC and invited Gumede to the Soviet

[6] See: *Africa Confidential*, Vol. 30, No. 15, July 28, 1989, p. 4.

capital where he was given a hero's welcome. So taken in and impressed by his Soviet hosts was Gumede that he became a valuable Soviet useful idiot, to cite Lenin's term. Upon his return to South Africa, he enthusiastically told crowds when he spoke: "I have seen the world to come, where it has already begun. I have been to the new Jerusalem."[7]

While Gumede was being feted by the Soviets in the "new Jerusalem", LaGuma was having serious talks with Bukharin about the situation in South Africa. At that time Bukharin was the leading light of the Comintern. The Comintern, as part of its effort to strike blows at the British Empire, was drafting plans to overthrow the British and Afrikaner in South Africa and form an "independent, democratic Bantu-Republic."

When Gumede and LaGuma returned to South Africa in February 1928, they brought back with them Moscow's marching orders: "South Africa must become an independent Native (Black) republic as a step towards a workers' and peasants' government".[8]

Stalin's directive was very explicit on what the SACP was to do: ". . . It must explain to the native masses that the black and white workers are not only allies, but are leaders of the revolutionary struggle of the native masses against the white bourgeoisie and British imperialism. A correct formulation of this task and intensive propagation of the chief slogan of a native republic will result not in the alienation of the white workers from the Communist Party, not in segregation of the natives, but, on the contrary, in the building up of a solid united front of all toilers against capitalism and imperialism.

". . . The party should pay particular attention to the embryonic national organizations among the natives, such as the African National Congress. . . . Our aim should be to transform the African National Congress into a fighting nationalist revolutionary organization against the white bourgeoisie and the British imperialists, based upon the trade unions, peasant organizations, etc., developing systematically the leadership of the workers and the Communist Party in this organization. The Party should seek to weaken the influence of the native chiefs . . . by developing peasants' organizations and spreading among them the influence of the Communist Party. . . ."[9]

At the same time Soviet leader Joseph Stalin ordered that all top executive positions in the SACP in the future be occupied by blacks.[10]

[7] Meli, p. 76.

[8] See: *South African Worker*, November 30, 1928.

[9] *The Communist International,* Vol. VI, No. 2, December 15, 1928.

[10] Pike, p. 167.

This bombshell had a stunning effect upon the SACP. On the one hand, as word of it spread, more blacks joined the party. On the other hand, the order sent shock waves through the white leadership of the Party and a split developed in the SACP.

In pursuit of this policy the SACP set about taking control of the ANC. They used classic Leninist strategy in doing it: ". . . If you want to help the 'masses' and win the sympathy and support of the 'masses', you should not fear difficulties, or pinpricks, chicanery, insults and persecution from the 'leaders' (who being opportunists and social-chauvinists, are in most cases directly or indirectly connected with the bourgeoisie and the police), but must absolutely *work wherever the masses are to be found.* You must be capable of any sacrifice, of overcoming the greatest obstacles, in order to carry on agitation and propaganda systematically, perseveringly, persistently and patiently in those institutions, societies and associations—even the most reactionary—in which proletarian or semi-proletarian masses are to be found. . . ."[11]

The Comintern's Black Republic resolution opened the SACP membership to blacks and the Party began recruiting members from existing black organizations into their ranks. Two organizations targeted by the SACP were the ANC and the only existing black trade union in South Africa, the Industrial and Commercial Union (ICU). (Even today these two areas still represent the vast bulk of SACP activity.) The Party gave special attention to individuals recruited from these organizations. They were trained by the SACP to achieve leadership positions in the organizations they belonged to.

One of the black ANC members who joined the SACP in 1928 was the militant J.B. Marks. He absorbed the lessons of Lenin well as he rose through the ranks of the ANC to become its general secretary in 1936. During most of the period (1930-1937), he was also a member of the political bureau of the SACP. Marks had been trained at the Lenin School in Moscow and when he died in Russia in 1972, the Soviets buried him with full honors befitting a hero of the Soviet Union.

The election of Eddie Khaile in 1927 as ANC secretary general had enabled him to exert a tremendous amount of influence on Gumede. Gumede and Khaile even visited the Soviet Union together and, as a result, Gumede took an increasingly pro-Soviet point of view. Pallo Jordan, current ANC National Executive Committee member and a member of the SACP, gives credit to Gumede and Khaile for radicalizing the ANC. It was they, claims

[11] Lenin, V.I., "Left-Wing Communism—An Infantile Disorder", *Selected Works One Volume Edition*, International Publishers, N.Y., 1971, pp. 541-542.

Jordan, who gave the ANC its anti-imperialist and class struggle posture.[12]

The "Black Republic" directive from Moscow had a transforming effect upon the SACP. From a small minority in 1924, blacks became the majority by the end of 1928. Although the rank and file of the SACP were predominantly black, the leadership was in the hands of the whites, as it still is today.

Moscow viewed the black surge of membership in its South African organ with some trepidation. They feared that the mass of poorly educated blacks joining the Party was not steeped enough in the tenets of communism and would weaken party doctrine and discipline, thus corrupting the principles of Marxism-Leninism.

The Comintern reacted by issuing a new order to the SACP to keep the party small as a select body of trained revolutionaries and work through larger mass organizations.[13]

In an attempt to set up a large mass organization as a front from which the SACP could operate, the SACP created the League of African Rights in mid-1929. Though the League was SACP-controlled, it outlined a policy that was broad enough to attract officials from other groups, including the ANC and the ICU. Before the year was over, Moscow changed its mind and sent a message to the SACP "ordering the immediate dissolution of the League."[14]

The coming to power of militant committed non-white communists in the SACP such as J.B. Marks indicated that trouble was brewing for some of the old guard. For now there was to be no toleration for anyone, no matter how long and devoted his past had been to the cause of communism in South Africa, if he deviated one iota from the Party line as laid down by Moscow. Purges followed as predictably as night follows day and many old-line communists such as Bunting, Bill Andrews, Solly Sachs and Bennie Weibren were purged from the party for such heretical acts as being "reform capitalists", "opportunists", "right-wing deviationists", "chauvinists" and other crimes against communism.[15]

Leaving no doubt of their crimes, and to indicate that a new group was in charge, Marks attacked Bunting in the SACP publication *Umsebenzi* saying he and the others purged were "wolves in sheep's clothing who deserved their expulsion from the communist party."[16]

[12] Jordan, Z.P., "Socialist Transformation and the Freedom Charter", *African Journal of Political Economy*, No. 1, 1986, pp. 148-150.

[13] Pike, p. 170.

[14] Roux, E., *S.P. Bunting*, The African Bookman, Cape Town, 1973, p. 144.

[15] Roux, p. 134.

[16] *Umsebenzi*, October 22, 1932.

The growing communist influence in the ANC alarmed the old guard leadership and at its 1930 national convention the ANC replaced Khaile and Gumede. The convention chose Pixley Seme, one of the founding fathers of the ANC as its new head.

Seme was not a revolutionary and he concentrated his efforts in trying to turn the ANC into a self-help organization for blacks.

The great depression had its effects in South Africa. Added to the misery of the economic slump, a severe drought hit the country causing large rural areas to become impoverished. This spurred a migration of farmers from the farms to the cities seeking work. The cities were already swollen with the unemployed and if ever social problems were ripe for exploitation by the Marxists, it was during this period of time.

Unfortunately for the communists, the recent purges had deprived the Party of its ablest people and the ANC was being led by its non-Marxist-sympathizing cautious, conservative old guard. The communists weren't able to take maximum advantage of the situation.

On the political scene the National Party of Hertzog merged with Smuts' South African Party to form the South African United Party, with Hertzog as Prime Minister and Smuts as Deputy Prime Minister. In addition to adopting a policy of looking out for the whites, they also maintained a very active anti-communist attitude.

Not all of Hertzog's members approved of the merger and an important splinter group broke away from his party. They called themselves the Purified National Party. Its leaders included future South African Prime Ministers D. F. Malan and J.G. Stryjdom. In 1948, this new party won the election in South Africa and has ruled the country ever since.

The communists did not roll over and play dead during the depression as they blamed the government then, as now, for every problem facing South Africa. But they were having little success either in radicalizing the masses or influencing liberal trade unions to pursue Marxist policies. Things got so bad for them that their propaganda organ, *Umsebenzi,* ran into financial trouble and soon ceased publishing. In 1939, the SACP moved its headquarters to Cape Town, where it remained until it was banned eleven years later.

Meanwhile the ANC began reassessing its policy direction after 1937 and, under the leadership of Makabane, who had recently been elected president general of the ANC, sought more effective forms of anti-government action.

The late 1930s also witnessed an influx of intellectual blacks into the ANC. They came from the small black middle class and had been educated either in missionary schools or abroad. These intellectuals originally refrained from participating in politics but were becoming more and more disenchanted with the leadership of the ANC and the discriminatory laws advocated by the coalition government of Hertzog and Smuts.

Consequently, young intellectual radicals like Anton Lembede, Nelson Mandela, Oliver Tambo, Walter Sisulu and others started casting a jaundiced eye at, and questioning the motives of, the whites.

These young blacks were well equipped to take over the leadership of the ANC and could redirect and reform the organization from within.

They made their move in 1940 when Dr. Alfred Xuma replaced Makabane as he was out of touch with the developments that were going on all around him within the ANC.

During this period of time other forces were at work in the world that were influencing the activities of the communists in South Africa. War clouds were gathering over Europe which the communists tried to exploit by drumming up public sympathy for the Soviet Union.

Hitler's invasion of Poland on September 3, 1939 provided the spark that ignited the Second World War. Both his Non-Aggression Pact with Stalin and the war caused splits in the South African government and caused major flip-flops in the SACP.

The question of whether or not South Africa should enter the war soon split the Hertzog-Smuts coalition. In the words of one historian, ". . . Hertzog maintained that it was a war between European powers which did not affect South Africa and was in favor of remaining neutral. Smuts, on the other hand, maintained that it was in South Africa's interest to enter the war as an ally of Britain."[17]

Smuts' view prevailed and Hertzog asked the British Governor-General to dissolve Parliament and call an election to choose a new government. The Governor-General refused and, instead, asked Smuts to form a new Cabinet which he did. Smuts then succeeded Hertzog and South Africa entered the war.

The communist party line was to oppose the war on the grounds that it was being fought to prop up the British Empire and thus maintain imperialism. They launched a nationwide anti-war effort. All this changed overnight when Hitler invaded Russia on June 22, 1941.

That event caused a complete turnabout in the attitude of the SACP. No longer was the war a defense of imperialism. Instead it became a people's war and no sacrifice was too great to save the Soviet Union from the evil clutches of Hitler. The Smuts government suddenly found itself with a new ally—the

[17] Muller, C.F.J. (ed), *500 years history of South Africa*, H.R. Academia, 1969, p. 440.

SACP. The Party was now riding high hitching its wagon to the patriotic feelings within South Africa to support their troops at the front. Between 1941 and 1943 the party membership quadrupled.[18]

At no period of its history, before or since, did the Party enjoy such good relations with the South African public as it did during World War II. Taking advantage of its popularity, the Party increased its efforts to infiltrate and seize control of unions and other mass organizations. The Party was hard at work spreading its doctrine of Marxism across South Africa by holding meetings and lectures and distributing masses of communist literature throughout the country.

The communists weren't the only group in South Africa that was moving forward. Under Xuma's leadership the ANC was showing a marked revival. The theoretical basis of this revival was furnished by Anton Lembede. Lembede developed an ideology based on the work of Marcus Garvey. It stressed the necessity of psychological liberation for the blacks, black solidarity, black pride, self-reliance and a go-it-alone attitude. Their course of action was more in line with the Ghandi-Garvey-Martin Luther King strategy of passive resistance than the strategy of violent armed struggle.

Lembede's version of black nationalism struck a responsive chord and served as a means to reach the awakening black masses. Under Lembede's guidance the ANC established its Youth League in 1943. It attracted the young black radicals such as Oliver Tambo and Nelson Mandela.

As part of Lembede's plan of "nation building" and to unify the black middle class with the workers, the Youth League embarked upon a radical program of action in 1949. The program called for civil disobedience, strikes, boycotts, and stay-aways (a very apt South African term for an organized work boycott designed to hurt employers by the simple fact of its labor not showing up for work). This new strategy launched the ANC down the path of extra-legal tactics, mass actions and the principle of non-cooperation.

Among those in leadership positions in the ANC Youth League were Nelson Mandela and Oliver Tambo. It is ironic to point out that during the early years of their involvement with the Youth League both Mandela and Tambo were extremely anti-communist. In fact in 1946, Mandela and Tambo tried to get the ANC to adopt a measure that would forbid any person from belonging to both the ANC and the SACP.

The proposal by these young turks was rejected, in large part, to spare the ANC embarrassment as several of the ANC hierarchy at that time were

[18] Pike, p. 191.

members of the SACP, the most prominent being J.B. Marks and Moses Kotane.

During this period Lembede's ideology of black nationalism was holding sway over the Youth League and Marxism-Leninism was finding barren soil. But not for long, as one of the Youth League officials, Dr. William Nkomo, soon started injecting Marxism into the mainstream of the Youth League.

Soon many members of the League became open Marxists, partially because of Nkomo but mostly because of the influence of one man—Moses Kotane. He had recently replaced Xuma as head of the ANC. At the same time as he took over the leadership of the ANC, Kotane was the general secretary of the SACP. Kotane's influence on the leaders of the Youth League soon became enormous: "There can be no doubt whatsoever that the work of Kotane and other Communists in the ANC allayed many of the fears of African nationalists about Communism as a 'foreign ideology'. There was nothing foreign about Kotane, a down-to-earth impressive personality whose love and loyalty to the African nation none ever had cause to question. The work of the Communists also helped to convince many Congressmen that class and national oppression in South Africa were closely allied, and recognition of this fact was reflected in many ANC policy documents in the subsequent decades."

"The co-operation between Lembede, the leading figure among young African nationalists, and Kotane at the conference was symptomatic of the greatly improved relations between individual ANC Youth League members and the Communist Party members of the ANC brought about by their common association in political action. . . .

"Many of the Youth Leaguers were to change their attitude towards Communists in the succeeding years; some were even to join the Communist Party, seeing in it a logical extension of the work they were doing in Congress. Before he died, at the tragically early age of 33, Lembede had also changed his attitude towards the Communist Party. 'They are workers, not just talkers', he admitted grudgingly to Kotane. Oliver Tambo, later to be acting President General of the ANC after the death of Chief Lutuli, today admits that it was acquaintance with Kotane which changed his ideas about the participation of Communists in the ANC. Tambo, who had been one of the sponsors of the anti-communist motions in the Transvaal ANC in 1945, first met Kotane at one of the annual ANC conferences in Bloemfontein which followed. . . ."[19]

The postwar years saw an increase in communist agitation which led to violence. The SACP tried every means possible to foment trouble. With

[19] Bunting, B., *Moses Kotane*, Inkululeko Publications, London, 1975, pp. 138-139.

thousands of recently released soldiers seeking work, plus the rising cost of living, it seemed fertile ground for the Party to exploit.

In April 1946, the African Mineworkers went on strike. Led by the communist J.B. Marks, 50,000 blacks eventually took part in the strike. It took the efforts of 1,500 policemen to contain the violence in which nine black miners were killed and scores injured. The strike was the largest upheaval orchestrated by the communists after the Second World War. It was, however, instrumental in leading to their partial downfall when the National Party took power after the 1948 elections.

During the same period of time a riot broke out in Durban between blacks and the Indians, who had a large community in the city. "Arising out of the chance striking of an African boy by an Indian shopkeeper, the riots enveloped most of Durban, as . . . Africans burned many Indian homes, all too often with their families inside."[20]

The Indians fought back and many pitched battles ensued between blacks and Indians: "The casualties were appalling, no less than 87 Zulus and 50 Indians being killed and nearly 1,100 injured. Slum conditions form the background to the riots and although communists were not always the instigators, there was little doubt that they were exploiting an explosive situation."[21]

A strong anti-communist theme was one of the features of the National Party's campaign against the Smuts government during the 1948 election campaign. It was one key factor in their victory.

During 1949, the ANC Youth League drafted a program condemning the National Party's apartheid program and called for action to fight it in the form of strikes and civil disobedience.

Dr. Xuma did not agree with all of the League's recommendations. Flexing its muscle within the ANC, the Youth League and its supporters engineered the ouster of Xuma and replaced him with J.S. Moroka. The mood of the ANC was becoming increasingly militant.

In 1949, South Africa was again racked by riots and demonstrations and the SACP was involved in them up to their proverbial necks. The new government was determined to do something about it.

Early in 1950, the SACP and the ANC decided to hold nationwide demonstrations for blacks but the South African government banned the demonstrations. The communists ignored the ban and widespread violence

[20] Cater, G.M., *The Politics of Inequality*, Thames and Hudson, London, 1958, p. 361.

[21] Kruger, D. W., *The Making of a Nation—A History of the Union of South Africa, 1910-1961*, MacMillan, Johannesburg, 1969, p. 256.

occurred on April 26, 1950 on the Rand. Eighteen people were killed and many were injured in the communist-sponsored demonstrations.

This was the last straw as far as the National government was concerned. When the National Party had come to power after the 1948 elections, it had established a Parliamentary committee to investigate the activities of the communists in South Africa. It submitted a report stating that communism constituted a national danger in South Africa.[22]

On May 6, 1950, the Minister of Justice, Mr. C.R. Swart, introduced the Suppression of Communism Bill in Parliament. It quickly passed and became law—the communist party in South Africa was no longer a legal entity.

The banning of the communist party in South Africa had important consequences as far as the so-called national liberation movement was concerned: "After the Communist Party was banned in 1950, African communists turned naturally to the ANC, of which most were already members, seeing it the best remaining outlet for their energies."[23]

Even though the new law had outlawed it, the SACP didn't just dry up and blow away. Instead, the party went underground, creating front organizations through which it continued operating.

The SACP used the banning to finally seal their pact with the ANC. At the same time the ANC executive council was moved to declare: "It (the Suppression of Communism Act) is primarily directed against Africans and other oppressed people and is designed to frustrate all their attempts to work for the fulfillment of their legitimate demands and aspirations."[24]

After the banning of the Communist Party, the communists moved rapidly to entrench their positions in, not only the ANC, but almost the entire opposition in South Africa. This was done by the formation of the Congress Alliance which was set up to lay the groundwork for drafting the basic revolutionary document in the continuing struggle for power in South Africa —the Freedom Charter.

[22] Pike, p. 265.

[23] Gerhart, G. M., *Black Power in South Africa*, University of California Press, Berkeley, 1978, p. 87.

[24] Bunting, p. 218.

5

CEMENTING THE SACP/ANC ALLIANCE

The Suppression of Communism Act sent the SACP underground with the strategy to infiltrate and take control of all kinds of national organizations. Their aim was to manipulate these groups for communist ends. They gravitated to national havens such as the African National Congress (ANC), the South African Indian Congress (SAIC) and the South African Congress of Trade Unions (SACTU). Since the communists were already members of these groups, the infusion of new communist blood from the banned SACP increased the influence the Party already had within them.

Previous South African governments had enacted legislation to control riotous agitation and behavior. The Riotous Assemblies and Criminal Law Amendment Act of 1914, the Bantu Administration Act of 1927 and the Riotous Assemblies Act of 1930, and other legislation, all were aimed at actual riot situations but didn't address the conspiratorial acts of those such as the communists, who planned and instigated the riots. The Suppression of Communism Act, and its succeeding amendments solved that problem.

As emergency situations arose in dealing with further communist-inspired action, the government added various amendments to the law. The 1951 amendment dealt with "communist persons" rather than "doctrines" as in the original 1950 law. The new law widened the scope to cover anyone who had professed to be a communist or had promoted the aims of communism.[1]

[1] du Toit, M.A., *South African Trade Unions: History, Legislation, Policy*, McGraw-Hill, Johannesburg, 1976, p. 18.

The 1951 amendment also applied retroactively to anyone who had ever been a communist.[2] The 1954 amendment prohibited publishing, recording or disseminating the writings or speeches of banned persons.[3] The 1962 amendment included "house arrests" under the coverage of the Act. Under these further amendments, banning orders covered a wide range of restrictions such as restricting a person to a specified area, town or even part of town, and allowing no communication of any type with another banned person.

The ANC Youth League's 1949 Program of Action led to a series of protest demonstrations which culminated in the ANC's Defiance Campaign of 1952. One of the leaders of the campaign was Nelson Mandela. He was in charge of recruiting "volunteers" to take part in the campaign.

The ANC's program of action called for a national work stoppage campaign. This idea led to a serious, as well as virtually the last, overt clash between the African nationalists and the communists within the ANC. The communists called for a strike in the Johannesburg area for May Day 1950, which Mandela and his allies felt was a blatant effort to pre-empt the ANC program in order for the communists to curry favor with black workers. The controversy escalated to violence as communist goon squads soon broke up non-communist meetings and the communists were, at the same time, being roundly attacked in ANC publications.

The communists retaliated in the war of words by criticizing the ANC's program as being crude. They tempered their criticism, however, with the admonition that communists should nevertheless support the ANC and guide it in the interests of unity of action. This unified action would be in opposition to racial discrimination and capitalism.

A coordinating committee was set up to plan the course of unified action. The committee included members of the Youth League, SAIC and SACP. The communists knew there were elements within the ANC that mistrusted them. In order to placate that opposition and pull its sting, the SACP sent Moses Kotane to Johannesburg as its secretary. He quickly established friendships with Mandela and Tambo and quickly convinced them he was really a nationalist.

In February 1951, the ANC, SAIC and the African Peoples Organization —a group representing the coloured in South Africa— called for a meeting of some thirty-two organizations in Cape Town. The object of the meeting was

[2] Rotbery, R. I., *Towards a Certain Future*, David Phillips Publishers, Cape Town, 1981, p. 38.

[3] Coetzee, J. A. G., *Industrial Relations in South Africa*, Juta & Co. Ltd., Cape Town, 1976, pp. 42-43.

to discuss options to follow in opposing the National Party government's new apartheid policy. A campaign of massive resistance was the principal fruit of the meeting. A joint Planning Committee was created to work out the organizational details of the resistance campaign. The committee members were: J.S. Moroka, J.B. Marks, Walter Sisulu, Dr. Y.M. Dadoo and Y.A. Cachalia. All but Moroka were communists.[4]

Pike points out: "In organizing the campaign, they envisioned forcing the government firstly to compromise with the organizers, and secondly, to arouse sympathy overseas for the 'oppressed' non-Europeans in South Africa."[5]

The organizers launched the Defiance Campaign on June 26, 1952. The ANC planned to get 10,000 volunteers to practice civil disobedience by violating laws which the ANC considered objectionable. The volunteers were to court arrest and imprisonment by their actions. The ANC reasoned that so many mass arrests would overcrowd the prisons. The police and judicial machinery would break down from being overwhelmed by the numbers it would suddenly have to cope with. Facing such chaotic conditions, the ANC thought, the government would be forced to modify the laws opposed by the ANC. In theory, it may have sounded like a plausible course of action, but reality turned out to be quite a different kettle of fish. The campaign ended about eight months later when the authorities arrested about sixty leaders of the ANC and SAIC—among them were a large number of known communists.

What had prompted the arrests was the fact that on several occasions the demonstrations had degenerated into ugly, violent riots that had resulted in serious loss of life and much destruction of property. After the ringleaders were arrested, the demonstrations abruptly stopped.

Although the Defiance Campaign failed in its goal to disrupt and change governmental apartheid policy, it did succeed in gaining thousands of new members for the ANC. This new influx of members had enabled the ANC, by 1952, to truly become a mass movement. Playing leading roles in the mass movement were the leaders of the soon to emerge Congress Alliance and the Communist Party.

The Defiance Committee had not achieved the ANC's goals, so it was back to the drawing board to plan their next move.

A prominent ANC member, Z.K. Mathews, returned from a visit to the USA in May 1953. He suggested that the ANC convene a national convention

[4] Pike, p. 280.

[5] *Ibid.*

composed of representatives of all of South Africa's racial groups to develop a plan of action. His idea was adopted by the Cape provincial conference of the ANC and was accepted by the national conference in December 1953.[6]

The organizers labeled the conference the Congress of the People (COP). It was supposed to represent a grassroots gathering of the people of South Africa and was scheduled to meet on June 25-26, 1955.

Within two months of Mathews' suggestion, activists formed two new national organizations: the South Africa Coloured People's Organization (SACPO) and the Congress of Democrats (COD)—an all white communist front. Both were to participate in the COP and became members of the umbrella group coordinating the COP—the Congress Alliance.[7]

These two new groups were formed as a direct result of suggestions by the ANC and SAIC that whites and coloureds ally themselves with the plan of the ANC.

The Suppression of Communism Act forced the known communists to leave the registered trade unions, causing the SACP to lose its influence in them. To overcome this loss, it created a new trade union movement in March 1955, the South African Congress of Trade Unions (SACTU).

SACTU was affiliated with the Soviet-controlled World Federation of Trade Unions (WFTU) and has received substantial aid from the World Council of Churches (WCC). It is thoroughly penetrated by communists and as a result of its banning it now operates from London, England and Lusaka, Zambia. Its legal counterpart in South Africa is the Congress of South African Trade Unions (COSATU), which plays a major role in the leftist-dominated Mass Democratic Movement within South Africa.

Not all whites opposed to the National Party government's policies were communists or communist-sympathizers. Many were genuinely concerned over the future course of black-white relations in South Africa. They had been active in the early anti-apartheid movement but were becoming alarmed over the growing communist influence in the movement and the growing polarization between the races in South Africa. They founded a new political party, the Liberal Party (LP) in South Africa. "The members of the party . . . wanted a multi-racial society in which all would have the vote. In this regard, they were therefore in agreement with the communists, but in other aspects they differed radically from them."[8]

[6] Bunting, p. 197.

[7] Kanit, T., & Carter, G.M., *From Protest to Challenge, Vol. III*, Hoover Institution Press, Stanford, 1972, p. 12.

[8] Muller, p. 496.

While some of the LP leaders claimed they were not communists, they tolerated the communist presence and at times cooperated with them. Within the LP there was a mixture of conservatives, moderates and even members of the SACP.

The SACP had instructed its members, upon its banning, that, "in order to prepare the ground for a violent national democratic revolution in South Africa, the SACP members would have to work with the Congress Alliance and the Liberal Party."[9]

The LP suffered one crippling election defeat after another and finally disbanded in 1968. Its only significance in the political history of South Africa was that, although most of its members claimed to be pacifists—as do so many liberals of today throughout the world—their attitudes and actions more often than not incited violence and promoted the causes of predominantly left-wing violent revolutionary organizations.

Lenin considered liberals as potential allies: "We welcome . . . the liberals . . . with our movement . . . support them by exposing all the despicable acts of the government and the local authorities, and try to induce them to support the revolution."[10]

In 1952 at the ANC's annual conference a black South African Zulu was named president of the organization. He was to gain international fame by being awarded the Nobel Peace Prize in 1961. Albert John Luthuli was the quintessential liberal behind whose back the socialists and communists could carry out their scheme of taking over the ANC.

Luthuli gained nationwide fame by using his position as Zulu Chief of the Grautville Reserve in Natal as a vehicle to give open support to the rioters and demonstrators during the Defiance Campaign.

In 1951, he became head of the Natal branch of the ANC. This brought him in conflict with the Nationalist government which ordered him to resign from the ANC. Luthuli refused and in November 1952 the government dismissed him from his position as one of the Zulu chiefs. His dismissal gave him nationwide publicity and this, coupled with his prior support of the Defiance Campaign, increased his stature immeasurably among the blacks. So much was his stature enhanced that at its annual conference the following month Luthuli was named president of the ANC. It was an office he would hold until his death in 1967.

Unlike the early Mandela or Tambo, Luthuli had no concern about

[9] Pike, p. 288; see also: Ludi, G., *Operation Q-018*, Nasionale Boekhandel, Cape Town, 1969.

[10] Lenin, V.I., *Collected Works, Vol. 5*, Moscow, n.d., p.79.

communists in either South Africa or the ANC. "There are communists in the South African resistance, and I co-operate with them," said Luthuli.[11]

Serving on the executive committee of the ANC when Luthuli became president were five communists including Moses Kotane. Luthuli was also a member of the World Peace Council, a noted international Soviet front. When the Soviet Union's most infamous mass-murderer, Joseph Stalin, died Luthuli sent a lengthy eulogy to Moscow lamenting the late dictator.[12] Although Luthuli professed not to be a communist,[13] he had a very blasé attitude towards them which allowed them to work unhindered within the ANC.

Luthuli continually clashed with the South African government and, as a result, was banned in 1952, again in 1954 and 1959. These bannings were important as they allowed de facto control of the ANC to pass from his hand into those who were sympathizers, collaborators or actual communist members of the ANC.

ANC policies were soon reflecting the increased communist influence within the organization. Black nationalism was being abandoned for multi-racialism for the simple reason that black nationalism couldn't be reconciled with the Marxian concept of class conflict. Multi-racialism, however, in the South African environment, was an essential precondition to the acceptance of the class analysis and that was how Marxists viewed the world. Marxists couldn't change their basic views to conform to the original nationalism of the ANC. Therefore, the ANC must change its views to bring them into conformity with the Marxists, and this is what they did.

The ANC moved to improve and increase its cooperation with other non-black organizations, in the spirit of multi-racialism. These included SAIC (by this time heavily infiltrated with SACP members), the all-white COD, the legal front of the banned communist party as its leadership was dominated by former members of the SACP, as well as the COP.

These three organizations and the ANC formally aligned themselves in a grandly named and promoted Congress Alliance. It was to organize and hold a mass meeting à la Mathews to approve a charter which was supposed to be the result of grassroots input generated by the Alliance. The meeting was to be held in Kliptown near Johannesburg to approve the document later known as the Freedom Charter.

[11] Luthuli, A., *Let My People Go*, Collins, Fontana Books, London, 1962, pp. 137-138.

[12] Harrigan, A., *Red Star Over Africa*, Nasional Boekhandel, Cape Town, 1964, p. 49.

[13] Luthuli, p. 137.

The grassroots involvement was a charade. Popular consultation did not shape the Charter. The dominant influence in the drafting of the Charter was the COD. The actual drafting was done by a small committee whose membership was kept secret from Luthuli.[14]

Jordon K. Ngubane, a founder of the ANC Youth League, threw cold water on the idea that Luthuli was the father of the Freedom Charter: "Luthuli himself had not known who had drafted the Charter. The bosses of the underground Communist Party did the planning and made policy decisions. They approached men like Luthuli and other non-communist leaders . . . to acquaint them with what had already been decided. . . ."[15]

After months of tireless preparation, much fanfare and organization, the Congress met. Instead of the anticipated 200,000, only 2,844 showed up from all over South Africa.[16] The organizers unveiled the Charter. Since Luthuli was banned and restricted to his abode in Natal, he was not at the meeting. Neither he nor Mathews, who had originated the idea of the Congress, nor Dr. Wilson Conco, Luthuli's deputy who presided over the Congress, saw a copy of the Charter before it was made public.[17]

The delegates acclaimed the Charter, clause by clause, by a show of hands. There was no discussion, no questions permitted, no mechanism for proposing, discussing or adopting amendments—just a here it is, take it attitude. The delegates took it exactly as presented.

Many today view the document as the blueprint for a future South Africa that expresses the desire for implementing human rights reforms in South Africa. Others, keeping in mind who were involved in its drafting are less enthusiastic about its contents. In fact if it is read in the context of the Marxist ideological worldview, the document is clearly riddled with Marxian solutions for South Africa's problems. As such, it becomes not a blueprint for freedom and progress but one for the normal tyranny, degradation and stagnation that go with a Marxist state.

The two most blatant, although certainly not the only, examples of Marxist phraseology are: "The national wealth of our country . . . shall be restored to the people. The mineral wealth beneath the soil, the banks and the monopoly industry shall be transferred to the people as a whole", . . . and,

[14] Campbell, K., *ANC: A Soviet Task Force?*, Institute For The Study of Terrorism, London, 1986, p. 36.

[15] Ngubane, J.K., *An African Explains Apartheid*, Frederick A. Praeger, New York, 1963, pp. 162-166.

[16] Muller, p. 497.

[17] Campbell, p. 36.

"imprisonment shall be only for serious crimes against the people, and shall aim at re-education and not vengeance."[18] Just such measures were put into practice by Pol Pot's Khmer Rouge regime in Cambodia. The whole world knows what happened in that tragic land.

If any proof were needed that the Freedom Charter is a blueprint for a Marxist South Africa consider the words of support for it by the SACP: "The Communist Party pledges its unqualified support for the Freedom Charter. It considers that the achievement of its aims will answer the pressing and immediate needs of the people and *lay the indispensable basis for the advance of our country along non-capitalist lines to a communist and socialist future.*" [emphasis added][19]

The SACP has not backed away from this position. Speaking on the occasion of the Party's 65th anniversary, July 30, 1986, Chairman Joe Slovo said: "We believe that the kind of victory to be aimed for in the coming struggle must provide a launching pad for the creation of conditions which will make it possible to work for a socialist future. . . . The main thrust and content of the immediate struggle continues to revolve around the Freedom Charter. . . . In expressing support for the Freedom Charter our 1962 Programme states that it is not a program for socialism but . . . at the same time, the Programme *insists the Freedom Charter will provide a basis for an advance to a socialist future.*" [emphasis added][20]

The ANC, in fact, has gone to great lengths to stress that the Freedom Charter is not a cry for socialism. It must do this or its support from Western sources would diminish. However, their writings on the Charter put that claim to rest as nothing more than a blatant lie.

Thabo Mbeki, a member of the ANC National Executive Committee, considered a "ANC moderate" and possible successor to Oliver Tambo as head of the ANC told listeners in a 1978 speech in Ottawa, Canada, how the ANC views the Charter in an ANC-liberated South Africa: ". . . we shall define our position as follows:

"• We are producers of wealth;

[18] Ludi, G., & Grobbelaar, B., *The Amazing Mr. Fischer*, Cape Town, 1966, p. 149.

[19] "The Road to South African Freedom: Programme of the South African Communist Party" adopted at the Fifth national conference of the Party, 1962; in: *South African Communists Speak: Documents from the History of the South African Communist Party 1915-1980*, Inkululeko Publications, London, 1981, p. 314.

[20] *South African Communist Party-African National Congress: An Alliance Forged in Struggle: Speeches by Alfred Nzo Secretary General of the African National Congress and Joe Slovo Chairman of the South African Communist Party at the 65th Anniversary Meeting of the South African Communist Party, London, July 30th 1986*, Inkululeko Publications, London, 1986, p. 9.

"• We produce this wealth for our own benefit to be appropriated by us, the producers;

"• The Aim of this production shall be the satisfaction, at an increasing level of the material and spiritual needs of the people;

"• We shall so order the rest of society and social activity, in education and culture, in the legal sphere, on military questions, in our international relations, etc, to conform to these goals."[21]

Behind the fog of Mbeki's rhetoric the message is clear: the Charter will be used by the ANC to establish a people's democracy—leftist jargon for a one-party socialist state.

Mbeki made that clear further on in his speech by issuing a call to revolution in clear, concise Marxist terms: "This is a call to revolution. This revolution is necessary, as Marx and Engels once said, 'not only because the ruling class cannot be overthrown in any other way, but also because the class overthrowing it can only in a revolution succeed in ridding itself of all the muck of ages and become fitted to found society anew.' "[22]

Alfred Nzo, Secretary General of the ANC, equated the concepts in the Freedom Charter with those motivating such totalitarian Marxist states as Angola, Ethiopia and Mozambique. "If many of the demands and concepts of the Freedom Charter have become essential elements of African and Asian states today, if they are already becoming living realities in the lives of the peoples of Angola, Mozambique, Ethiopia and other African countries dedicated to a new social order free from discrimination and exploitation, it is because our freedom struggle is an integral part of the world-wide struggle against racism, colonialism and imperialism, for peace, independence and social progress."[23]

The people of Angola, Ethiopia and Mozambique obviously aren't too impressed with the "concepts of the Freedom Charter" in their respective countries. They are living in misery, plagued by famine and are conducting liberation wars to rid themselves of their hated Marxist masters and their version of the Freedom Charter.

Finally, and not to belabor the point: "The South African Communist Party, whose members are striving not only for national liberation but finally for the destruction of the capitalist system itself, also agree with the demands

[21] Mbeki, T., "The Historical Injustice," *Selected Writings on The Freedom Charter, 1955-1985*, African National Congress, London, 1985, pp. 46-47.

[22] Mbeki, p. 49.

[23] Nzo, A., "The Freedom Charter, A Beacon to the People of South Africa", *Selected Writings on The Freedom Charter 1955-1985*, African National Congress, London, 1985, pp. 62-63.

of the Freedom Charter, for they are quite aware that the black working class needs freedom from national oppression. Led by the ANC in alliance with the SACP, our people demand nothing less than complete transfer of political power to the people, which implies the immediate overthrow of racist autocracy, of the colonial state of national domination and its replacement by a state of the whole people.

"To establish such a people's democratic republic in South Africa, it is absolutely necessary that the political sovereignty be vested in a revolutionary people's assembly. . . . It is in pursuance of this political goal, one which cannot come about unless our democratic revolution has achieved complete victory over the apartheid regime, that our revolution is aiming at political seizure of power.

"A people's assembly that can have the power to create a new constitution for South Africa, . . . can only be an outcome of a victorious mass insurrection, a conquering political and military force of the armed masses led by the African National Congress and the People's Army, *Umkhonto we Sizwe*. It is this kind of assembly alone, born of a revolutionary victory by the whole people, that is capable of achieving the aims of the Freedom Charter and subsequently of defending the new state of people's democracy against racist and imperialist counter-revolution."[24]

Similar sentiments have led to misery, loss of freedom and genocide throughout the world where kissed by the curse of Marxism.

Given the overwhelming support and endorsements of the Freedom Charter by those who advocate a totalitarian system for South Africa, it is reasonable to conclude that the Charter is a blueprint for a communist-style freedom. "When the ANC/SACP Marxist-Leninist alliance asks you for freedom they do it because it is your concept and principle. When you ask them for freedom they will not grant you real freedom, because it has never been one of their concepts or principles."[25]

Most of this activity was going on in response to the Nationalist government's institutionalizing apartheid, or separate development based on

[24] Mzala (a Zulu word for friend), "The Freedom Charter and Its Relevance Today", *Selected Writings on The Freedom Charter 1955-1985*, African National Congress, London, 1985, pp. 91-92.

[25] Booyse, W.J., "A Critique of Crucial Concepts in The Freedom Charter", *Southern African Freedom Review, Vol. II, No. 1,* International Freedom Foundation, Washington, D.C., 1987, p. 18. This is an excellent analysis of the main points of the Freedom Charter; see also: Campbell, K., "A Commentary on the Freedom Charter", in, *ANC: A Soviet Task Force?*, Institute For The Study of Terrorism, London, 1986, pp. 36-43. These two studies make it clear that the Charter is heavily dosed throughout with Marxian concepts.

racial segregation. Legislation to implement apartheid included the Mixed Marriage Act of 1949, which prohibited interracial marriage; the Population Registration and Group Areas Act (1950), which classified a person as to race—white, black or coloured—and restricted areas of habitation for each group, the most noted being the black homelands; the Separate Amenities and Bantu Education Acts (1953), which segregated public accommodations and set up a separate education system for the blacks and coloureds.

It goes without saying, that the Nationalist government at that time firmly believed, and had an overwhelming mandate in 1953 from the white electorate, that black domination in South Africa was not acceptable.

While the first two Nationalist Prime Ministers, D.F. Malan (1948-1954) and J.G. Stryjdom (1954-1958) were in office, it was never suggested that the black homelands would develop into semi-autonomous states. Both viewed the whites as being the guardians of the blacks and that this situation would be the case far into the future.

Even the future Prime Minister, who is viewed in the West as the father of apartheid, Dr. H.F. Verwoerd, who as Minister of Native Affairs in 1951 gave the homelands a greater measure of self-rule, expressly denied that his policy would lead to independent black states.

Shortly after becoming Prime Minister in 1958 he changed his tune. He conceded that his policy could lead to the creation of a number of independent black states in South Africa. This has actually happened although no one outside of the South African government recognizes them as independent entities.

Verwoerd defended this switch with the argument that he preferred a small white South Africa to a large black South Africa.

It was against this background that events were taking place in South Africa involving both blacks and whites. Yet, in spite of their claims, the ANC/SACP course of action was not only opposed by the whites, but there was black opposition to it as well. In fact the opposition rose to a point that a split occurred, shattering the unity facade of black opposition to the white government in South Africa.

Let us now turn our attention to that split.

6

ANC—PAC SPLIT

The Congress Movement didn't stop its activity with the adoption of the Freedom Charter. In 1958, it once again decided to mount a new campaign, this time in cooperation with the South African Congress of Trade Unions (SACTU). The campaign was centered around advocating a minimum wage for black workers. If this wage demand wasn't met, the SACTU and the Congress would call a nationwide strike.

Government opposition and a lack of interest by black workers doomed the strike to an embarrassing failure for its organizers.

In 1958, the ANC revised its constitution to incorporate the Freedom Charter in it. This didn't sit too well with the Africanists in the ANC. They sarcastically claimed the mania for the Charter in the ANC had resulted from, ". . . vodka cocktail parties of Parktown and Lower-Houghton. (These were high-class Johannesburg white suburbs where several communist party white members resided.)"[1]

Their bitterness at the shape of events taking place in the ANC led a group of the Black Power advocates within the ANC to attempt a takeover of the organization. They were led by Robert Sobukwe, a lecturer at Witswatersrand University, in Johannesburg. He had joined the ANC Youth League in 1948 and had been an outspoken supporter of the Defiance Campaign. His appointment to the university teaching post did not cool his ardor for revolutionary politics. He was soon committed to the Black Power agenda

[1] Gerhart, p. 156.

and was advocating an all-black position for the ANC. He was opposed to opening ANC membership to other race groups in South Africa.

Matters came to a head at the November 1958 meeting of the Transvaal ANC conference. After a heated confrontation at the meeting including accusations that the ANC leadership were people of "leftist inclination" and that the organization was blind to emerging African nationalism, the ANC expelled the Africanists.

Sobukwe then formed the Pan African Congress (PAC). Its aim was to set up a government of black Africans, run by black Africans for black Africans. The other oppressed groups, in Sobukwe's view, should emulate the PAC and unite on their own and fight as a separate racial group—the Indians should form an all Indian group and the Coloureds an all coloured group.

Sobukwe was a dynamic figure and a powerful orator. Under his leadership the PAC, in a year's time, was almost as powerful and popular as the ANC.

The ANC didn't like this new turn of events one bit. A bitter rivalry quickly developed as both organizations vied with one another for influence and power among the blacks. "When in December 1959, the ANC decided to start a campaign of resistance against the pass laws on 31 March 1960, the PAC decided to begin a similar protest campaign ten days earlier, on 21 March 1960."[2]

Not only was there rivalry between the two groups but both groups detested each other.

"The PAC has made a lot of noise internationally but very little inside South Africa . . .", said Francis Meli, SACP member and editor of the ANC's monthly magazine *Sechaba*.[3]

"The PAC claimed 'to be the direct heir and legitimate successor to the original Congress which was founded in 1912'. This they justified claiming that the ANC has been undermined by the birth of the multi-racial Congress Alliance in the 1950's, and was finally destroyed when it adopted the Freedom Charter. . . ."[4]

The ANC accused the PAC of ". . . breaking the broad democratic front of patriotic forces which the ANC was painstakingly built *(sic)*. . . ."[5]

Not only that, the PAC was committing ideological heresy because ". . . there was no class analysis . . ." and ". . . negating our experiences and our

[2] Muller, C.F.J., *500 Years South African History*, H.R. Academia, Pretoria, 1969, p. 499.

[3] Meli, F., *South Africa Belongs to Us; A History of the ANC*, p. 137.

[4] *Ibid.*

[5] Meli, pp. 138-139.

contribution to the African revolution and therefore moving against the tide of history and the African revolution. . . ."[6]

The ANC's Walter Sisulu chimed in by condemning the PAC and suggesting they were in cahoots with the ruling National Party: ". . . It would be foolish to imagine that a wave of black chauvinism, provoked by the savagery of the Nationalist Party (and perhaps secretly encouraged and financed by it too) may not some day sweep through our country. . . ."[7]

The PAC, in turn, accused the ANC of being a "union of the exploiters and the exploited"[8] and that the ANC has " betrayed the material interests of the African people. They have sacrificed these interests upon the political altar of an ungodly alliance, an alliance of slave-owners, slave driver and slave"[9]—the essence of foreign involvement in African affairs. Furthermore, the PAC charged, black members and leaders of the ANC were "self-confessed lackeys and flunkies of the white ruling class and the Indian merchant class" *[still creating problems in black politics in South Africa —ed.]* led by a " white pseudo-leftist directorate."[10]

The ANC has committed the ultimate sin, in the PAC's view, by being nothing more than Soviet stooges under the leadership of the white-led SACP. Their claimed alliance was actually working against the interests of the people of Azania, the PAC's name for South Africa.

"Enthusiastically taking up the Soviet line, the SACP and the ANC energetically avoided and backhandedly attacked all the upsurges among the Azanian people between 1956 and 1961. Instead of waging people's war, the SACP and ANC actively promoted reliance on the United Nations for the solution to imperialist oppression in Azania. . . ."[11]

Such accusations back and forth led each group to come up with new tactics in order to outdo the other.

This rivalry was to lead to a tragic event as the PAC took an immediate militant stance against the government which meant the ANC and its allies had to follow suit.

[6] Meli, p. 139.

[7] Meli, p. 140.

[8] Meli, p. 137.

[9] *Ibid.*

[10] *Ibid.*

[11] "Revisionism and Southern Africa: An Expose of the African National Congress and The South African Communist Party", Revolutionary Reprints, No. RR 102, Revolutionary Communist Party, USA, Chicago, n.d., p. 8.

Violent demonstrations and strikes became common occurrences as the SACP, the ANC and the PAC cadres were doing their utmost to turn every possible incident into physical confrontation and conflict in order not to lose face with their supporters and risk losing their support to one of their rivals.

The fateful step was taken when both organizations decided, as mentioned earlier, to organize an anti-pass law campaign for 1960.

The PAC's plan was to escalate and use the campaign so that it would peak in 1963, when the government would collapse, so they reasoned, and an African Socialist Democratic state would be installed in its place.

It didn't go according to plan.

In January 1960, a rioting crowd killed a policeman in Cato Manor, a black township in Durban. On March 21st the anti-pass law campaign crossed its Rubicon and tragedy struck. It happened at Sharpesville, a black township near Vereeniging, where fifty-nine years before the peace treaty had ended the Boer War.

A crowd numbering about 10,000 blacks descended upon the local police station. The crowd had been stirred up by fiery oration and advanced on the station armed with sticks, clubs, bottles, knives, spears, iron pipes, *pangas* (an African version of the machete) and other weapons.

In 1961, there were standing orders allowing the police to use their firearms when the safety of the police station was threatened. This gave the commander in charge the discretion to decide what constituted the minimum force necessary to control the situation. Unfortunately, words such as "minimum force" were difficult to define in the presence of an excited mob. Even when properly handled, mob control is a difficult job at best. And not every mob is properly handled. Viewing the chanting, frenzied crowd advancing on them, the handful of officers at the station panicked and opened fire. When the shooting stopped, 69 blacks were dead and 178 were wounded.[12]

The Sharpesville shootings reverberated throughout South Africa and around the world. Riots and protests erupted in the black townships such as Soweto and Langa.

Both the ANC and PAC leadership seized on the tragic event to advance their own agendas. The ANC even blamed the PAC as the cause of the incident.[13] Both groups called for a national day of mourning and urged blacks

[12] See: *Rand Daily Mail*, March 22, 1961.

[13] "Revisionism and Southern Africa", p. 9; see also: Vermaak, C., *Red Trap*, APB Publishers, Johannesburg, 1966, p. 40.

to stay away from work. The PAC was able to mobilize 25,000 blacks to attend a protest in Cape Town.

The government swung into action. On March 30th it declared a state of emergency in sixty percent of the country's magisterial districts. The National Party government quickly enacted the Unlawful Organizations Act (No. 34 of 1960) which, on April 8, 1960, permitted the banning of both the ANC and the PAC. Along with this legislation, the government placed a ban on public meetings, which lasted from March 24th until the end of June, 1960.

These measures had their effect and the riots and violence quickly subsided. By the end of August the state of emergency had been lifted in South Africa.

The government took legal action against the leaders of both organizations and sentenced many to prison.

The banning of the ANC and PAC following in the wake of the Sharpeville incident brought severe worldwide criticism upon the government of South Africa.

The banning of the ANC forced it to revise its strategies and tactics. It opted to launch a revolutionary war against the South African government.

7

UNDERGROUND

As the decade of the 1950s drew to a close the SACP, ANC and their radical front organizations found themselves either in exile or forced to go underground. Those who eventually chose to go underground included Nelson Mandela. He had been a leading organizer of the ANC and soon would be on the run from the law. The prevailing attitude was to continue the struggle in South Africa in the form of mass demonstrations, boycotts and strikes on the one hand, but at the same time to prepare militants to resort to violence.[1]

Other ANC leaders beside Mandela who went underground were Walter Sisulu, the secretary general of the ANC, and Govan Mbeki, a member of the ANC National Executive Committee. SACP members who decided to continue operations in cooperation with the ANC included Joe Slovo. Slovo was a solid pro-Soviet communist who later allegedly achieved a high rank in the KGB. He was the mastermind behind the ANC terror campaign.

Others were architect Lionel Goldberg, who, with Arthur Goldreich, was a member of the ANC high command and its soon to be formed military wing; and Harold Wolpe, a high ANC intelligence official, to name just a few.

Goldreich and Wolpe had known each other since the late 1940s when Wolpe had been a lecturer in Sociology at Witswatersrand University and Goldreich was chairman of the Liberal Students' Association. They were dedicated communists whose goal was the overthrow of the South African government and its replacement with a Marxist-Leninist regime.

[1] Pike, pp. 348-349.

They travelled extensively throughout the world to meet and get advice from international terrorist leaders about overthrowing the South African government. During their travels they also solicited financial support to carry out their plans.

The ANC strategy to operate underground was part of the Mandela Plan. It was a classic communist revolutionary strategy. Black townships were divided up into zones, each having a local revolutionary committee appointed by the Regional Command of the ANC.[2] Members recruited into the organization were sworn to secrecy and had to be prepared to die for the cause.

The Sharpeville shootings in April focused world outrage on South Africa and the ensuing violence had led to the banning of the ANC. The ANC seized upon the incident to generate support throughout the world for its cause. Jack Simons, an exiled white member of the SACP, said, "It was the shooting that made March 21st a red letter day. The shots echoed round the world, caused a panic in ruling circles, . . . unleashed a storm of criticism of racial policies. . . ."[3]

In December 1960, the ANC leaders assembled at a clandestine meeting in Johannesburg to chart a course of action for South Africa's planned change from a British Dominion to an independent republic. They set up a Continuation Committee of African leaders as a new front for the ANC. The Committee planned an "All-African Conference" in Pietermaritzburg on March 25 and 26, 1961. Nelson Mandela was one of the guiding geniuses behind this new meeting.

The All-African Conference passed a resolution to call a three-day stay-at-home strike to coincide with the Republic Day celebrations planned on May 29-31st when South Africa would become an independent republic.

It didn't take long for the authorities to get wind of the plan. Soon after the conference a warrant was issued for Mandela's arrest and he disappeared from sight into the ANC's underground.

The underground ANC was hard at work. In June 1961, they convened at a secret meeting place inside South Africa to organize a terrorist war campaign in the country. The ANC's military wing, *Umkhonto we Sizwe*—Spear of the Nation—was born.

In July 1961, the ANC needed a base from which to plan and coordinate their new militant terrorist plan of action. They purchased a small farm, called Lilliesleaf, located in the Rivonia area near Johannesburg. The small

[2] See: Meli, F., p. 153.

[3] Meli, p. 140.

farm contained a large house and other outbuildings on twenty-eight acres of land. The ANC immediately turned the house into a command post where Mandela and his colleagues were soon at work devising the master plan for the revolutionary takeover of the country.

The well-known South African communist, Michael Harmel, using the fictitious name Jacobson, purchased the Lilliesleaf farm, saying he needed it for his brother-in-law who was sick and needed peace and quiet.

The purchase documents were drawn up by another communist, Harold Wolpe. He was a junior partner in the legal firm of James Kantor and Partners. Harmel bought the property bought in the name of Navin (Pty) Ltd. At the time of the deal, Wolpe was a member of *Umkhonto we Sizwe.*

The ANC also bought two other properties in the Johannesburg area. One was another farm, Travallyn, which the ANC was to use as an ordnance depot where they would make bombs, hand grenades and landmines for their revolutionary war in South Africa. The third, in the suburb of Mountain View, was to be a safe-house and hide-out for ANC terrorists on clandestine missions in the country.

Goldreich took over control of Lilliesleaf farm. He was a militant communist who had been trained in the theory and practice of revolution and terrorist warfare by the Chinese Communists. He was also one of the authors of Operation MAYIBUYE, the ANC's terror plan for South Africa.

Goldreich had travelled to Red China and, carried away by his passion for communism, had negotiated with East German, Russian and Chinese officials for aid to the ANC. Part of his "aid" would be learning about explosives techniques which could be used in South Africa in the ANC's future terror war.

Towards the end of 1961 *Umkhonto we Sizwe* set up a branch in Natal and headquarters in Durban. The communist members of the command included all races and gave each other military titles: "Comrade Captain" Curnick Ndlovo, a black, Second-in-command, Comrade Billy Nair, an Indian and "Comrade Lieutenant" Ronnie Kasrils, a white. All were members of the communist party and their job was to recruit terrorist fighters from the ranks of SACTU and the ANC.

A technical committee was established, under the guidance of a white communist, Harold Strachan. Its prime function was to manufacture bombs for the Natal branch of *Umkhonto we Sizwe.* The ANC sent Strachan to Durban to prepare a campaign of violence scheduled to start on December 16, 1961. Strachan had also trained other groups of ANC terrorists, including one in Port Elizabeth.

On January 11, 1962, Mandela slipped out of the country and travelled to

Dar es Salaam on a false Ethiopian passport identifying him as David Motsamayi. During the first week in February he attended, as part of a six-man ANC delegation, the Pan African Freedom Movement conference in Addis Ababa. He even addressed the conference on February 3, 1962.

After the conference his travels took him elsewhere in Africa for meetings with the leaders of the Algerian and Moroccan terrorist organizations. He paid particular attention to the Algerian underground movement, studying its structure and tactics. He also was keenly interested in the methods employed by the French to try and crush the Algerian rebellion and the counter tactics used by the rebels. He absorbed these lessons for incorporation in the war plans of the ANC in South Africa.

In notes he made during his visits to the Algerians he said: "It is absolutely important that the person preparing the revolution be unknown. Let legends be built up. . . . To the people and the world the uprising must assume the character of a popular revolutionary movement. To the enemy it must appear as an uprising of a few only. . . . There must be perfect harmony between the external delegation of the revolutionary movement and the High command . . . traitors and informers should be ruthlessly eliminated."[4]

Among the African leaders Mandela met were Julius Nyerere of Tanzania, Haile Selassie of Ethiopia, Ben Bella and Belcacim Krim of the Algerian resistance and Milton Obote of Uganda.[5] All would provide either training, base locations or financial and moral support for the planned ANC terror campaign in South Africa.

Mandela's grand tour also included Great Britain where he met with Hugh Gaitskell, the leader of the left-wing British Labour Party.[6] Then it was back to Africa for more meetings and terrorist training in Algeria before returning to South Africa.[7]

On Mandela's return he sent out the call to the ANC's regional branches asking them to recruit candidates for overseas terrorist training.[8] But, at the same time, he warned his colleagues that most of the leaders of the independent black states whom he had met were opposed to communism; therefore, he told them that "recruits undergoing training must never reveal the fact that they were communists." Instead Mandela stressed to the regional

[4] Strydom, L., *Rivonia Unmasked*, Voortrekkerpers, Johannesburg, 1965, p. 107.

[5] Meli, F., p. 149.

[6] Meli, F., pp. 149-150.

[7] Meli, F., p. 150; see also: Benson, M., *Nelson Mandela, The Man and the Movement*, W.W. Norton & Co, New York, 1986, p. 114.

[8] Benson, p. 115.

branches how "recruits from South Africa could be sent to camps (in Algeria) to train as guerrillas;" and that Haile Selassie had offered to pay the way for recruits to come to Ethiopia and train. Other countries, he indicated, would also help: Cuba would help and outstanding recruits with the proper educational qualifications would even go to East Germany for their specific training.[9]

After a meeting between Mandela and the ANC's Natal Regional Command, a member said: "Mandela went on to tell us about his meeting with the Chief Commander of the Algerian Army, who supported communism. This man had taken him to see a training camp on the border between Algeria and Tunisia. He told Mandela he was anxious to help him. . . . Recruits from South Africa could be sent to this camp to be trained as guerrillas. They would even be supplied with arms."[10]

The first four batches of recruits left South Africa in July 1962. The recruits were driven to the Botswana border in two Volkswagen Combis. They were dropped off near the border, crossed it on foot and made their way to Lobatse. From there they travelled to Bulawayo in then Rhodesia (now Zimbabwe), on to Lusaka in Zambia, through Tanzania to Nairobi in Kenya, and from Nairobi they went by air to Dabrazid in Ethiopia.[11]

At Dabrazid the recruits underwent an intensive three-month course in all aspects of terrorist warfare ranging from the use of handguns to the laying of landmines and the preparation of booby traps and ambushes. They were also taught how to use heavier weapons such as anti-tank guns and bazookas.

After completing their training they were sent back to South Africa by way of Rhodesia with the mission for each of them to select and train fifteen recruits inside South Africa. However, on their return trip to South Africa, nine were arrested by Rhodesian police and handed over to the South African authorities.

They were trained to recruit terrorists to carry out a massive ANC terror operation in South Africa no later than the end of May 1963, the second anniversary of South Africa becoming independent.

Code-named "Operation MAYIBUYE" (Muyibuye is a Zulu word meaning "return"), it was a complex, six-part detailed plan to seize power in South Africa. The main thrust of the revolt would be sabotage and attacks by

[9] Pike, p. 349.

[10] "Africa Hijack", SABCTV, 1989.

[11] Vermaak, C., *Bram Fischer, The Man With Two Faces*, APB Publishers, Johannesburg, 1966, p. 74.

terrorists supplied with sufficient arms and ammunition to sow terror throughout the country.

The first part was a candid admission that a general revolt leading to a total war against the South African government was not possible.

"Rather, as in Cuba, the general uprising must be sparked off by organized and well-prepared guerrilla operations, during the course of which the masses of the people will be drawn in and armed. We are faced with a powerfully armed modern state with tremendous industrial resources, which can, at least in the initial period, count on the support of three million whites.

"The following plan envisages a process which will place in the field at a date fixed now, simultaneously in preselected areas, armed and trained guerrilla bands, who will find ready to join them local guerrilla bands with arms and equipment at their disposal. It will further coincide with a massive propaganda campaign both inside and outside South Africa, and a general call for unprecedented mass struggle throughout the land, both violent and non-violent. In the initial period, when for a short while the military advantage will be ours, the plan envisages a massive onslaught on preselected targets which will create maximum havoc and confusion in the enemy camp, and which will inject into the masses of the people and other friendly forces a feeling of confidence that here is at last an army of liberation equipped and capable of leading them to victory."[12]

The second part of the plan defined four rural areas of South Africa where the guerrillas were to trigger the revolution. They were the Mzimkulu area near Port Elizabeth; the Port Shepstone area; North Western Transvaal on the border with Botswana; and North Western Cape on the border with South West Africa.[13]

Part three gave details of the planned insurrection:

"1. There would be a simultaneous landing of four groups of thirty men by ship or air. They would be armed and equipped to fight for at least a month.[14]

"2. Initially they would be split up into platoons of ten men each to operate continuously within a specific area and linking up with pre-arranged local groups.[15]

"3. Simultaneously with the landing of the groups of 30, and continuing

[12] "Africa Hijack."

[13] *Ibid.*

[14] Pike, p. 379.

[15] *Ibid.*

thereafter, there would be a supply of arms and other war material to arm the local population which was to integrate with the guerrillas.

"4. On landing, a detailed planned attack on pre-selected targets with a view to taking the enemy by surprise, creating the maximum impact on the population, and creating as much chaos and confusion for the enemy as possible.

"5. Temporary bases would be chosen in the pre-selected areas from which the guerrillas could attack and to which they could later retreat.

"6. Before the operation started a political authority would have been established in secrecy in a neighboring friendly territory, from where the internal and external aspects of the struggle would be supervised. This body would be known as the Provisional Revolutionary Government."[16]

Part four concerned itself with the internal organization of the uprising. Once again the planning of the SACP/ANC alliance was detailed. "Our target is that on arrival the external force should find at least 7,000 men in the four main areas ready to join the guerrilla army in the initial onslaught. These will be allocated as follows: Eastern Cape—Transkei, 2,000; Natal-Zululand—2,000; North Western Transvaal—2,000; and, North Western Cape—1,000.

"To realize our target in each of the main areas . . . it is proposed that auxiliary guerrilla/sabotage units in the four main areas be set up before and after the commencement of operations.

"They may engage in activities that may serve to disperse the enemy forces, assist to maintain the fighting ability of the guerrillas as well as draw in the masses in support of the guerrillas."[17]

Parts five and six of the plan dealt with the gathering of intelligence necessary to the guerrilla forces—such as the location of police and military posts and bases and the logistics involved in landing and supplying the guerrillas. In addition the plan made provision for the local manufacture of arms and explosives. Local production requirements were for 48,000 land-mines, 210,000 hand grenades and 1,500 time devices for bombs.[18] The significance of these figures will become apparent in the chapter on the Rivonia trial.

The SACP/ANC approach, as evidenced in this plan, displays an exceptional similarity to the Guevara/Debray model of revolutionary warfare. In Debray's words, the revolutionary "foco" has to serve as "the

[16] Pike, p. 379.

[17] "Africa Hijack."

[18] Pike, p. 380.

'small motor' that sets the 'big motor' of the masses in motion."[19]

According to Fox, the "foco" should "create and direct the revolutionary front."[20]

The actions of the ANC guerrilla groups were thus destined to act as stimuli to bring about a fast reaction from the population that would lead to an escalation of the steps necessary to follow in successfully carrying out a revolutionary war. These stimuli would enable the ANC to bypass the lengthy processes of politicization and mobilization of the masses which are crucial first steps to take in following the classic path of conducting a guerrilla war.

On August 5, 1962, Mandela, disguised as a chauffeur,[21] was arrested near Pietermaritzburg for illegally leaving South Africa. He was subsequently sentenced to five years in prison for passport violations used in his illegally leaving the country.

Early in 1963 an incident occurred that caused a major governmental crack-down on terrorist groups in South Africa. On February 2, 1963, POQO —meaning "pure", the military wing of the PAC, murdered five whites near the Bashee River bridge in the Transkei.

The leader of the PAC, Robert Sobukwe, was in prison and the instructions for these killings and others undertaken by POQO had come from his second-in-command, Potlako Leballo. He was running POQO from offices in Maseru, the capital of neighboring Lesotho.

Although it was not involved in the Bashee River atrocities, the ANC decided to capitalize on the notoriety and horror the killings had stirred up in South Africa. Soon afterward a pamphlet printed by the ANC was stuffed in the mail boxes of white homes. It read: "LISTEN WHITE MAN! Five whites were murdered in the Transkei, another hacked to death in Langa. . . . Sabotage erupts every other week throughout the country, now here, now there. The whites are turning vicious and panicky. . . . At this rate, within a year or two South Africa will be embroiled in the second, bloodier, more furious, Algerian war. SABOTAGE AND MURDERS MULTIPLIED LAST YEAR. SABOTAGE AND MURDER WILL NOT CEASE. You are now facing an indefinitely long future of terror, uncertainty and steadily eroding power. You will keep a gun at your side, not knowing whom to trust. Perhaps the street-cleaner is a saboteur, perhaps the man who makes your tea at the

[19] Debray, R., *Revolution in the Revolution? Armed Struggle and Political Struggle in Latin America*, Monthly Review Press, New York, 1967, p. 156.

[20] Fox, I.O. , "The Cuban Theory of Revolutionary War: The Faith, The Fallacies, and The Heresy", *RUSI Journal*, Vol. 122, No. 4, December 1977, p. 26.

[21] Benson, pp. 116-117.

office has a gun. . . . You will never be safe and you will never be sure. YOU WILL HAVE LAUNCHED A WAR YOU CANNOT WIN."[22]

The Bashee River killings weren't the only act of terror Leballo had in mind. The PAC planned a Night of Death for April 8, 1962. Members of 150 PAC cells throughout the country had been ordered to carry out a mass uprising whose objective was the indiscriminate killing of white men, women and children.

But just a few days before the PAC's "Night of Death" a South African policeman visiting Maseru in Lesotho met a foreign agent who had broken into the PAC offices and photographed documents containing hundreds of names and addresses of operatives inside South Africa. Prints from the films revealed the plans for the event and indicated that Leballo would soon be sending out orders for its launching.[23]

Every border crossing from Lesotho into South Africa was quickly placed under strict surveillance. Soon Leballo's secretary and another woman crossed the border into the Orange Free State. They were carrying a briefcase containing the letters to launch the terror campaign.

Near Ladybrand in the Orange Free State the two couriers were intercepted and the briefcase confiscated. After deciphering the letters, almost the entire South African POQO network was arrested, totalling more than 3,000 people.[24] It was a setback from which the PAC would never fully recover and which left the SACP/ANC alliance established as the firm front runner in the revolutionary stakes.

The crackdown and roundup of anti-government activists caused the ANC to abort Operation MAYIBUYE scheduled to take place the following month.

It did not make them cancel their plan of terrorist violence, just postpone it to a future date.

In fact the underground SACP/ANC headquarters at Lilliesleaf farm was going full blast preparing for the upcoming revolution in South Africa. Unfortunately for the ANC their plans were soon to become further derailed.

[22] Strydom, L., *Rivonia Unmasked*, Voortrekkerpers, Johannesburg, 1965, p. 12.

[23] Pike, p. 356.

[24] *The Star*, July 17 & 18, 1963.

8

THE RIVONIA TRIAL

The SACP/ANC underground headquarters was still operating secretly in Rivonia. It also happened to be the hideout of Walter Sisulu and the site for the ANC's clandestine "Radio Liberation" broadcasts.

Meanwhile, the ANC's plan to carry out Operation MAYIBUYE was moving forward. In July 1963, Dennis Goldberg made an arrangement with Mrs. N. Weinberg of Houghton in Johannesburg to use her house as a mail drop for letters arriving there addressed to D. Williams.[1]

Under the name of Williams, he negotiated through the mails the purchase of equipment necessary for making explosives. He sought bids from two Johannesburg lumber yards for enough wood to make 48,000 containers —exactly the number of landmines stipulated in the MAYIBUYE plan.[2]

Using the same alias, Goldberg approached two different iron foundries getting quotes for casting 210,000 iron molds—exactly the number of hand grenades needed for the plan.[3]

The grenades and landmines would have been made at the ANC's ordnance depot and second hideout, Travallyn farm.

In response to a reward offer for information as to the location of the SACP headquarters, an informant contacted the police on July 3, 1963. He claimed he knew where the headquarters of both the ANC and the SACP were located and added that Walter Sisulu was hiding out there.

[1] "Africa Hijack", *op. cit.*

[2] *Ibid.*

[3] *Ibid.*

The informant did not know the exact address but thought he could guide the police there from Rosebank, a northern suburb of Johannesburg.

It took the informant and the police a week of searching the posh suburb areas north of Johannesburg before he was able to identify Lilliesleaf farm in Rivonia as the site.

The police questioned neighbors and got interesting information. According to neighbors the owner of the farm was a man named Arthur Goldreich and his place was known in the neighborhood for its "drinking and mixed parties."[4]

On July 11, 1963, senior police officials gave permission to Lieutenant van Wyk, the investigating officer, to take a counterinsurgency unit (the core of this unit later became the Bureau of State Security—BOSS, now National Intelligence—NI) and raid the farm. At about three P.M., hidden in a rented laundry van, the raiding party of fourteen policemen and a police dog entered the property. Halfway up the drive they were met by a black who told them "there's nobody home."[5]

Making a quick on-the-spot decision, Lieutenant van Wyk ordered his men to get out of the van and storm the house and the other outbuilding on the farm. Their catch was impressive: the raid scooped up some of South Africa's top SACP/ANC members.

In a thatched cottage which the police first entered there were six men: three blacks, two whites and an Indian. They were Walter Sisulu, Govan Mbeki, Ahmed Kathrada, Lionel Bernstein, Bob Hepple and Raymond Mhlaba.[6]

In the main building the police arrested the ANC's communist terrorist warfare specialist Dennis Goldberg. In the ensuing search of the buildings, the police found more than 200 incriminating documents and the components of a radio transmitter and a radio mast.[7]

Next to one of several duplicating machines the police found a tin can with a clear fingerprint which turned out to be that of Harold Wolpe. Wolpe was not at Lilliesleaf at the time of the raid. When he heard what had happened he tried to flee the country but was arrested near the Botswana border on July 17, 1963.[8]

Later in the day other SACP/ANC alliance members such as Arthur

[4] Pike, p. 376.

[5] *Ibid.*

[6] de Villiers, H.H.W, *Rivonia—Operation Mayibuye*, A.P.B., Johannesburg, 1964, p. 4.

[7] Pike, pp. 376-378.

[8] Pike, p. 378.

Goldreich and his wife Hazel unsuspectingly returned to the farm where they too were arrested.[9]

Many SACP and ANC leaders, deciding that discretion was the better part of valor, fled the country, escaping one jump ahead of the police. Among those were Oliver Tambo, Joe Slovo, Moses Kotane, Ronnie Kasrils, J.B. Marks and Johannes Modise.

The communists organized a jail break for their comrades Wolpe and Goldreich. Communist money was used to smuggle Wolpe, Goldreich and two Indian communists, Moolla and Jassat, out of the country.[10] The escape was possible because a young constable at the jail was in financial difficulties and accepted a bribe to help the prisoners escape.[11]

Hundreds of lesser fry in the SACP/ANC alliance were scooped up, tried and imprisoned as a result of evidence found at the Rivonia farm. For example, Bruno Mtoto was a prominent member of *Umkhonto we Sizwe* in Natal. Unfortunately for him, he was not a member of the group's high command. He had to stay behind and face the music. Special escape plans were only for the privileged and the rich and not for the rank and file. "We the poor fools were left to nurse their baby", said Mtoto in his book, *The Road to the Left*.[12]

Eventually, the escapees travelled to London, arriving in the British capital on September 23, 1963. During a press conference that same day Goldreich vigorously denied any knowledge or involvement in acts of sabotage. He claimed such stories were disinformation to malign the self-proclaimed "freedom fighters" in the eyes of the world.

At the same press conference, agreeing with Goldreich, were two other SACP/ANC escapees, Oliver Tambo, now president of the ANC, and Joe Slovo, chief of staff of *Umkhonto we Sizwe*.

Thus, Goldreich, Wolpe, Tambo and Slovo were not among the accused when the Rivonia Trial, as it became known, began in Pretoria supreme court on October 9, 1963. It would be a long trial ending, finally, on June 11, 1964.

The roll-call of the accused read like a Who's Who of the SACP/ANC alliance. Those who went on trial were: Nelson Mandela, Walter Sisulu, Dennis Goldberg, Govan Mbeki, Ahmed Kathrada, Lionel Bernstein,

[9] *Ibid.*

[10] Pike, p. 382.

[11] *Ibid.*

[12] de Villiers, L., *South Africa A Skunk Among Nations*, International Books, London, 1975, p. 70.

Raymond Mhlaba, James Kantor, Elias Motsoaledi, Andrew Mlangeni and Bob Hepple.

Mandela and his ten co-defendants were charged on four counts:

- One count under the South African Suppression of Communism Act No. 44 of 1950, charging that the accused committed acts calculated to further the achievement of the objective of communism;
- One count of contravening the South African Criminal Law Act (1953), which prohibits any person from soliciting or receiving any money or articles for the purpose of achieving organized defiance of laws and country; and
- Two counts of sabotage, committing or aiding or procuring the commission of the following acts:

1) The further recruitment of persons for instruction and training, both within and outside the Republic of South Africa, in:
   (a) the preparation, manufacture and use of explosives—for the purpose of committing acts of violence and destruction in the aforesaid Republic, (the preparation and manufacture of explosives, according to evidence submitted, included 210,000 hand grenades, 48,000 anti-personnel mines, 1,500 time devices, 144 tons of ammonium nitrate, 21.6 tons of aluminum powder and a ton of black powder);
   (b) the art of warfare, including guerrilla warfare, and military training generally for the purpose in the aforesaid Republic;
      (ii) Further acts of violence and destruction, (this includes 193 counts of terrorism committed between 1961 and 1963);
      (iii) Acts of guerrilla warfare in the aforesaid Republic;
      (iv) Acts of assistance to military units of foreign countries when involving the aforesaid Republic;
      (v) Acts of participation in a violent revolution in the aforesaid Republic, whereby the accused, injured, damaged, destroyed, rendered useless or unserviceable, put out of action, obstructed, with or endangered:
         (a) the health or safety of the public;
         (b) the maintenance of law and order;
         (c) the supply and distribution of light, power or fuel;
         (d) postal, telephone or telegraph installations;
         (e) the free movement of traffic on land; and
         (f) the property, movable or immovable, of other persons or of the state.[13]

[13] *The State v. Nelson Mandela et al*, Supreme Court of South Africa, Transvaal Provincial Division, 1963-1964, Indictment.

Dr. Percy Yutar, the State prosecutor, read the indictment, which in part said: "The accused deliberately and maliciously plotted and engineered the commission of acts of violence and destruction throughout the country. . . . The planned purpose was to bring about in the Republic of South Africa chaos, disorder and turmoil which would be aggravated, according to their plan, by the operation of thousands of trained guerrilla warfare units deployed throughout the country at various vantage points. These would be joined in the various areas by local inhabitants as well as specially selected men posted to such areas. Their combined operations were planned to lead to confusion, violent insurrection and rebellion, followed, at the appropriate juncture, by an armed invasion of the country by military units of foreign powers."[14]

Hepple was released on October 29th, after having agreed to turn State's witness. However, soon afterwards, he fled the country.

Ten thus remained before the court. All the defendants pleaded not guilty to charges of sabotage and acts of violence including aid to foreign powers trying to invade the country. However, the State's case was very strong. As the prosecutor said after the case: "So strong was the documentary proof that it was barely necessary to adduce oral testimony in support of the various allegations made by the State, and for that reason I called as witnesses less than one half of the number of persons from whom statements had been taken by the police.

"For that very reason too, I deemed it sufficient to set out in three of the four volumes comprising the State's concluding address a factual analysis of the documentary exhibits and the oral testimony without any comment whatsoever.

"In my view the documents spoke more eloquently than I could ever hope to do by way of critical comment. No wonder then that during the course of a hearing for bail, I declared that never in all my experience had the police presented me with a stronger case against an accused than in this case!"[15]

At the conclusion of the State's case, a motion was made by the defense for the dismissal of James Kantor on the grounds of lack of evidence against him. The motion was granted and Kantor was released.

Evidence submitted by the State during the trial proved without any doubt that Mandela and his fellow defendants incited and promoted violence in South Africa. It also included over a hundred maps showing proposed targets for *Umkhonto we Sizwe* guerrillas to attack. They included adminis-

[14] Pike, p. 388.

[15] "Africa Hijack", *op. cit.*

tration buildings in the black townships, and black leaders opposed to the ANC, and black policemen.[16]

The first witness called by the defense was Nelson Mandela. He refused to take the oath which, in South African jurisprudence, meant he could not be cross-examined by the prosecution.

Mandela's defense had conceded during the trial:

(1) that Mandela was one of the founders of *Umkhonto*, the military wing of the ANC;

(2) that he was a member of the National Executive of the ANC;

(3) that he toured Africa during the first half of 1962, and that during his tour:

  (a) he received military training in Algeria;

  (b) he made arrangements for members of *Umkhonto* to receive military training and;

  (c) he solicited and received funds for *Umkhonto*.

(4) that he requested the National Executive of the ANC to assist the military wing in the transportation of recruits, and approved of its decision to allow its secretariat and external missions to be used for this purpose."[17]

Instead of being cross-examined, Mandela submitted a lengthy statement which he read to the court. He admitted that he had been actively involved in the Defiance Campaign and that the ANC had continued to operate underground after it had been banned in 1960. He also admitted playing a prominent role in creating *Umkhonto we Sizwe*.

Nor did Mandela deny plotting sabotage, but admitted that *Umkhonto* had been responsible for a number of acts of sabotage as set out in the indictment. This was, he claimed, as a result of changing policy within the ANC that now allowed properly controlled acts of violence.

Mandela denied that the ANC was a tool of the SACP. He admitted, however, there was close cooperation between the two groups and that certain black communists had joined the ANC. They had, he admitted, served on regional, provincial and even national committees of the ANC.

However, two documents, which Mandela admitted that he had written,

[16] De Villiers, H.H., *Rivonia*, Afrikaanse Boekhandel, Johannesburg, 1964, pp. 72-73.

[17] *Ibid*, pp. 35-36; A later report from Australia about the Rivonia trial said: "At no time during the trial did the defense challenge the authenticity or authorship of the documents submitted. On the contrary, the defense stated that 'in the face of the overwhelming bulk of evidence against his clients', it would be 'futile to refute any of the charges.' "—from an article in *Intelligence Survey*, July 1983, pp. 7-8, as quoted in Pike, p. 413, n. 10.

which were part of the evidence in the trial showed Mandela wasn't being entirely candid.

The future South Africa envisaged by Mandela was, and still is not a Periclean democracy. It is a classless socialist society created by means of a violent revolution.[18] He stated in *How To Be A Good Communist* that: "In our own country, the struggles of the oppressed people are guided by the South African Communist Party and inspired by its policies. The aim of the SACP is to defeat the Nationalist Government and to free the people of South Africa from the evils of racial discrimination and exploitation and to build a classless or socialist society in which the land, the mines, the mills and factories will be owned by the State. Under a Communist Party government South Africa will become a land of milk and honey."[19]

"In South Africa, a communist party member must take part in mass struggles initiated by the South African Communist Party, the Congress Movement, or by the political bodies with the liberation movement. The people of South Africa, led by the communist party, will destroy capitalist society and build in its place socialism. . . . Hence the transition to socialism and the liberation of the working class from the yoke cannot be affected by slow changes or by reforms as reactionaries and liberals often advise, but by revolution. One must, therefore, be a revolutionary and not a reformist."[20]

His preference for communism shows up in his other writings. For example in his book *The Struggle is my Life* (International Defense and Aid Fund for Southern Africa, London, 1986), he blasted the chief capitalist country, the United States: "[T]oday, American imperialism is a serious danger to the independent states in Africa and its people must unite before it is too late and fight it out to the bitter end. . . .

"The future of this continent lies not in the hands of the discredited regimes that have allied themselves with American imperialism."[21]

[18] See: interview with Nicholsa Bethal, *The Mail on Sunday*, January 27, 1985. During this interview Mandela told Bethal: "Personally I am a socialist and I believe in a classless society." During the Rivonia trial Mandela also stated ". . . without violence there would be no way open to African people to succeed in their struggle,"; see: Booyse, W., *Getting Beyond the Mandela Smoke Screen*, International Freedom Review, International Freedom Foundation, Vol. 1, No. 2, 1988, p. 37n.

[19] Mandela, N., *How To Be A Good Communist*, unpublished document entered as evidence in the Rivonia trial, and is part of the court record. Mandela acknowledged to *Washington Times* columnist John Lofton that he wrote this document, see: *Washington Times*, August 22, 1985.

[20] Strydom, L., *Rivonia Unmasked*, Voortrekkerpers, Johannesburg, 1965, pp. 104-105.

[21] Mandela, N., *The Struggle is my Life*, International Defense and Aid Fund for Southern Africa, London, 1986, pp. 76-77.

He classifies those desiring an open society and a market economy as counter-revolutionaries and calls for communists everywhere to ". . . fight to destroy capitalist society and to replace it with socialism, where the masses of the common people, irrespective of race or color, will live in complete equality, freedom and happiness. They seek to revolutionize society and are thus called revolutionaries. Those who support capitalism with its class divisions and other evils, and who oppose our just struggles to end oppression and exploitation, are called counter-revolutionaries."[22]

With the escalating effort during the 1980s to make Nelson Mandela a saintly crusader for peace and justice in South Africa, it is well to ponder his own words: "The cause of communism is the greatest cause in the history of mankind because it seeks to remove from society all forms of oppression and exploitation, to liberate mankind to ensure peace and prosperity to all."[23] Communism's peace, however, is the peace of the grave. It is crumbling throughout the world, yet Mandela still clings to its barbaric tenets.

One may argue that Mandela wrote those words over a quarter of a century ago and he may have changed his mind since then. He still fiercely defends the SACP/ANC alliance even today: "No dedicated ANC member will ever heed the call to break with the SACP. . . . What man of honor will ever desert a life-long friend at the insistence of a common opponent and still retain a measure of credibility among his people?"[24]

It is interesting to note that Amnesty International, no right-wing pro-South Africa organization by any stretch of the imagination, doesn't consider Nelson Mandela a political prisoner. In a letter to the Finnish newspaper *Helsingen Sanomat*, September 13, 1985, Amnesty International pointed out: "AI ascertained that Mandela had participated in planning acts of sabotage and inciting violence, so that he could no longer fulfil the criteria for the classification of political prisoners. At the end of his trial, Mandela delivered a speech wherein he said that after all his peaceful action he had concluded that the only chance for a change in SA was through violence."[25]

Walter Sisulu, unlike Mandela, gave evidence under oath. He denied he was a communist but admitted that his views had been influenced by socialism.

[22] Mandela, N., *How To Be A Good Communist*, p. 2.

[23] Mandela, N., *How To Be A Good Communist*, p. 10.

[24] Rusher, W., "Unlocking what future Course? Posturing and precedent" *The Washington Times*, February 7, 1990.

[25] Campbell, K., *ANC: A Soviet Task Force?*, Institute For The Study of Terrorism, London, 1986, p. 58.

He claimed that "Operation MAYIBUYE" was just a contingency plan. It had been submitted to the ANC high command for discussion but had not been approved. He said the guerrilla weapons were to be kept in reserve until the revolution had been launched.

Sisulu saw nothing wrong with sabotage and admitted he wouldn't hesitate to resort to it if he considered it necessary. He readily admitted that its widespread use would inevitably escalate to insurrection and civil war.[26]

On June 11, 1964, the presiding judge, Justice Quartus de Wet, delivered the verdict. Mandela, Sisulu, Goldberg, Mbeki, Mhlaba, Motsoaledi and Mlangeni were found guilty on all four counts. Kathrada was found guilty on only one count—the second, and Lionel Bernstein was found not guilty.

In passing sentence Justice de Wet said: "I have heard a great deal during the course of this case about the grievances of the non-white population. . . . I am by no means convinced that the motives of the accused are as altruistic as they wish the court to believe. People who organize a revolution usually plan to take over the government, and personal ambition cannot be excluded as a motive. The crime of which the accused have been convicted, the crime of conspiracy, is the essence of high treason. The State has decided not to charge the crime in this form. . . . I have decided not to impose the supreme penalty, which in a case like this would usually be the penalty for such a crime. But consistent with my duty, that is the only leniency which I can show. The sentence in the case of all the accused will be one of life imprisonment."[27]

The trial had raised an international furor and calls for amnesty poured in calling for the release of the accused. During the trial the Special Apartheid Committee of the United Nations asked the United Nations Security Council to try to "save the lives" of the accused. The Security Council complied by demanding amnesty for all so-called political prisoners in South Africa.

While the international press condemned South Africa for the trial, within South Africa even the most liberal and left-wing press approved the verdict. The leftist *Rand Daily Mail* said: "The sentences pronounced by Mr. Justice de Wet in Pretoria yesterday at the conclusion of the Rivonia trial were both wise and just."[28]

The leader of the opposition, Sir de Villers Graaf, who frequently condemned the government's apartheid policy, praised the verdict in Parliament. "I want to say quite clearly that we of the Opposition want it on record, so that not only this House will know but that the outside world will

[26] Pike, p. 393.

[27] Judge's remarks in passing sentence, *The State v. Mandela.*

[28] *Rand Daily Mail,* June 17, 1964.

know too, that we are convinced that the verdicts in the trial were just, that they were necessary, and that they were right in view of the actions to which the accused themselves pleaded guilty. I want to say that if I have any regret, then my only regret is that they were not charged with high treason."[29]

The Opposition leader's sentiment were shared by most South Africans during that period of time.

Nelson Mandela and his fellow revolutionaries began their life sentences on June 12, 1964.

Soon after the trial was over, Mandela's defense attorney, Bram Fischer, was arrested and charged in 1965 under the Suppression of Communism Act. Fischer was the mastermind behind the SACP bag of subversive tricks.

Largely on the testimony of an undercover police officer, Gerard Ludi, who had infiltrated the SACP and had become one of Fischer's inner circle of SACP confidants, Fischer was convicted and sentenced to life imprisonment.

By 1965 most active SACP and ANC members were either in jail or had fled the country. The SACP/ANC's armed struggle had come to a screeching halt in South Africa.

[29] de villiers, L., *South Africa A Skunk Among Nations*, p. 74.

9

ANC SHIFT TO ARMED STRUGGLE

After the banning of the African National Congress (ANC) and the Pan African Congress (PAC), the communist element in the Congress Alliance began to openly advocate an armed struggle by means of revolutionary warfare to achieve the Alliance's goals.

Before going into the ANC/SACP strategy on revolutionary war, or what the Soviet Union terms "wars of national liberation", a brief overview of revolutionary war theory is in order. The SACP/ANC's adaptation of revolutionary war will be discussed in greater detail elsewhere in this work.

The first thing to stress is that revolutionary and guerrilla war are not the same. The reason why lies in the tactics used. The American counter-insurgency expert, Dr. R. H. Shultz, Jr., points out, "Revolutionary warfare strategy employs ancient military tactics in conjunction with political and psychological techniques to transfer governmental power as a prelude to the transformation of the social structure. The objective is to impose a new regime on the society through a protracted conflict strategy."[1]

Sarkesian describes revolutionary warfare as "the forcible attempt by a politically organized group to gain control or change the structure and/or politics of the government, using unconventional warfare integrated by political and social mobilization, resting on the premise that the people are both the targets and the actors."[2]

[1] Shultz, R.H., Jr., *The Soviet Union and Revolutionary Warfare*, Hoover Institution Press, Stanford, 1989, pp. 2-3.

[2] Sarkesian, S.C., "Revolutionary Warfare: An Introduction", in *Revolutionary Guerrilla Warfare*, ed. by S.C. Sarkesian, Chicago, Precedent Publishing, Inc., 1975, p. 7.

In other words, revolutionary warfare aims to overthrow the existing government by a coordinate mixture of political, social, economic, psychological, diplomatic and military means. It depends upon winning the support of the population, in part by promising a better or more acceptable form of society, but accomplishes it, or tries to, largely through intimidation and armed propaganda.

Revolutionary warfare involves using an illegal political organization whose program does not call for reforming the existing targeted regime, but challenges its basic legitimacy and seeks to replace it. The revolutionary struggle adopts an ideology which serves as its justification and guidance for the conduct of its revolution.

At the second congress of the Soviet Comintern in 1920 Lenin said that revolutions in the so-called colonial world, now known as the Third World, would pass through two stages: the stage of national independence, led by the bourgeoisie, and the second stage would be the socialist revolution, led by the communists, which would lead to a proletarian dictatorship.[3]

Lenin's theory of revolution is a logical outgrowth of his Marxist worldview. He believed that society was made up of two classes in conflict—the exploiters and the exploited. Revolution, according to him, was the only way to end this conflict. Thus, for him, the principal and basic means of transferring power from one class to the other is by revolution.[4]

Lenin, however, believed that the conditions most favorable for revolution were to be found in the industrialized nations with their centers of urban workers. It was here that capitalism was developing to its maximum because of the concentrations of economic and political power. This enabled the bourgeoisie to utilize the forces of capitalism to further their ends which resulted in the further exploitation of the working class. Here Lenin's main actors, the exploiting bourgeoisie and the exploited proletariat would interact according to his revolutionary script. In short, his theory is predicated on taking place in advanced industrial countries, not backward Third World countries in Africa.

How to capitalize on the post-World War II phenomenon of the colonial powers shedding their colonies and explain it in terms of Marxism-Leninism required some mental gymnastics by Soviet intellectuals. Some modification of Lenin's theory was necessary in order to give an ideological basis for Moscow's support to revolutionary movements in developing countries. The Soviet intellectuals were up to the task.

[3] Second Congress of the Communist International, New Park, London, 1977, pp. 110-111.

[4] Lenin, V. I., *Collected Works*, Vol. 6, Progress Publishers, Moscow, 1978, p. 33.

They hitched their modifications on Lenin's concept that a colony's desire to be liberated is based on the right of nations to self-determination.[5]

From this, Soviet intellectuals have expanded Lenin's revolutionary concept to include the various forms of national liberation struggles against colonial occupations that were taking place in the Third World. Now these struggles could be brought under the theoretical umbrella of Marxism-Leninism.[6]

The first phase of the Leninist blueprint is to set up a broad democratic movement composed of various anti-government groups which become united into a progressive movement whose goal is to seize power and restructure society. In the South African context this would be made up of anti-apartheid and anti-imperialist forces united in a mass movement designed to overthrow the existing South African government.

Only when Lenin's first phase is finished can the second phase—the socialist revolution—begin. This involves moving the society from one of capitalism to one of communism. This is done in the name of the working class by their vanguard party—the Communist Party.

In Lenin's second phase, the alliances formed during the first phase are dismantled or eliminated as the communists consolidate their grip on power. The non-communist groups allied with the communists in the first phase must be abolished or eliminated as they could quickly become rallying centers for opposition to communist rule. Or, in the jargon of Leninism, they could develop into counter-revolutionaries. This is totally unacceptable to the communists.

The two phases can neither be isolated nor separated. Lenin said: "We all categorize bourgeois revolutions and socialist revolutions, we all insist on the absolute necessity of strictly distinguishing between them. However, can it be denied that in the course of history individual particular elements of the two revolutions become interwoven?"[7] As his words indicate, Lenin considered revolution as a continuous process.

Lenin's phases reflect his revolutionary process in a broad scope. To look at the revolutionary process in depth more is needed and a fuller analysis can

[5] See: Lenin, V. I., *Imperialism, the Highest Stage of Capitalism*, Foreign Language Press, Peking, 1975, p. 146.

[6] See: Zotov, V., *Lenin's Doctrine on National Liberation, Revolutions and the Modern World*, Progress Publishers, Moscow, 1983, p. 20; and: Pavlenko, A., *The World Revolutionary Process*, Progress Publishers, Moscow, 1983, p. 6.

[7] Lenin, V.I., *Selected Works*, Vol. 1, International Publishers, New York, 1954, pp. 511-512.

be made if one adds two more processes to the Lenin model—a political phase and an ideological phase. We will go into greater detail on these phases later in this work. Suffice it to say, the revolutionary program of the SACP/ANC reflects, with these modifications, such a Leninist approach.

The 1950 banning of the SACP drove it underground and capable party cadres took cover in existing legal organizations such as the ANC. Given their organizational skills, dedication, a willingness to work and a deep commitment to their ultimate ideological goal of a communist South Africa, these cadres became leading lights in the ANC. They quickly rose from within the ranks of the Congress to leadership positions.

The underground existence of the SACP placed it in an admirable position when the government banned the ANC in 1960. The communists in the ANC were best suited both by experience and training to lead the ANC in the post-1960 era of underground resistance.

The ace the SACP had up their sleeve, which greatly enhanced their role, prestige and influence within the ANC, was their ability to open doors of opportunity for the Congress. Through the SACP the ANC had access to the Soviet Union support apparatus—financial as well as military.[8] Because of their connection with the SACP, ANC members received terrorist training at Soviet facilities, were given massive amounts of monetary assistance and were plugged into the Soviet Union's worldwide propaganda network.

By casting their lot with the Soviets the ANC had turned their back on the West. The SACP alliance with the ANC closed the ANC to other ideological influences. The Party alone was to provide the ideological and political theory guidance to the organization. The Social Democrats in Sweden, who over the years have contributed large amounts of financial assistance to the ANC, until recently had repeatedly failed to attract a single ANC candidate with offers of political education in Sweden, in spite of numerous invitations. Political education was the exclusive domain of the Party and its Soviet allies, and they regarded social democracy as a heresy.[9]

The Soviet Union has maintained a direct interest in southern Africa since the early 1960s. It originally involved itself in the struggle of the African people to rid themselves of Portuguese colonialism. After the demise of the Portuguese colonies it directed most of its energies in the region to supporting and keeping in power the Marxist parties that had seized power in Mozambique and Angola. As part of that maintenance, they included support to revolutionary movements involved in trying to establish Marxist

[8] See: Sparks, A., "South Africa's White Communist", *The Washington Post*, July 14, 1985.

[9] *Africa Confidential*, Vol. 31, No. 1, January 12, 1990, p. 2.

rule in South West Africa/Namibia[10] and the Republic of South Africa.

Although Moscow often denies it, most of the military and financial aid to the ANC has come from the Soviets and their surrogates. The Soviets funnel most aid to the ANC through the Organization of African Unity's (OAU) liberation committee.[11] This is why Soviet Foreign Ministry spokesman Yuri Afanasyn could claim in May 1986 that "the Soviet Union gave no military assistance to the ANC."[12] This ploy enables the USSR to deny responsibility where convenient, while ingratiating itself with much of African political opinion as orchestrated by the OAU.

The Soviet Union, its surrogates and front organizations, all took up the cause of the ANC. This gave the Congress publicity, prestige, diplomatic, military and financial support. Equally important, it provided the ANC with an international forum for it to conduct political warfare against the South African government. All this was done by the simple expedient of selling the ANC soul to the Soviet Devil, brokered by the SACP.

The Soviet Union's early and continuing active support of the United Nation's Special Committee with Regards to the Implementation of the Declaration on the Granting of Independence to Colonial Countries—better known as the Committee of 24—allowed it to carry out political warfare against the West in the United Nations. The Soviets and their surrogates worked hard within the committee and, as it became more militant and anti-Western, the committee was able to play an important role in the UN General Assembly's continuing support and interaction with the ANC.

The Soviets' aid was, and still is, neither altruistic or one sided. Support to the ANC allows Moscow to posture as the friend of the down-trodden, willing to help "liberate" the "oppressed" people while they are actually becoming slaves to a more repressive "people's democracy". By exploiting groups such as the ANC, Moscow is able to promote its policies under the guise of peace, racial equality and support for the masses to a much wider audience. These groups also provide a means, and here is where part of the pay-back for Soviet support comes in, for criticizing and isolating its main enemies strategically, politically and morally. The ANC, for example, constantly blasts the West, especially the United States, accusing it of

[10] For a detailed account of Soviet meddling in South West Africa/Namibia, see: Norval, M., *Death in The Desert: The Namibian Tragedy*, Selous Foundation Press, Washington, D.C., 1989.

[11] Vanneman, P., "The Soviet Union and the African National Congress of South Africa: What is the Relationship?", *Coexistence* 26, 1989, p. 274.

[12] BBC SWB SU 8265/A5/1, May 22, 1986.

whatever evil the Soviets are touting at the moment, yet it appears as a separate non-Soviet voice offering the criticism. Likewise, the ANC, like all good obedient Soviet fronts, defends on the world stage unpopular aggressive Soviet actions such as the invasion of Afghanistan.

All this resulted from the SACP/ANC alliance and is part of the revolutionary war strategy to be used against the hated capitalists.

The International Freedom Foundation notes, "The ANC is a tactical vehicle for the SACP, which does not need to control the ANC numerically. Their control is assured via the strategic positioning of SACP members within the top structure of the ANC. . . ."[13]

The influential London-based newsletter, *Africa Confidential*, says that SACP domination of the ANC is extensive: "So pervasive is Party influence that it is hard to distinguish Party from non-Party in the ANC as all and sundry speak one language, Marxism. The oft-repeated allegations of tensions between Party and non-Party is a lie. . . ."[14]

The ANC continues to receive most of its moral and material support from the Soviet Union and other communist bloc countries through its alliance with the SACP.

The Soviet Union regards the ANC as a so-called liberation movement. Soviet revolutionary doctrine requires that it must be aided and supported to seize power in South Africa by any means—including violence. Thereafter a second phase of revolution, mentioned earlier, commences. During this second phase the role of the so-called liberation movement (the ANC) will diminish and all opposition to the revolution will be eliminated. This will be necessary to achieve the ultimate aim—a Marxist/Leninist dictatorship of the proletariat under the guidance of the most important organ of the State, the SACP.

Should the SACP/ANC succeed, the Soviet Union will have attained its ultimate and most prized strategic goal in Africa.

[13] Booyse, W.J., "The Revolutionary Program of the South African Communist Party", *International Freedom Review*, Vol. 2, No. 1, Washington, D.C., 1988, p. 51.

[14] *Africa Confidential, op. cit.*, p. 2.

The National Executive Committee of the ANC

(as of 1988)

Name	Position	Ethnic Origin	Member SACP
1. Oliver Tambo	President	Xhosa	✓
Nelson Mandela	Deputy President (As of 1990)	Xhosa	
2. Alfred Nzo	Secretary General	Xhosa	✓
3. Thomas Nkobi	Treasurer General	Ndebele	✓
4. Thabo Mbeki	Director: Dept. of Information and Publicity	Xhosa	✓
5. T.M. Hani (aka Chris)	Chief of Staff: Umkhonto we Sizwe	Xhosa	✓
6. Daniel Thloome	Chairman: SACP	Sotho	✓
7. Johnny Makatini	Director: Dept. of International Affairs	Zulu	✓
8. Henry Makgothi	Director: Dept. of Education Deputy Secretary General, SACP	Tswana	✓
9. Simon Makana	Chief Representative to the USSR	Xhosa	
10. Gertrude Shope	Secretary of the Womens Section,SACP	Sotho	✓
11. Stephen Dhlamini	President: South African Trade Union	Zulu	✓
12. John Nkadimeng	General Secretary: South African Trade Union	Sotho	✓
13.Joe Modise	Commander: Umkhonto we Sizwe	Tswana	✓
14. Mzwandile Piliso	Director: Department of Manpower and Development	Xhosa	✓
15. Robert Manci (aka Conco)	National Executive Council Representative in Tanzania	Xhosa	
16. Jacob Zuma	Member: Politico Military Council	Zulu	✓
17. Joe Nhlanhla	Director: Department of Intelligence and Security	Sotho	✓
18. Joe Slovo	Member: Politico Military Council; General Secretary: SACP	White	✓

The National Executive Committee of the ANC

(as of 1988)
Continued

Name	Position	Ethnic Origin	Member SACP
19. S. R. Maharaj (aka Mac)	Member: ANC Political Committee	Indian	✓
20. Aziz Pahad	Prominent Member: ANC/SACP	Indian	
21. Reginald September	Political Committee Treasurer; Prominent Member: ANC/SACP	Coloured	✓
22. H. Loots (aka James Stuart)	Secretary: External Co-ordinating Committee	Coloured	✓
23. Francis Meli	Editor: Sechaba	Xhosa	✓
24. Pallo Jordan	Head: Research Section of the Dept. of Information and Publicity		✓
25. R. Motsoane (aka Ruth Mompati)	Administrative Secretary: Treasurer General's Office; Member: Dept. of International Affairs; and the Women's Section	Tswana	
26. Sizakele Sigxhashe	Second-in-Command: Dept. of Intelligence and Security (DIS); Head: Research Section of DIS	Xhosa	✓
27. Anthony Mongalo	Secretary: Presidential Office		
28. Steve Tshete	National Commissar: ANC	Xhosa	
29. Ronnie Kasrils	Chief of Staff for Intelligence: Umkhonto we Sizwe	White	✓
30. Stanley Mabizela	Representative in Zimbabwe	Xhosa	
31. Sindiso Mfenyana	Representative in East Germany	Xhosa	
32. Jackie Selebi	Member: Youth Section	South-Sotho	
33. Timothy Mokoena	Political Commissar: Umkhonto we Sizwe	Zulu	
34. Jacqueline Molefe	Chief of Staff for Communications: Umkhonto we Sizwe	Zulu	
35. Josiah Jele	Member: National Executive Committee		

10

THE MOROGORO CONFERENCE

In April, 1969 the African National Congress (ANC) held an important conference in Morogoro, Tanzania. This conference would rank in importance for the SACP/ANC alliance as the so-called Congress of the People meeting in the mid-1950s.

The main task of the conference was to decide how the ANC would seize power in South Africa. The conference decided that waging a people's war would be the road to power for the SACP/ANC alliance, and discussed proposals aimed at successfully bringing about the overthrow of the South African government by a national liberation movement led by the SACP and the ANC.

The chairman of the SACP, J. B. Marks, chaired the Morogoro Conference. Moses Mabhida, later to become the Party's general secretary, assisted him.

The conference grappled with what it considered the central problem of the movement, ". . . of reaching the fighting front and the means of communication between external center and the home front. . . ."[1]

The conference approached the problem in a typical Marxist fashion and its solutions were riddled with hackneyed Marxist terminology such as "people's war", "imperialism" and "oppressed peoples", etc. The final document containing the resolutions adopted by the conference became the doctrine of the SACP/ANC war of terror it was planning to launch in South Africa—a typical Marxist-Leninist subversive war that has become part of

[1] Meli, pp. 163-164.

the tragic history of the second half of the twentieth century. They were determined to wage a long revolution.

The Marxist, Francis Meli, editor of the ANC's journal *Sechaba*, said, "History, including contemporary history, has demonstrated that the overriding determinant in a people's war of liberation is not the military, economic or manpower resources of imperialism (important though these may be) but the intensity and protracted nature of the conflict. . . ."[2] In other words, if the SACP/ANC's war of terror were violent enough and long enough, then the "imperialists", personified by the South African government, would eventually fall to the revolutionaries.

The conference turned its attention to decide on the ways and means of conducting its violent, protracted "people's war" in order to bring the South African regime to its knees.

One way was to attract more "soldiers" to the ranks of the revolutionaries. To do this the ANC made one of its most important decisions at the conference—to open its ranks to non-blacks.

As Meli said: "One of the major decisions of the Morogoro Conference was that non-African political activists and cadres should be integrated into the ANC's External Mission. The alliance between the ANC and other organizations, notably the South African Indian Congress, the Coloured People's Congress, the Congress of Democrats and the South African Congress of Trade Unions (SACTU) had evolved and changed in a constant process of search and renewal. This alliance, as the political opposition in South Africa, offered the only real alternative policy to that of the white supremacists and, indeed, the only realistic alternative government. . . .

"Every step along the road to unity had had to be fought for bitterly, not only in direct struggle of the movement against the racist regime, but also against the forces of conservatism, prejudice, anti-communism, racism, suspicion, and hostility which centuries of colonialism had sown among the various social, religious, class and racial divisions of the South African population."[3]

As egalitarian as this decision may seem, it is important to notice the few non-blacks that joined the ANC were all SACP members. They included Joe Slovo, Yusul Dadoo, Jack Simons, Reg September and others. This new policy had the effect of increasing the presence and clout of the communist presence in the ANC.

The outcome of the discussions over how the SACP/ANC alliance

[2] Meli, p. 164.

[3] Meli, p. 165.

would organize itself to carry out its self-appointed revolutionary mission was contained in a document, "Strategy and Tactics of the ANC", adopted by the conference.

It was a pipe-dream document full of optimism for extending the guerrilla war to the classic mobile phase which would lead to the collapse of the South African government. This would be done via a three-phase program: the initial guerrilla phase would comprise acts of armed propaganda —sabotage, landmines and car bombs; the second phase would be the equilibrium phase in which strong *Umkhonto we Sizwe* units would engage the government's forces in mobile warfare; and the third phase would culminate in a general offensive which would coincide with the collapse of the South African economy, the demoralization of the government's security forces and the isolation of the government.[4]

In point of fact, the document was nothing more than an imitation of the SACP's 1962 program, "The Road to South African Freedom". The ANC's document was allegedly written by Joe Slovo and Joe Mathews of the SACP.[5]

This is not surprising when one examines the document and considers Slovo's role, until recently, of running the ANC's military wing, *Umkhonto we Sizwe*. The Strategy and Tactics document was drafted by someone, or a group of people, who had a sound knowledge of communist revolutionary war doctrine. It reeks of Marxist revolutionary rhetoric. In fact Bunting, in his account of the conference, claimed the document was originally called "The Revolutionary Programme of the ANC".[6]

As Bunting also points out: "The Communist Party conducted its own independent activity during this period, holding several meetings of its Central Committee. . . . Both the ANC conference at Morogoro and the Communist Party augmented committee meeting revealed once again how the development of both organizations went hand in hand, the one complementing the other in the fulfillment of the national democratic revolution."[7] A cynic might suggest that instead of complementing one another, one was dictating to the other. At any rate, the Marxist influence was extremely evident in the finished product of the Strategy and Tactics document. It looked and sounded just like a regurgitated version of the

[4] See: Hough, M., "Revolutionary Warfare in South Africa," *Strategic Review*, Institute for Strategic Studies, University of Pretoria, Pretoria, January 1986.

[5] "South Africa:The Party faithful", *Africa Confidential*, Vol. 31, No. 1, January 12, 1990, p. 2.

[6] Bunting, B., *Moses Kotane*, Inkululeko Publications, London, 1975, p. 281.

[7] Bunting, p. 282.

SACP's 1962 document. An example, one of many, will show the similarities between the two documents:

The SACP's 1962 program, "The Road to South African Freedom", states: "As its immediate and foremost task, the South African Communist Party works for a united front of national liberation. It strives to unite all sections and classes of oppressed and democratic people for a national democratic revolution to destroy White domination. . . . The destruction of colonialism and the winning of national freedom is the essential condition and the key for future advances to the supreme aim of the Communist Party: the establishment of a socialist South Africa, laying the foundation of a classless, communist society."[8]

The ANC's "Strategy and Tactics", adopted at Morogoro seven years later, said: "The struggle of the oppressed people of South Africa is taking place within an international context of transition to the Socialist system, of the breakdown of the colonial system as a result of national liberation and socialist revolution, and the fight for social and economic progress by the people of the whole world."[9]

Although the wording of the two documents is not exactly the same, the message is similar and loaded with Marxist phraseology. The influence of the SACP is clear and overwhelming.

Another important decision taken at the conference was the establishment of a group within the ANC to oversee and manage the day-to-day activities of the so-called liberation struggle in South Africa. This group was called the Revolutionary Council.

Meli tells us why the ANC created the Revolutionary Council: ". . . The machinery was created to deal professionally and adequately with internal reconstruction and propaganda, planning of the commencement of sustained guerrilla operations and the injection back home of our trained personnel to form the core of the armed force. This was also meant to correct the imbalance between the work of the movement externally and internally; to correct our priorities and to bring home the idea of the primacy of the internal needs and the fact that the only possible justification for the existence and activity of the ANC outside the country was as an adjunct of the needs of the situation at home. . . ."[10]

[8] "The Road to South African Freedom", programme of the South African Communist Party adopted at the fifth national conference of the Party held inside the country in 1962, in: *South African Communists Speak*, Inkululeko Publications, 1981, p. 286.

[9] "Strategy and Tactics", adopted at the ANC Consultative Conference, Morogoro, Tanzania, 1969, p. 2.

[10] Meli, p. 164.

The ANC formed the Revolutionary Council, active until 1983, composed of blacks, whites, Coloured and Indians, essentially to oversee the activities of *Umkhonto we Sizwe*. It quickly fell under the control of the communists, as Joe Mathews became its first secretary. Helping Mathews exercise control was the fact that all non-black members of the Council were SACP members.

The conference also announced the formal alliance between the SACP and the ANC. This was nothing new but now they were announcing the fact to all the world. This was, however, an important event within the ANC because it effectively closed the doors to any other ideological influence except Marxism. In such a closed environment the Party ruled the roost and could extend the tentacles of its control throughout the ANC without worrying about any other competing non-Marxist heresies.

Oliver Tambo, the head of the ANC, was the only one in a position to challenge the Marxists if he so desired. He had worldwide stature and prestige and was in a position to oppose the Marxists. He didn't, but the Party wasn't taking any chances. The Party controlled him by keeping him trotting around the globe on exhaustive rounds of diplomatic visits. This kept him out of the day-to-day administrative and political goings on within the ANC. This was ably handled by his presidential staff, which has become a SACP fiefdom.[11]

The SACP arrogantly argues the necessity for their control and use of the ANC (which the SACP styles as "the mass national movement") in their own publications. They base arguments on the haughty belief, endemic to all communist parties, that the working class can rarely, if ever, bring about a revolutionary transformation on its own. It requires the Party to guide it.

The African Communist states, "The achievement of the aims of the National Democratic Revolution demands a broad alliance of all classes and strata. In organizational terms the Liberation Alliance is expressed through the liberation front headed by the African National Congress. The ANC is a broad mass national movement which attracts to its ranks all Africans and other revolutionaries, whatever their class origins. . . . The ANC correctly continues to retain its character as a broad national movement.

"Marxism/Leninism teaches that the Party of the working class has the leading role in the struggle. The need to give correct guidance to the revolutionary cause does not imply that the party must insist on projecting itself as the public 'leader' of every step in the unfolding of the conflict. The question of whether it is correct for the Party to strive to place itself

[11] *Africa Confidential*, Vol. 31, No. 1, p. 2.

exclusively at the head of the different stages of the revolutionary upsurge depends upon the conditions of a particular struggle at each of these stages and the precise role of the class which it represents. This most advance class of our epoch can rarely, if ever, bring about a revolutionary transformation on its own. It works at all times with social forces. If correct leadership of the democratic revolution requires the strengthening of the national movement as the major mass organizational force, then this is precisely the way in which a party exercises its leading and vanguard role in the real (and not vulgar) sense of the term."[12]

The ANC conference at Morogoro had the end result of consolidating the SACP's grip on the ANC. The ANC had become another communist front, similar to the South Vietnamese National Liberation Front—the Viet Cong—a supposedly nationalist organization open to all but where the important key posts were all held by communists.[13] The communists were thus in a position to direct the organization so that it would aid the communists as they try to impose a Marxist regime in the future in South Africa.

This was confirmed when the ANC expelled the Gang of Eight—eight blacks expelled for their opposition to the communist presence in the hierarchy of the ANC. One of them, Ambrose Makiwane, charged that "The trouble the African people have at present is that our strategy and tactics are in the hands of, and dominated by a small clique of non-Africans."[14] He blamed this on "the disastrous Morogoro Consultative Congress which opened ANC membership to non-Africans."[15]

The Gang of Eight made public their disagreement with the ANC in an extensive memorandum released in London on December 11, 1975. They complained that there was an absence of democratic consultation within the organization, that the traditional ANC policies and ideology had been diluted, and that the SACP, whose leaders were white, had effective control of the ANC.[16]

These charges were similar to those in the late 1950s during the

[12] *The African Communist*, No. 87, Fourth Quarter 1981, pp. 32-35.

[13] Campbell, K., *ANC: A Soviet Task Force?*, p. 49.

[14] "Soviet, East German and Cuban Involvement in Fomenting Terrorism in Southern Africa", *Report of the Chairman of the Subcommittee on Security and Terrorism to the Committee on the Judiciary*, United States Senate, Ninety-seventh Congress, Second Session, November 1982, Washington, D.C., p. 7.

[15] *Ibid.*

[16] *Ibid.*

ANC-PAC split. The passage of time had not rid the ANC of its African nationalist forces. By now, though, the communists were in control and, as Makiwane and his friends found out, the ANC leadership had no truck with those who disagreed with its policies.

With their controlling influence over the ANC, the SACP could now turn its attention to waging the revolutionary war in South Africa.

ANC recruits at an ANC terrorist training camp in Zambia.

Edendale, a black township near Pietermaritzburg, has been the scene of violent clashes between the ANC/UDF alliance and *Inkatha,* the Zulu political and cultural organization of Gatsha Buthelezi.

A mobile SAP police station in Umbali.

ANC terrorism at work—the Pretoria Church Street car bomb blast in 1983.

ANC sabotage efforts on railroad tracks in South Africa.

The ANC's "armed struggle"—blowing up electrical transmission line pylons.

"With our boxes of matches and our necklaces we shall liberate this country."—Winnie Mandela, April 13, 1986. An example of how the ANC and Winnie Mandela will liberate South Africa by means of the necklace.

Durban Daily News/Peter B.G. Duffy, Photographer

The ANC's contempt for religious values, as evidenced by their attempt to necklace the Christ figure in a Durban churchyard.

Afrikaanse Pers Publikasies

The ANC 's underground headquarters at Lilliesleaf Farm in Rivonia, a northern suburb of Johannesburg. Note the radio antennas on the roof.

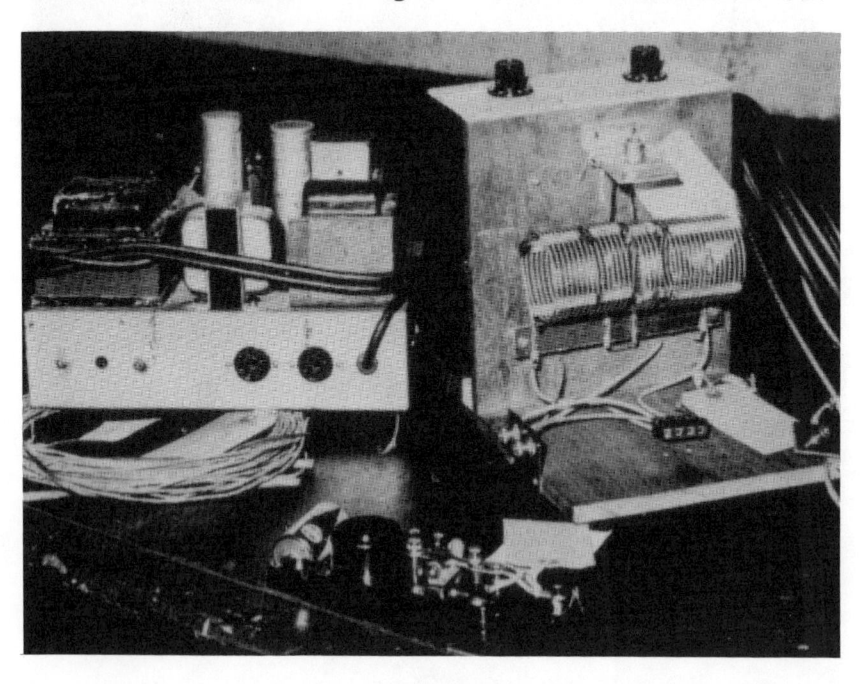

Afrikaanse Pers Publikasies

Shortwave radio transmitter used by the ANC found at Lilliesleaf Farm.

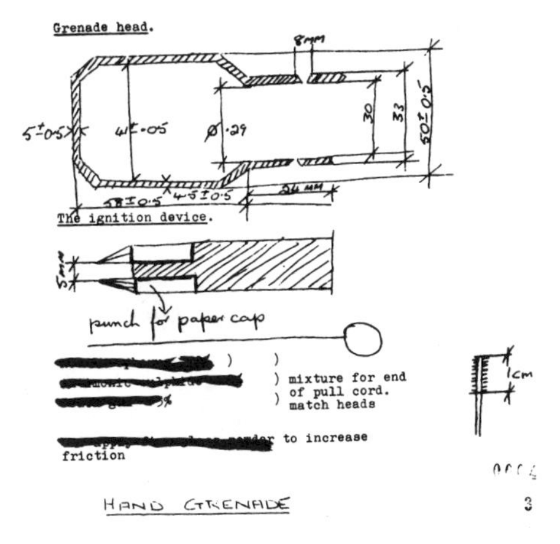

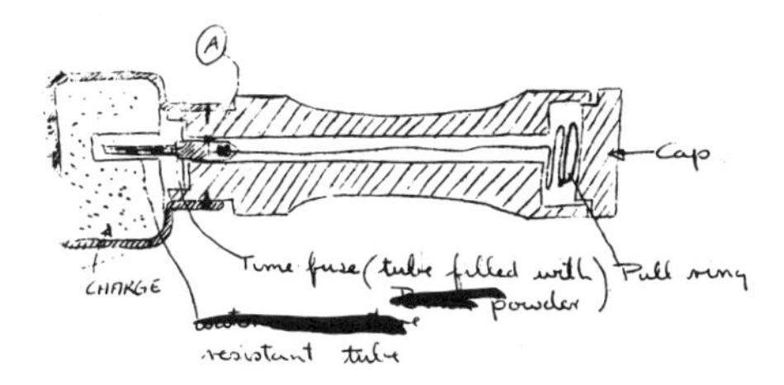

ANC plans for manufacturing hand grenades found in the documents at Lilliesleaf Farm.

Voortrekkerpers

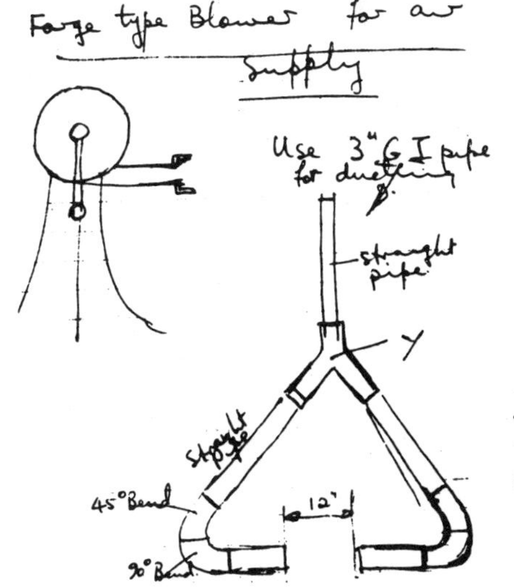

Plans for a forge for making homemade arms found in the documents seized from the ANC headquarters at Lilliesleaf Farm.

Voortrekkerpers

Voortrekkerpers

ANC homemade gasoline bombs. Note the delayed action device inserted in the open can on the left. These were found at the ANC headquarters at Lilliesleaf Farm.

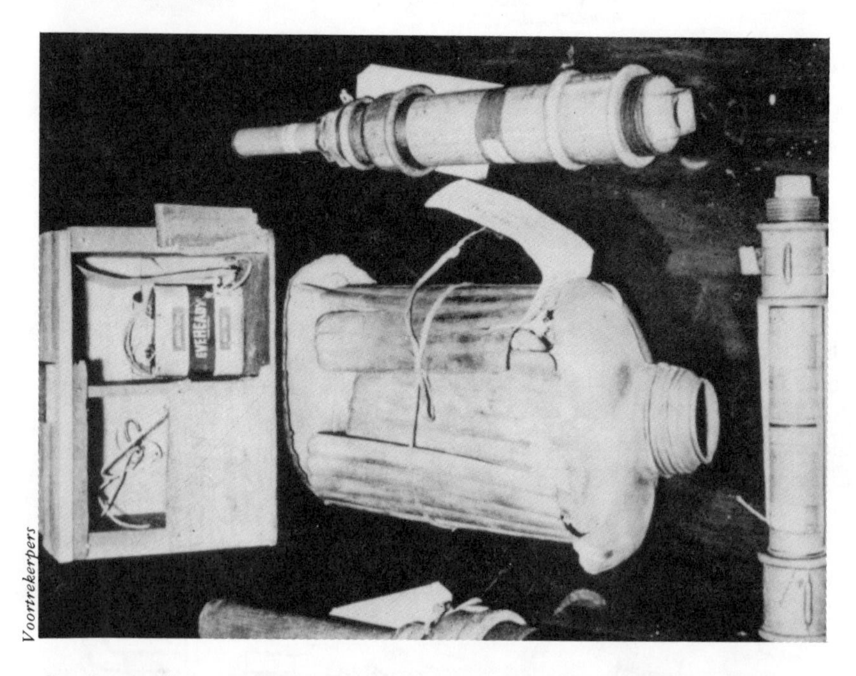

Voortrekkerpers

Crude, deadly weapons made by the ANC terrorists at Lilliesleaf Farm. In this photo are a hand grenade, pipe bombs and a landmine.

Ronnie Kasrils, an influential member of both the ANC and the SACP, is a strong proponent of the ANC's armed struggle.

ANC President Oliver Tambo.

Chief Alert Luthuli, ANC head who saw no problem in working with communists.

Beeld

Aerial view of rampaging rioters during the 1976 Soweto riots.

Rapport

Armed rioters during the 1976 Soweto riots.

Beeld

Dr. Melville Edelstein, a physician who devoted his practice to giving aid and comfort to his black patients in Soweto, was brutally murdered by those he sought to help. Note the warning "Beware" marked on the wooden box beside the body.

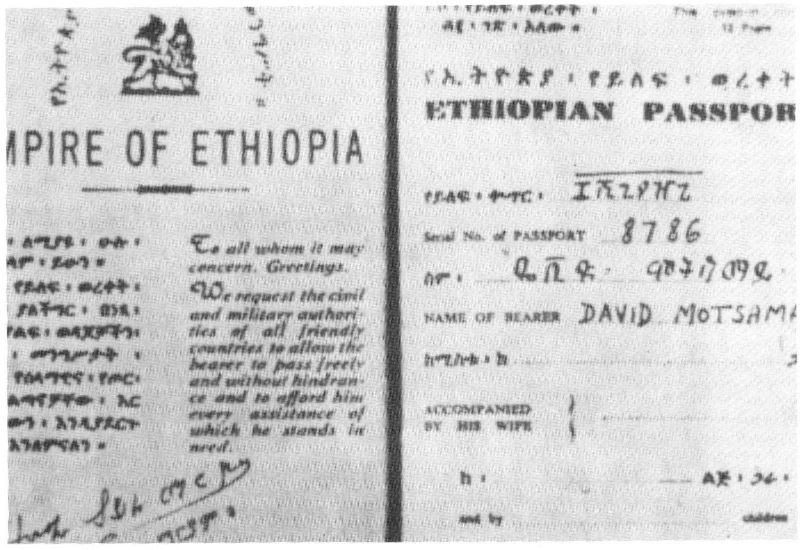
MPIRE OF ETHIOPIA

To all whom it may concern. Greetings.
We request the civil and military authorities of all friendly countries to allow the bearer to pass freely and without hindrance and to afford him every assistance of which he stands in need.

ETHIOPIAN PASSPOR

Serial No. of PASSPORT 8786

NAME OF BEARER DAVID MOTSAM

ACCOMPANIED BY HIS WIFE

and by children

Afrikaanse Pers Publikasies

Nelson Mandela's forged passport used in his travels around Africa where he received terrorist training. The passport was issued by Emperor Haile Selassie of Ethiopia and was found in Mandela's possession when he was arrested.

The electrified security fence along the Northern Transvaal border between South Africa and Zimbabwe.

The Limpopo River separates South Africa from Zimbabwe, which provides sanctuary and support for ANC terrorists.

The Beit Bridge across the Limpopo River is a key transportation link for South Africa's northern neighbors. Goods to and from these must pass over this vital link. Closing this bridge would shut down the economies of Zambia and Zimbabwe.

A solitary South African soldier on guard duty on the Beit Bridge.

A sudden rain storm has flooded a dip in the road from Messina to Weipe in the Soutspansburg Military District in the Northern Transvaal. This area is a favorite infiltration route for ANC terrorists infiltrating into South Africa. Nor are the terrorists adverse to planting landmines on this dirt road.

Wildlife, ostriches and a cheetah, in the thick bush country of the Northern Transvaal.

Wide World Photos, Inc.

Moammar Qadaffi—"We consider ourselves comrades in arms."—Nelson Mandela's remarks to Qadaffi May 18, 1990.

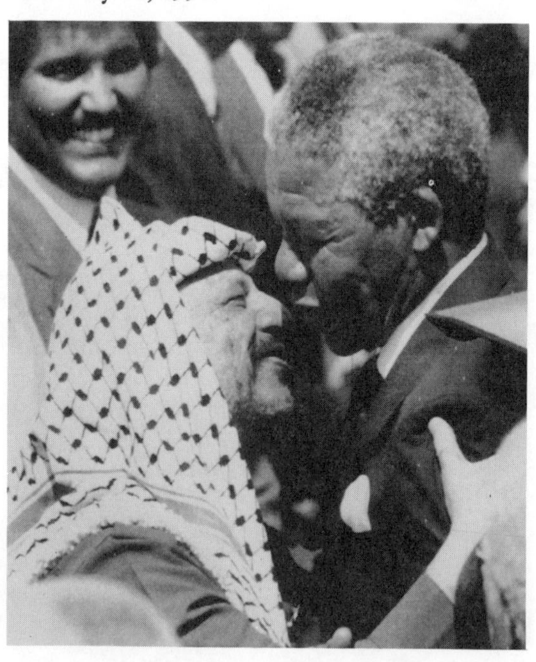
Wide World Photos, Inc.

Mandela lovingly embraces Yassir Arafat, another "comrade in arms."

NELSON MANDELA'S

Wide World Photos, Inc.

Fidel Castro—"There is one thing where that country stands out head and shoulders above the rest—that is in its love for human rights and liberty." —Nelson Mandela's remarks on Cuba.

Wide World Photos, Inc.

Solidarity—Mandela and South African Communist Party boss Joe Slovo at a SACP rally in South Africa.

GALLERY OF HEROES

A typical picturesque Zulu *kraal* in Natal.

UDF graffiti in Umbali, a black township near Pietermaritzburg.

ANC graffiti in Edendale, a strife-torn black township in Natal.

UDF headquarters in Pietermaritzburg.

Part of the international isolation pillar of the ANC/SACP revolutionary strategy—an anti-apartheid demonstration in London.

Black workers learning to become bricklayers by means of a government program.

The Star

Joe Slovo, General Secretary of the SACP, addresses a rally in Mitchel Plains, near Cape Town.

ANC/UDF directed violence during the 1984-86 unrest in South Africa. The whip-wielding person in the foreground is one of the "comrades" whose job is to persuade, via the whip if necessary, the township residents to particpate in the violence.

The Star

Nelson Mandela giving the ANC/SACP clenched-fist salute at a rally in Soweto.

The Pan African Congress national executive committee in September 1959. PAC founder, Robert Sobukwe, is in the front row, second from the left.

The Star

Spears and other crude, but deadly, weapons abandoned by rioters who marched on the police station at Sharpeville, after they were fired on by the police.

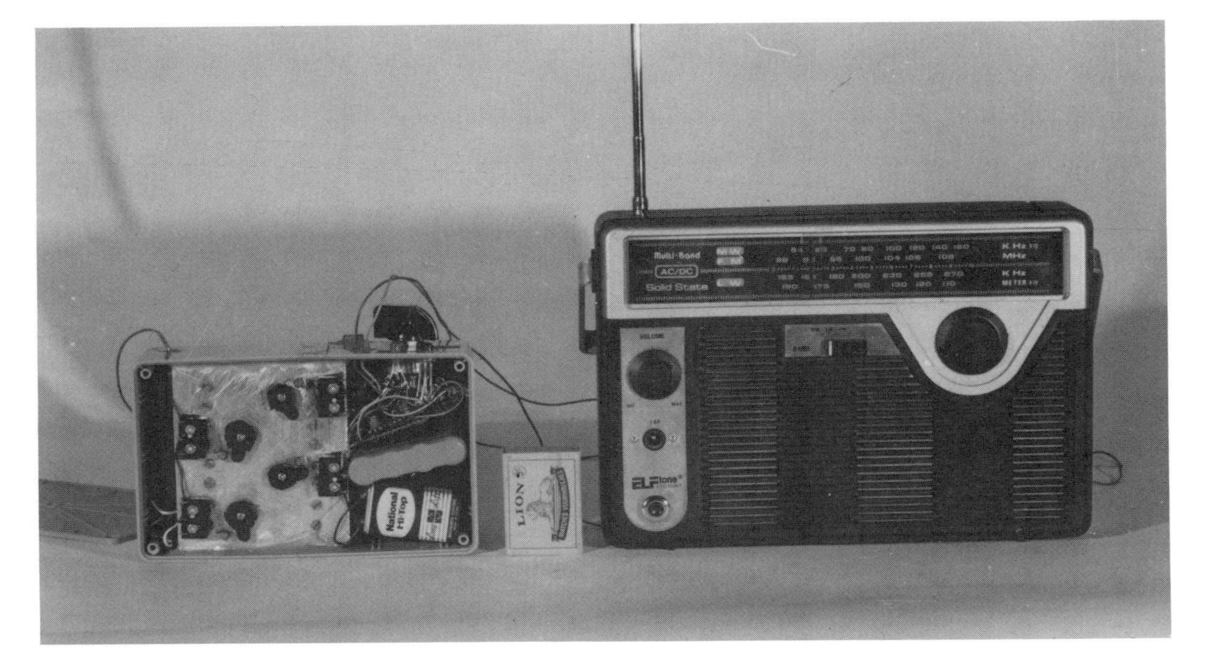

The transmitter and receiver for a radio-detonated bomb smuggled into South Africa by the Dutch citizen Klaus de Jonge. He was an ANC courier who transported weapons into South Africa for use by ANC terrorists. He was caught, escaped and sought refuge in the Dutch Embassy, which gave him asylum, thus becoming an international celebrity for the ANC/SACP cause.

Burning vehicle during the 1984-86 ANC-inspired unrest in South Africa.

Wide World Photos, Inc.

Ideological soulmates, Jesse Jackson and Nelson Mandela.

Wide World Photos, Inc.

Left to right: Joe Slovo, General Secretary SACP, Chris Hani, Chief of Staff, *Umkhonyo we Sizwe*, Joe Modise, military commander, *Umkhonyo we Sizwe*.

Captured Soviet-Supplied Weapons

1. 10 RPG 7 projectile
2. 10 RPG 7 Propellant Charge

3, 4. 1 RPG 7 Launch Tube

5. 9 Limpet Mine

6, 7, 8, 9. 1 Luger Pistol with 2 Magazines

10. 1 x A.K.M.S. Rifle
11. 1 x A.K.M.S. Rifle
12. 2 x R.G.D. 5 Handgrenades
13. 5 x 71 Handgrenades
14. 3 x RG. 42 Handgrenades

Captured Soviet-Supplied Weapons

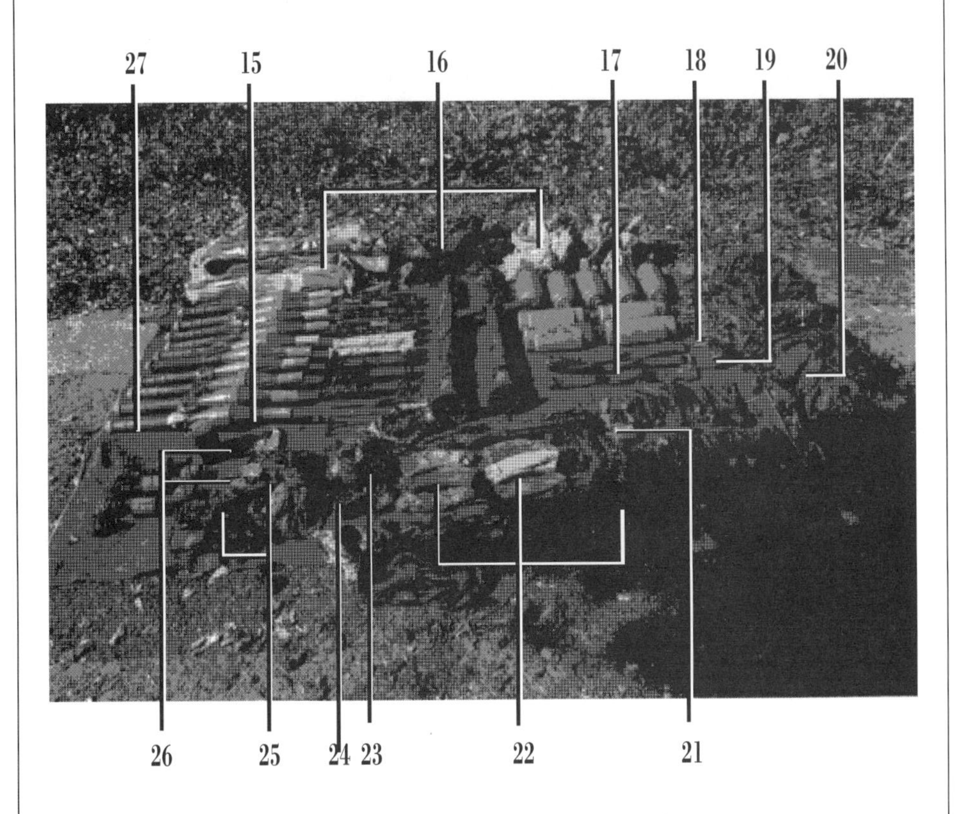

15. Cleaning Kit for RPG 7 Launch tube
16. Plastic bag in which articles were packed
17. 3 Limpet Mine carrying straps
18. 9 Limpet Mine ignitors
19. Percussion caps for limpet mine ignitors
20. Plastic refuse bag in wich articles were covered
21. 3 boxes, each containing 25 9mm rounds
22. 8 AK 47 magazines-each carries 10 rounds
23. 10 boxes, each containing 20 7.62mm rounds
24. 1 box containing 10 7.62mm rounds
25. 2 optical sights with containing bags for RPG 7 launcher tubes
26. 2 Handgrips for RPG 7 launcher tubes
27. 1 sealed tin containing 10 hand grenade ignitors
28. Shows the hole after weapons and explosives were removed

Reuters/Beckmann

Old habits die hard; Walter Sisulu still supports the communists.

Al Venter

Two victims of the PAC terrorist wing POQO massacre at the Bashee Bridge.

Isandhlwana, the site of the massacre of the 1st. Battalion, 24th (2nd. Warwickshire) Regiment of the British Army by the Zulus on January 22, 1879, during the Anglo-Zulu War of 1879.

Monument honoring the defenders of Rorke's Drift located in the cemetery at Rorke's Drift. Here the British redeemed their honor lost at *Isandhlwana.* Though outnumbered forty to one, the small force withstood the constant Zulu attacks. More Victoria Crosses (eleven) for gallantry were awarded as a result of this battle than any other in British military history.

Like the guillotine of the French Revolution's reign of terror, the burning tire has become a symbol of terror in the ANC/SACP's war of terror in South Africa.

11

ANC DOLDRUMS

Although the ANC had adopted the SACP's blueprint for using an armed struggle to seize power in South Africa, translating that plan into reality proved to be a different matter. So far their track record in conducting a revolutionary war has been pretty shabby.

Operation MUYIBUYE was the first step in the process along the road of revolution in South Africa. Hoping to emulate Fidel Castro's success in Cuba, the SACP/ANC alliance decided that its guerrillas would be the spark that touched off a mass uprising inside South Africa.

The operation's tactical approach followed the Guevara/Debray model of revolutionary war. The basic assumption under this model is that it is not necessary for a revolutionary climate to be formed before launching a revolutionary armed struggle. The proper climate can be created by the revolutionaries themselves. The first thing the revolutionaries must do is to establish a small armed cadre (the "foco"). Popular support wasn't necessary during the early stages of the revolution; it would come later, after the guerrillas had begun their campaign. The action of the "foco" would create a reaction from the population favorable to the advancement of the revolution.[1]

The "foco" theory was a dismal failure in Latin America as revolutionaries there failed repeatedly to create powerful revolutionary movements. Yet so strongly did its creators believe in the theory that, like Don Quixote chasing windmills, they pursued it to the bitter end. Guevara was killed and

[1] Evans, E., *Wars Without Splendor*, Greenwood Press, New York, 1987, pp. 61-63; and, Porzecanski, A.C., *Uruguay's Tupamaros*, Praegers Publishers, New York, 1973, pp. 14-15.

Debray captured in 1967 while trying to apply their strategy in a hopeless attempt to overthrow the Bolivian government.[2]

As in Latin America, the ANC "focos" were exceptionally vulnerable to the activities of police security forces. The general political apathy among the black population made the police task much easier. All the agitators and leaders were either in jail, in exile or burrowed deep in the underground. The revolutionary front was in shambles. (One of the purposes of the Morogoro conference was to attempt to regroup the revolutionary front.)

The outlawed ANC and PAC were limited to small scale acts of sabotage inside South Africa. Attempts to infiltrate small groups of terrorists to conduct small-scale operations usually ended up in quick arrests of the would-be guerrillas by the security forces.

The departure of the ANC and PAC, because of the banning, jailing and exile of their leaders, created a political vacuum among the blacks in South Africa.It was not long, however, before a new group stepped into this vacuum and political activity resumed among the blacks.

The new group came from among black students. They had sought to vent their political steam by playing a role in the white anti-government National Union of South African Students (NUSAS) but quickly became disenchanted with the typical white liberal paternalistic attitude it exhibited. Finally, in December 1968, they formed the South African Student's Organization (SASO) as a national organization of student representatives from the black universities. The first president of SASO was Steve Biko, a medical student at the University of Natal.

The year 1968 was a period of worldwide student unrest. In the United States, the student anti-war campaign was in full swing on college campuses, creating turmoil throughout the American college system. Students were also heavily involved in the anti-war marches and demonstrations in cities all over the United States. Student revolts in France had almost ousted the DeGaulle government, and student rebellions were occurring in West Germany as well.

These events affected the growing number of students in South Africa. The number of black pupils in the urban areas had more than doubled in the ten years since 1960 as the demands of industry and commerce grew by leaps and bounds for trained skilled labor.[3] This naturally led to an increase in the

[2] For an eyewitness account of Guevara's last days see: Rodriquez, F. I., & Weisman, J., *Shadow Warrior*, Simon & Shuster, New York, 1989, pp. 157-171.

[3] Johnson, S., "The Soldiers of Luthuli: Youth in the Politics of Resistance in South Africa", from: *South Africa No Turning Back*, ed. by Shaun Johnson, McMillan Press Ltd., London, 1988, p. 100.

number of students attending the black universities in South Africa. As the black school population continued to increase by roughly 100 percent every five years from 1970 on, it loomed large as a potential political force.

Biko was an extraordinary talented and important figure in the history of black opposition to apartheid. He was the founding father of Black Consciousness in South Africa, a credo preaching black unity and black self-reliance. Black Consciousness owed much to both the exclusive Africanism of the PAC and the Black American Civil Rights movement.

Biko was a charismatic figure and a superb orator possessing an extraordinary gift of leadership. "He had at that time extraordinary magnetism. His hold on his all-black audience was almost frightening; it was if they were listening to a new 'messiah' ", said Biko's friend Aelred Stubbs.[4]

Biko stressed that his idea of Black Consciousness was in reality "an attitude of the mind, a way of life". Blacks needed "group cohesion and solidarity" so they could wield the economic and political power they already possessed but didn't realize they had.

He popularized the slogan: "Black man, you are on your own" and argued that blacks could only prepare themselves for physical liberation by ridding themselves of psychological subservience—black self-esteem had to be engendered as a prerequisite for the revolution.[5]

Biko stressed the importance of black unity and wanted blacks to distance themselves from white liberals, such as the South African journalist Donald Woods, who claimed to be an intimate friend of Biko and wrote a book about him.

Biko warned: ". . . The biggest mistake the Black world ever made was to assume that whoever opposed apartheid was an ally. For a long time the Black world has been looking at the governing party and not so much at the whole power structure as the object of their rage. In a sense the very political vocabulary that the Blacks have used has been inherited from the liberals. Therefore, it is not surprising that alliances were formed so easily with the liberals.

"Who are the liberals in South Africa? It is that curious bunch of non-conformists who explain their participation in negative terms; that bunch of do-gooders that goes under all sorts of names—liberals, leftists, etc.

[4] Biko, S., *I Write What I Like: A Selection of his Writings edited with a personal memoir by Aelred Stubbs*, C.R., London, 1978, p. 158.

[5] Robinson, S., "After the Biko movie, will the real Donald Woods stand up?", *Sunday Times*, September 20, 1987.

These are people who argue that they are not responsible for White racism and the country's 'inhumanity to the Black man'; these are the people who claim that they too feel the oppression just as acutely as the Blacks and therefore should be jointly involved in the Black man's struggle for a place under the sun; in short, these people who say that they have Black souls wrapped up in the White skins. . . ."[6]

The Black Consciousness Movement (BCM) was formed to carry the banner of Biko's Black Consciousness ideology in South Africa. It swept the non-white campuses in South Africa like wildfire. So fast did it grow and so large did it become, almost overnight, that it became a serious headache for the SACP/ANC alliance. As it grew and grew, it would, if unchecked, outstrip the banned alliance's attempts to control it, no matter how hard they tried.

Supporters of the BCM were widespread, ranging from genuine Black Africanist nationalists of the old PAC stripe who hated the whites to those who merely despised the policies of the government. The BCM umbrella was so widespread that it could collapse or grow depending upon the political climate of the moment. Besides, the leaders were blacks and not white intellectuals such as those who controlled the SACP. The black leaders of the BCM showed no inclination to turn over the leadership reins to whites, be they communists or not.

This independent nature was not promising material for creating a communist-led revolution in South Africa. This, however, didn't stop the SACP from trying to infiltrate and take over the BCM. The SACP became more alarmed as the posts on the various committees that kept springing up to carry forward the BCM were being filled with genuine black nationalists who were not sympathetic to the communists. The SACP tried to form communist cells within these committees in order to influence and guide them but their efforts failed, largely due to the efforts of Biko, Abram Tiro and Harry Kengwekhulu.[7]

The SACP/ANC alliance didn't like the situation one bit. Through its organ, *Sechaba*, the ANC unleashed a furious attack on the BCM and its leaders. Throughout 1977 *Sechaba* routinely ran articles attacking the BCM as being "backed by the West", or, as Alfred Nzo, secretary general of the ANC called them, "new allies of imperialism" and "substitutes for the Bantustan

[6] Dube, D., *The Rise of Azania The Fall of South Africa*, Daystar Publishing, Lusaka, Zambia, 1983, p. 90.

[7] McClure, P., "Through the Looking Glass: The South African View", in, Venter, Al J., *Challenge: Southern Africa within the African Revolutionary Context*, Ashanti Publishing Ltd., Gibraltar, 1989, p. 422.

leaders."[8] To make sure they got the message Nzo said, "some of those who only yesterday were hailed as the new revolutionary upsurge inside our country are now important allies of imperialism against the ANC."[9]

In addition to their general attacks on the BCM, the ANC tried to discredit its most visible and popular leader, Steve Biko. According to *Sechaba* (first quarter, 1977), Steve Biko was tied in with British liberals and, by implication, to U.S. imperialism, a most heinous crime in the eyes of the communist-dominated ANC.[10] (Of course the ANC quickly changed its tune after Biko's death and tried to claim Biko and his BCM as one of their own. For example *Sechaba* editor Francis Meli claims: "The BCM was part of the broad forces fighting together with, and not in competition with, the ANC, against colonialism, racism and exploitation in South Africa. . . ."[11])

In spite of SACP/ANC opposition and fears, the BCM spread to other parts of the black community. As a result a non-student adult wing, the Black People's Convention (BPC), was founded in July 1972.

The government cracked down on the BCM in 1973, blaming a wave of strikes on the influence of the BCM and its leaders. They banned Biko and seven other leaders. Biko could no longer speak publicly and was restricted to King Williams Town in the Eastern Cape.

Inflation and a strained economy brought forth a wave of strikes and unrest in South Africa from 1973-1976. These strikes showed a growing militancy on the part of the strike leaders which many claimed was the result of the spreading influence of the Black Consciousness Movement.

The leaders of the movement became more defiant, more uncompromising in their demands, and more militant in their rhetoric after 1973. The government reacted to this situation by banning or detaining dozens of the leaders. Others left the country in exile. Things were beginning to look bleak for the BCM.

However, in 1974 an event occurred in a neighboring country that caused joy and exultation within the movement. The Portuguese government had been overthrown by a leftist coup and it was only a matter of time before they turned power over in Mozambique to the Marxist FRELIMO guerrilla movement. On September 25, 1974, the South African Students Organization (SASO) and the BPC defied a government ban and held a "Viva FRELIMO" rally in Durban, celebrating the Marxist victory in Mozambique. The police

[8] *Revisionism and Southern Africa*, Revolutionary Communist Party (USA), Chicago, nd, p. 14.

[9] *Ibid.*

[10] *Ibid.*

[11] Meli, p. 182.

moved in and arrested many of the black participants. A two-year trial resulted that finally concluded on December 15, 1976. The evidence in the trial consisted primarily of Black Consciousness pamphlets, articles and other writings. The accused were charged with, among other things, conspiracy to use unconstitutional or violent means to bring about a revolutionary change. The leaders of the rally were convicted and some were sentenced to prison.

Biko didn't let the banning stop his political activity. He founded the Eastern Cape Branch of the BPC and worked as its branch secretary until forbidden in 1975.

The police arrested and jailed Biko on numerous occasions during the period 1975 through 1977. During his last jailing in 1977 he died on September 12th, as a result of beatings he received while in detention. During his various imprisonments Biko's friends and supporters organized campaigns to have him released. The ANC opposed these campaigns, stating that there were more well-known people in jail much longer than Biko had been, who were more worthy of freedom.[12]

The escalating militant mood among blacks culminated in the Soweto riots that broke out on June 16, 1976. This outbreak of violence was bigger than the famous one at Sharpesville some sixteen years earlier.

The triggering factor in the outbreak of the rioting was one of language: the requirement that Afrikaans was henceforth be the language of instruction in the schools. Afrikaans is one of South Africa's two official languages, English is the other. Blacks did not want to learn Afrikaans, a problem that still exists today. (Black students in the universities—especially in the Black Universities—study their lessons either in one of South Africa's many black languages or in English. This puts them at a disadvantage in South African society because of the fact that most business and governmental affairs are conducted in Afrikaans.)

On June 16th a protest march held in Soweto by black pupils protesting the use of Afrikaans escalated into violence. The police had made attempts to break up the demonstrations and were met by stone-throwing youths. The police opened fire and rioting erupted all over Soweto.[13] The rioting quickly spread to other black townships in South Africa. By the end of June, the official death toll was 140, with more than a thousand injured, 900 arrested and a huge amount of property damaged or destroyed.

Even the SACP/ANC alliance was caught off guard by the massive civil disobedience. The ANC declared that the riots came as " a complete surprise

[12] "Revisionism and Southern Africa", p. 14.

[13] *Rand Daily Mail*, June 17 & 18, 1976.

for everybody" and that the ANC "was not prepared for these events."[14] Experienced political agitators and others found themselves swept up in the wave of youthful thuggery and rioting.

Zulu workers in the mines on the Rand saw their living quarters ransacked and in some case burnt down by the youthful mobs. They retaliated in typical Zulu fashion by forming *impis* and hunted down the arsonists, murderers and rioters and dispensed Zulu-style justice. Not surprisingly, the unrest quickly died down in that area.

A government-appointed Commission of Inquiry failed to find conclusive proof of SACP/ANC involvement with the student rioters. However, they certainly found ample proof that they tried their best to fan the flames once the violence started. There was conclusive evidence that the ANC and SACP quickly published and distributed a large number of pamphlets that played a part in inciting the rioters to continue with their depredations after the initial outbreak of violence.

However, Henry Pike in his *History of Communism in South Africa* shows that the KGB was aware as early as two months before the riots that trouble was coming to South Africa. He describes an extraordinary meeting in London between the white South African communist, Joe Slovo, and a former secret lover (secret from his wife, that is) of his living in South Africa. Slovo's twenty-year affair with the woman had produced a son, who also attended the meeting in Trafalgar Square in London between the two old lovers. Slovo warned his former mistress to leave South Africa immediately, as there was great trouble coming there in the middle of the year.[15]

When Slovo's great trouble came it obviously was more than even he imagined, as the SACP/ANC was forced into trying to ride the back of a rampaging tiger and keep up with events instead of leading them.

As the rioting subsided, thousands of youths anticipated the coming crackdown and left the country, with many ending up joining the exiled ANC or PAC. Those joining the ANC became ready recruits for *Umkhonto we Sizwe*.

The exodus of youth from South Africa into the waiting arms of the ANC alarmed the SACP and demonstrated the depths to which the movement had fallen since the Rivonia trial. So few recruits had flocked to the standards of *Umkhonto we Sizwe* in the interim that the party disbanded its commissariat in 1970. Now they were being flooded with recruits and, in

[14] *Sechaba*, January 1987, pp. 21-22.

[15] Pike, p. 483.

order to ensure ideological purity in the new recruits, the Party quickly revived the commissariat.

According to *Africa Confidential*, "The Party dispatched Dr. Francis Meli, a Central Committee member, to be the first political commissar of the Nova Katenga camp in Angola, the Sandhurst of a whole generation of the post-Soweto *Umkhonto we Sizwe* officer corps. The Party underpinned this drive for ideological purity with the appointment of Andrew Masondo, also a Central Committee member, as National Commissar of the ANC to ensure that even those outside the army were within the Party's ideological orbit. Meli was impatient with the street-wise Sowetans under his charge. . . . He was reassigned to the editorship of *Sechaba*, the official journal of the ANC. . . . The fatherly Marks Shope, a veteran Party man and ex-secretary general of the South African Congress of Trade Unions (SACTU) was brought in to replace Meli at Katenga. It was Shope, later assisted by Jack Simons, who converted the Black Consciousness-inclined Soweto youth to Marxism. . . ."[16]

Other recruits scooped up by the ANC were taken to training centers run by the SACP/ANC in Angola, Mozambique and Zambia. The ANC sent the better and more politically reliable trainees to camps in Libya, the Soviet Union, Cuba, East Germany and Nigeria.

The movement was finally accumulating the needed cannon-fodder to use in their violent revolution in South Africa. At long last, it seemed possible for the SACP/ANC to get out of their doldrums and begin the task of executing their grandiose plans, made at Morogoro, to violently seize power in South Africa.

[16] *Africa Confidential*, Vol. 31, No. 1, p. 2.

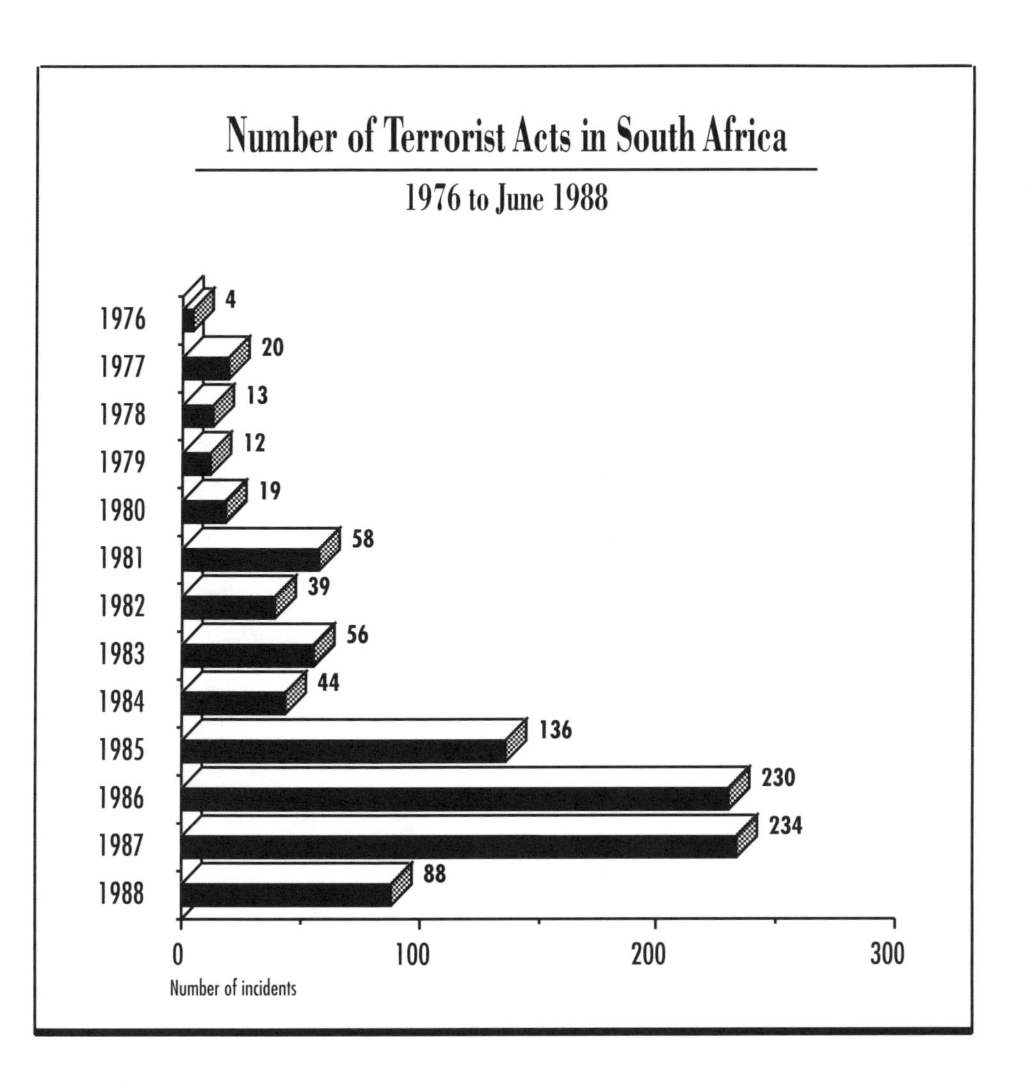
Number of Terrorist Acts in South Africa
1976 to June 1988
1976
1977
1978
1979
1980
1981
1982
1983
1984
1985
1986
1987
1988
4
20
13
12
19
58
39
56
44
136
230
234
88
0
100
200
300
Number of incidents

12

YOUTH IN THE SACP/ANC REVOLUTIONARY WAR

Youth are valuable for a variety of functions in the Marxist worldview. One of their most useful and obvious tasks is to be the soldiers on the battlefield in the revolutionary war. It has been said that war is a job for the young and it is no secret that geriatrics are not found in abundance in armies throughout the world—even guerrilla armies.

In spite of the general contempt for human life that permeates Marxism-Leninism, they look on youth as something more than just cannon-fodder.

Ever since the Bolsheviks seized power in Russia in 1917, the youth have taken their place, along with the workers, as a vital cog of any communist revolutionary movement formed to seize power and impose a Marxist-Leninist totalitarian dictatorship on the unfortunate targeted country.

The importance of youth in the communist revolutionary scheme of things is a constant theme running from Lenin down to the present SACP/ANC alliance. Lenin said: "In a certain sense, it is the youth that will be faced with the actual task of creating a communist society."[1] The reason, said the late Marxist dictator of Mozambique, Samora Machel, is that "young

[1] Lenin, V.I., *Collected Works*, Vol. 31, p. 253.

people represent the greenhouse, the nursery, out of which will emerge the cadres of all kinds that are needed to build an advanced socialist society."[2]

This "Greenhouse Effect" Machel fondly spoke of is especially important for any ideological movement. The necessity to perpetuate and insure the survival of the movement in the future requires the capturing of the hearts and minds (a very important slogan in revolutionary war) of youth at an early age in order to mold them into the future leaders and fighters of the movement.

It is well to keep in mind that it was young turks that came from the ranks of the ANC Youth League—Nelson Mandela, Oliver Tambo and Walter Sisulu, to name just three—that led the ANC into using violence, the so-called "armed struggle" to attempt to attain its goals in South Africa.

Youth are very malleable because, if they haven't reached maturity, they often are not able to conceptualize the difference between right and wrong. It is for this reason that young people between the ages of ten and eighteen can kill and hate without showing the same remorse that their elders would.

History is full of tyrants who took advantage of this: Lenin and Stalin used teenagers as executioners in their war against the Russian people; Mao's Red Guards, some under 12 years old, ran amok throughout China during the Cultural Revolution killing thousands and Pol Pot used teenagers in Cambodia to rid his communist utopia of so-called reactionaries and counter-revolutionaries.

The ANC also considers youth as a powerful tool in their revolutionary strategy in South Africa. This should surprise no one, considering the Marxist-Leninist influence that guides the ANC's revolutionary campaign in South Africa. To better understand the ANC's use of youth we should look at their mentor's (the Soviet Union's) view on the role of youth in revolutionary war.

The Soviets give a high priority to the training and indoctrination of youth. They are considered the key, as Lenin's doctrine shows, to the continuation of communist rule in the Soviet Union. The Soviets also see them as important players in carrying out the worldwide communist revolution in the drive to destroy capitalism.

On the home front the Soviets start the youth indoctrination process early—as soon as they start school. Soviet children are taught to hate capitalism and to love the Soviet state.

As the children grow older they pass through the Communist Youth

[2] *Samora Machel, An African Revolutionary, Selected Speeches and writings*, Barry Munslow, ed., 1985, p. 180.

League. Here the message they learned in their elementary schooling is reinforced and expanded. Again, its role is to serve the Soviet state and the Communist Party. The International Freedom Foundation points out, "The party regards the youth as a great creative force in the Soviet people's struggle for communism. . . . The Young Communist League organizations must concentrate on educating the youth in a spirit of utmost devotion to their country, the people, the communist party and the communist cause. . . . It is the sacred duty of the YCL to prepare young people for the defense of their socialist country. . . . The YCL educated the youths in a spirit of strict adherence to communist moral principles and standards. . . ."[3] In other words, the Soviet idea is to make sure that only orthodox communist views of things are taught to their young so that is all they'll ever know. This makes them easier to control as they pass into adulthood and, hopefully, it will insure the continuation of the communist domination in the Soviet Union.

Under the guidance and control of the KGB, the Soviet Union exports its process of warping the minds and souls of youth throughout the globe by infecting them with the virus of Marxism-Leninism.

Youth groups have played key roles in prior communist revolutions in Latin America, Asia and Africa. It doesn't take much imagination to figure out that the SACP/ANC alliance have also given youth a high degree of priority in their terrorist war in South Africa.

The Soviets accomplished this task through foreign communist parties or front groups. As an additional bonus, they gain a worldwide network that can be used as an auxiliary to further Soviet aims and ambitions when and where the Kremlin desires.

Party cadres give these groups a thorough grounding in the theory and practice of Marxism in all its aspects, including military training. The cadres expect the youth to be active in the communist party or front group in their home with the view of subverting it and installing a communist regime, or working to keep an existing Marxist government in power. These young people are the future revolutionaries and/or leaders and they are programmed to follow the lead and guidance of Moscow.

The two most important Soviet-sponsored youth front groups are the World Federation of Democratic Youth (WFDY) and the International Union of Students (IUS). Both groups work together and host worldwide meetings of youth who gather together for pep talks on communist doctrine and to blast the West for whatever current "evil" the Soviets are promoting at the time.

[3] Davies-Webb, W., 'The Role of Youth in Revolutionary Warfare", *International Freedom Review*, Vol. 1, No. 1, 1987, pp. 22-23.

Among the favorite recruiting and indoctrination meetings are the so called World Youth Festivals. These festivals have been a staple diet feeding Moscow's worldwide crusade for Marxism-Leninism since the Second World War. They are lavishly funded, largely by the Soviet Union, and draw a large audience. The festival held in Moscow in 1985 drew 20,000 youths from all over the world at a cost of around $100 million.[4]

In addition to the youth festival extravaganzas staged by the WFDY and the IUS, they dispense "solidarity funds" to young people, primarily from the Third World. These funds are usually in the form of scholarships which enable the recipients to study at schools or training centers located in either the Soviet Union or one of its surrogates. A special preference in the selection of beneficiaries of this largesse goes to youth from Third World "liberation movements."

Those selected learn the intricate skills necessary to be a good terrorist along with the usual heavy dose of Marxist political theory. Even those training in areas not directly involved in terrorist military training, such as management and administration, can't escape getting the training heavily dosed with Marxist indoctrination.

The front organizations also give a further special preference to members of the youth wing of communist parties the world over—the Young Communist Leagues—as well as members of youth wings of leftist liberation movements.

The key elements, as the Kremlin views them, are indoctrination and control. They are synergistic. A thoroughly indoctrinated individual is more easily controlled. He will follow the orders and direction of his controller more readily than one not indoctrinated with the ideology of the group, be it a Japanese corporation in Japan or a Marxist-Leninist communist party anywhere on the globe.

Youth are a critical component of liberation movements because these movements often have non-communist elements in them—genuine nationalists, for example. The more thoroughly the communists can penetrate such movements, the better positioned they become either to control them prior to seizure of power, or, if successful, to eliminate the non-communist elements after victory.

The ANC makes no bones about the importance of youth. At its Kabwe Consultative Conference, held in Zambia June 16-23, 1985, its report, the *Commission on Cadre Policy, Political and Ideological Work,* said, "The youth is an important section of the fighting forces in our struggle. The young

[4] "Influence and the media—The Greater Peril", *Now*, January 30, 1981, p. 31.

generation constitutes the future. For the future of any revolutionary movement, it is important to give particular attention to the development and participation of youth in the struggle for liberation.

"The position that our youth has come to occupy in the mass democratic struggle in our country has made the task of organizing and educating the young even more important."[5]

In addition, the ANC Kabwe Conference recommended that:

- The ANC should establish cores in existing youth organizations;
- They should pay particular attention to organizing youth of all national groups i.e. Indian, coloured and whites;
- The ANC must be in charge of the process: "We have to consciously guide the process of building youth organizations with the aim of making the working youth and the unemployed youth the backbone of youth organizations. . ."[6]
- The ANC must also subvert religious and cultural youth groups. "We need to educate the youth in religious and cultural organizations to translate their religious beliefs toward the rejection of apartheid as a heresy and greater involvement in the struggle for liberation. The culture of youth organizations should reflect our culture of resistance and struggle."[7]

Two constant themes run through the above recommendations: subversion and control. The ANC, through its youth wing, must subvert existing groups to the ANC's way of thinking and it must control these groups.

The ANC's consistent attitude towards youth pre-dates the Kabwe conference's setting it out as formal doctrine. The former SACP General Secretary, Moses Mabhida, spelled it out during an address to an ANC youth conference in Mazimba, Tanzania in August 1982: "We are faced with a formidable task in our country, it is the task of organizing and mobilizing our people. The youth in this respect has got an important role to play, to spread the world of revolution in all corners of our country. To all citizens of our country, they have got to symbolize the spirit of resistance, the spirit of fighting."[8]

The SACP, however, insists that the youth must be properly indoctrinated before they can become good revolutionaries: "Educational training must

[5] "Commission on Cadre Policy, Political and Ideological Work", ANC document, June 1985, p. 9.

[6] "Cadre Policy", pp. 9-10.

[7] "Cadre Policy", p. 10.

[8] *The African Communist*, First Quarter, No. 92, 1983, p. 83.

be seen as an integral part of the liberation process."[9] But it is not reading, writing and arithmetic the SACP has in mind. "Without the promotion of a revolutionary consciousness among the students and youth generally, the educational training of our young people would lack one of the most important elements necessary for bringing about meaningful revolutionary social change in South Africa."[10]

This is the SACP/ANC's "people's education"—revolution before education. The SACP/ANC alliance is more concerned with getting foot soldiers for the revolution than raising the educational level of the youth of South Africa. It is a callous attitude at best.

A most disturbing aspect of the SACP/ANC strategy to mobilize the youth for their revolutionary program is that, through their "comrades", they are rapidly creating a lost generation of children who, turned against their parents, relish the excitement of violence and wanton destruction. They have roamed the streets of the black townships in "death squads" meting out their brand of revolutionary justice via the infamous "necklace treatment" against those who oppose their fanatical behavior. They dance, sing and cheer as their victims die agonizing deaths by stabbing, stoning or burning. They are egged on by Nelson Mandela's wife Winnie, the Madame DeFarge of the SACP/ANC revolution as she exhorts them to greater atrocities as she did at a public funeral on April 13, 1986: "With our boxes of matches and our necklaces we shall liberate this country."

In spite of the outcry from civilized nations that her statement evoked, Winnie didn't back away one iota from it. Later in 1986, she told a group of young people: "I want to remind you about the power you have . . . the weapon you are using, the necklace."[11]

Like the guillotine of the French Revolution's reign of terror, the necklace has become a symbol of the SACP/ANC's similar reign of terror in the black townships of South Africa. The sight of burning used tires evokes a shudder and is a reminder that a fiery, agonizing death at the hands of howling mobs of young men is as close as the nearest junk yard or street corner in the black townships. This is the SACP/ANC's school of life for the black youth of South Africa.

The SACP/ANC are devoting a considerable amount of their resources

[9] *Sechaba*, July 1984, p. 10.

[10] *Ibid.*

[11] Roux, H., "The Young People of South Africa and Revolution: From Soweto 1976 to the Necklace of the 1980's", *How Revolutionaries Use Children*, Lone Tree Publications, Halfway House, 1988, p. 20.

to their youth wing as it dovetails nicely into the general scheme of their revolutionary doctrine. As you read on you will see for yourself the important role the SACP/ANC-directed youth play in the terror campaign in South Africa.

It is time we examined more closely the SACP/ANC's theory and practice of revolutionary war in South Africa.

13

SACP/ANC REVOLUTIONARY STRATEGY

Mao Tse-tung said that if a poorly equipped and trained revolutionary force wishes to fight a modern army, ". . . the only way to win ultimate victory lies in a strategically protracted war."[1] In order to win such a war the revolutionaries must grind down the targeted government and reverse the power relationship.[2] Or, as the ANC says, ". . . the revolutionary movement must always be ready to seize power by arms, for the seizure of state power can only take place when the balance of power swings in its favor."[3] This can be done by sapping the government's strength with the "cumulative effect of many campaigns and battles"[4]; while building their own strength by mobilizing the support of the people, establishing bases, and capturing equipment; and, by gaining outside political and, if possible, military support.[5]

[1] Mao Tse-tung, "On the Protracted War", *Selected Works*, Vol. II, International Publishers, New York, 1954, p. 180.

[2] McCuen, J.J., *The Art of Counter-Revolutionary War*, Stackpole Books, Harrisburg, PA, 1966, p. 30.

[3] Mtungwa, M.K., "The Road of Struggle That Leads To Freedom", *The African Communist*, No. 87, Fourth Quarter, 1981, p. 70.

[4] Mao Tse-tung, "Strategic Problems in the Anti-Japanese Guerrilla War," *Selected Works*, Vol. II, International Publishers, New York, 1954, p. 125.

[5] McCuen, p. 30.

The SACP/ANC communist leadership, although having their differences, all talk the language of Marxism and are, in this day of *perestroika*, Stalinist in their thinking.[6] Their revolutionary theory, though in practice it resembles Mao, Giap or Guevara/Debray, has evolved out of Lenin's two-stage theory of revolution, as mentioned earlier.

The SACP/ANC alliance's revolutionary assault on South Africa actually will take four steps, or phases: the democratic phase, the socialist phase, the political phase and the ideological phase.

In the democratic phase the revolutionaries will organize the masses around the revolutionary cause. While organizing the masses, the cadres set up revolutionary organizational structures—cells, block committees, etc.—to control the population. The aim will be the mobilization of all sectors of the population in support of SACP/ANC activity and ideology. This total mobilization process will assume the proportions of a "total war" effort in which the cadres regulate and control all aspects of public and private life in support of the revolutionary cause.

By means of propaganda and coercion the masses are to be slowly and systematically mobilized to participate in violent resistance to the government. From this a people's army will be formed to wage the armed struggle with the assistance of anti-government organizations which the SACP/ANC revolutionary alliance have formed and used as national fronts.

After the victory of the revolutionaries, the assault on capitalism begins in earnest and the socialist phase begins. The key facet of this phase is that the social structure and prosperity of the collective is raised above the rights, freedoms and thoughts of the individual. It is, however, the elite of the vanguard SACP/ANC alliance that determines the criteria of the rights and privileges of the people. As a result, the decision-making and the reins of power are being consolidated into fewer and fewer hands. The noose is being tightened around the throat of capitalism and soon it is destroyed.

The revolution then proceeds to the next stage—the political phase. In this phase party cadres form a one-party totalitarian communist state by the brutal elimination of all political opposition. In this phase the SACP/ANC alliance would either be severed to the detriment of the ANC, or the ANC would transform itself into the new Communist Party of South Africa, under the leadership of the Marxist members of the ANC and old SACP. All non-communist ANC officials would be purged and the reins of power would be held firmly in the hands of the elite of this so-called communist vanguard of the revolution.

[6] *Africa Confidential*, Vol. 31, No. 1, January 12, 1990, p. 3; see also: "South Africa: The Party's dilemma", *Africa Confidential*, Vol. 31, No. 9, May 4, 1990, pp. 1-2.

The Four Phases of Communist Revolution

1. Democratic Phase-

- Masses organized around the revolutionary cause;
- Control the population by means of revolutionary structures;
- Mobilize the masses, create "Peoples Army";
- Form front groups to use in National Front against government.

2. Socialist Phase-

- The social structure and prosperity of the community is raised above the rights, freedoms and thoughts of individuals leading to a destruction of individualism.

3. Political Phase-

- Form a one-party communist state and eliminate political opponents.

4. Ideological Phase-

- Communist ideology rules all aspects of society.

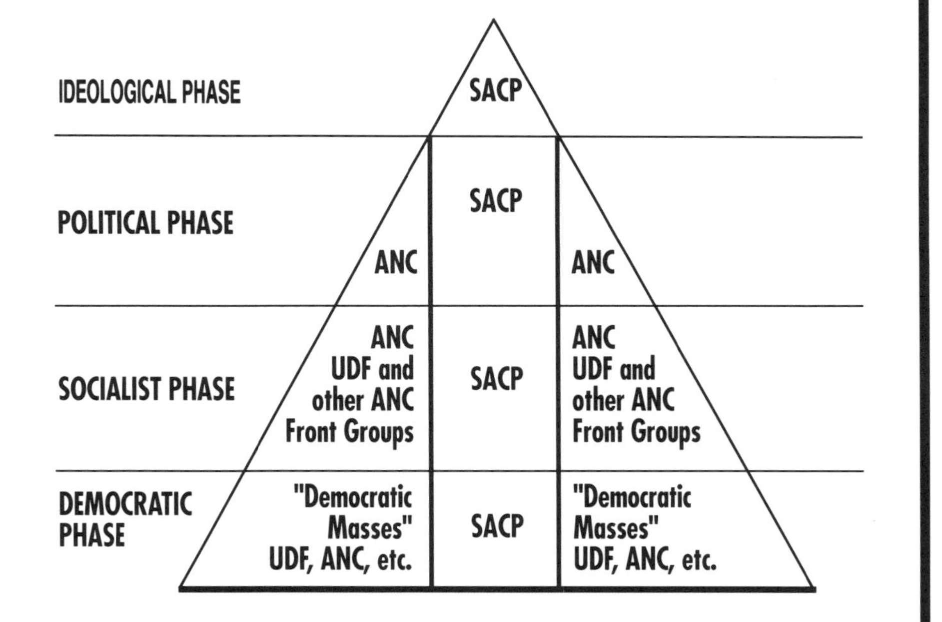

Participation in the revolution and government during the four phases of the communist revolution

After this phase, the final ideological phase can be established in South Africa—the usual Marxist utopia leading to the so-called withering of the State, that re-occurring fantasy that keeps springing from the fevered brows of communists throughout the ages. In actual fact, an unmitigated Dark Age would set in over another former free area of the globe.

On a theoretical level, this is how the SACP/ANC alliance plans to bring their brand of "freedom" to South Africa.

As the diagram shows, as each stage ends and another begins, fewer and fewer people are involved in the formulation and conduct of policy in the "Brave New South Africa". In the democratic phase, the masses are involved; in the socialist phase the elite of the SACP/ANC alliance and their front organizations (controlled by the alliance) determine and implement policy; in the political phase only the SACP and ANC are involved; and, finally, in the ideological phase the SACP emerges at the peak of the power pyramid.

The central power core, however, of all phases, as shown by the diagram, is the SACP. It appears small at the beginning but as the phases progress it grabs more and more power until finally, as it has long planned, it becomes the state.

The Rivonia trial brought to light the SACP/ANC revolutionary strategy outlined in their plan for MAYIBUYE. The Rivonia trial and the general lack of preparation by the ANC prevented the launching of Operation MAYIBUYE. Nevertheless, in the words of one expert, ". . . it still forms the basis for some ANC activities. . .",[7]especially in organizational activities of the ANC such as forming revolutionary cells inside South Africa, a process that is rapidly being advanced due to the recent unbanning of the SACP and ANC.

The ANC, however, has re-evaluated its love affair with the "foco" strategy because, like a reluctant lover, it cannot lead to success. The "foco" strategy, according to current ANC thinking, fatally down plays the vital connection between the armed guerrilla struggle and the various forms of mass activity essential to mobilizing the people in support of the revolution.

There is merit to the ANC's thinking says General Stadler, ". . . if 'foco' activities are destined to bring about accelerated mobilization, as in the case of 'operation Mayibuye', since the revolutionary 'foco's' would be exceptionally vulnerable to security force action due to their relative weakness. The 'foco' can therefore be eradicated before mass participation becomes a reality and subsequently, the revolutionary process is deprived of its source of origin. If

[7] Stadler, H.D., "The Revolutionary campaign Against the RSA", address by Maj. Gen. H.D. Stadler, SAP, to Institute for Strategic Studies, University of Pretoria Conference on South Africa and the Changing Security Environment, Pretoria, September 7, 1989.

actions are implemented by the 'foco' on a lower level of intensity and as part of the politicizing context, it can fulfill an important role in bringing about . . . popular participation in the revolutionary offensive. Such popular participation as part of the intensified context can in an escalated form give rise to guerrilla warfare of a higher degree of intensity than the original 'foco' activities."[8]

The Seventh Congress of the SACP stressed this same theme in its report: ". . . that the mission which exile gave us—to build the underground, to put ourselves back into the situation—looks for the first time like the beginnings of a reality. . . . The pledge of the 7th Congress must be for each and every one of us to dedicate ourselves to the underground in everything we do."[9]

Following the Soweto riots of 1976 and the resulting influx of recruits joining the ANC, the SACP/ANC alliance moved towards an intensification of their people's war in South Africa. Events unfolding in Southeast Asia strongly influenced the decision. The ANC studied the Vietnam War closely to see if the communist tactics used there could be adopted for use in South Africa.

In 1978, Oliver Tambo led an ANC delegation to Hanoi to study North Vietnamese revolutionary tactics used against the French, Americans and South Vietnam.[10] From this study, they concluded that the armed struggle must be combined with a variety of political actions in order to attack South Africa's military, economic and social strengths with any degree of success. The ANC said, ". . . There are a number of conclusions which can be drawn from the experience of other peoples, the understanding of which is indispensable in the analysis and planning of people's war in our own circumstances. . . . The Vietnamese experience tended to confirm our own belief that the armed struggle must be based on, and grow out of, mass political support and it must eventually involve all our people. All military activities must at every stage, be guided and determined by the need to generate political mobilization, organization and resistance, with the aim of progressively weakening the enemy's grip on his reins of political, economic, social and military power, by a combination of political and military action."[11]

[8] Stadler, *ibid.*

[9] "Build The Home Front! A Salute to the Underground From The 7th Congress" *Umsebenzi*, Special Congress Issue, March 1989, p. 4.

[10] *The Star*, August 21, 1987; see also: Mazala, "Building People's Forces for Combat", *Sechaba*, November 1984.

[11] *Ibid.*

Among the political activities that would work hand-in-glove with the armed struggle would be mass mobilization of the people, strengthening both the fronts inside and out of the country and stirring up protests on a variety of causes.

This type of activity flows naturally from the ANC's own definition of a "people's war". They wrote in *The African Communist*, "By people's war we mean a war in which a liberation army becomes rooted amongst the people who progressively participate actively in the armed struggle both politically and militarily, including the possibility of engaging in partial or general insurrections. The present disparity in strength between the enemy forces and our own determines the protracted nature of the struggle . . . such a struggle will lead inevitably to a revolutionary situation in which our plan and aim must be the seizure of power through a general insurrection (or whatever other ways might present themselves)."[12]

The SACP/ANC plan of action for their "people's war" rested on four pillars, which ANC President Oliver Tambo described as, "The all round vanguard activity of the underground structures; the united mass action of the peoples; our armed offensive; spearheaded by *Umkhonto we Sizwe*; and the international drive to isolate the apartheid regime and win worldwide moral, political and material support for the struggle."[13]

The key is politicizing, organizing and mobilizing the population. The South African communists point out, "The policy of armed struggle constitutes a vital part of the liberation movement's strategy. But, as we have always stressed, it is a strategy which can only take effective shape if it is rooted in the broadest possible mobilization and organization of our people. It is politics which is in command and it is politics which determines the nature and level of armed activity at every stage."[14]

The brain directing and controlling this whole process is the vanguard —the SACP/ANC alliance with the ANC being the visible public vehicle, while the SACP remains in the shadows. The National Executive Committee (NEC) of the ANC is the elite within the movement that not only decides policy, but oversees it as well. Thus it exercises total control as both a policy making and administrative body.

As mentioned elsewhere, the SACP influence on the ANC is overwhelming,[15] and thus it runs the ANC not from a position of numerical

[12] *The African Communist*, No. 84, First Quarter, 1986, p. 32.

[13] Tambo, O., *Sechaba*, March 1984, p. 4.

[14] *The African Communist*, No. 80, First Quarter, 1980, pp. 36-37.

[15] See also: *Africa Confidential*, Vol. 31, No. 1, January 12, 1990, pp. 1-4; *Africa Confidential*, Vol. 31, No. 9, May 4, 1990, p.2; Booyse, W. J., "The Revolutionary Program of the South African Communist Party", *International Freedom Review*, Vol. 2, No. 1, 1986, pp. 43-44.

ANC's Four Pillars:

Peoples' War Strategy

Mobilization of the Masses
to Participate in the Struggle

Organization- Develop a Political Underground System
inside South Africa

Armed Struggle: Revolutionary Terror and Violence
By Military Wing, Umkhonto we Sizwe

International Isolation of South Africa on All Fronts:
Economic, Cultural, Sports

strength but from the strategic positioning of SACP members within the NEC of the ANC.

As Dubula states in *The African Communist*, ". . . If correct leadership of the democratic revolution requires the strengthening of the national movement as the major mass organizational force, then this is precisely the way in which a party exercises its leading and vanguard role in the real (and not vulgar) sense of the term. This is the way in which Vietnamese Communists exercised their vanguard role in relation to the FLN [Viet Cong —ed.] during the liberation struggle, and it is also the way in which the early Cuban Communists related to Fidel Castro's July 26th Movement. *As long as the party does not lose its independence and its separate identity as a political vanguard of the working class, its projection of the ANC as the body leading the alliance of class forces in our struggle is in no way inconsistent with the Party's role as a vanguard organization of the working class.*" [emphasis added][16]

The NEC is a classic example of what McCuen terms "unifying the effort in a revolutionary struggle." It is . . . "the basic principle behind all effective revolutionary strategy, tactics, planning, and organization."[17] This unity of effort requires a unified command and since revolutionary war involves both military and political activity, the unifying agent must be a practitioner of both skills. This is a process the communists have developed to a high degree and have included in virtually every modern revolutionary movement in which they are involved. It requires dedicated, skilled individuals working for a common purpose to carry it out. In the words of Mao Tse-Tung, ". . . The idea of fighting a guerrilla war at haphazard means nothing but making a game out of it—the idea of an ignoramus in guerrilla warfare. The operations in a guerrilla area as a whole or the whole operation of a single guerrilla detachment or guerrilla corps must be preceded by the most comprehensive planning possible, which is the preparatory work for all kinds of activities. Questions of how to grasp the situation, to define the tasks, to disperse the forces, to carry out military and political training . . . should all be carefully considered and thoroughly worked out by guerrilla leaders. . . . Without this there could be no initiative, flexibility or offensive."[18]

The *key* element of the SACP/ANC revolutionary program is the

[16] Dubula, S., "The Two Pillars of our Struggle", *The African Communist*, No. 87, Fourth Quarter, 1981, p. 34.

[17] McCuen, J., *The Art of Counter-Revolutionary War*, p. 69.

[18] Tse-tung, Mao, "Strategic Problems in the Anti-Japanese Guerrilla War", *Selected Works*, Vol. II, p. 131.

ANC: Strategy

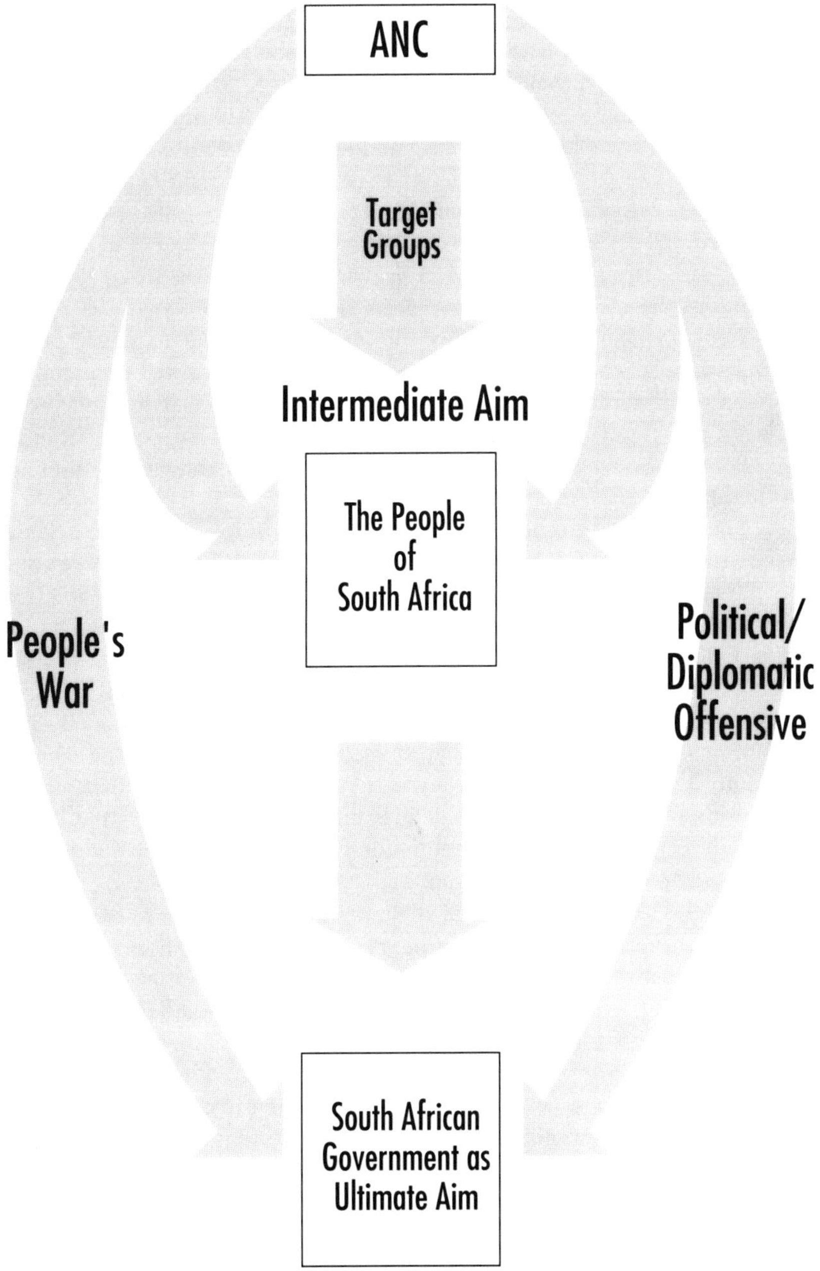

ANC

Target Groups

Intermediate Aim

The People of South Africa

People's War

Political/ Diplomatic Offensive

South African Government as Ultimate Aim

political pillar. The ANC regards it as its strategic dimension. The political pillar serves a revolutionary organization as its bible, which not only justifies its struggle, but also provides a guideline for ways of taking concrete political steps for executing the revolutionary process.

We must not make the mistake and equate this emphasis on political activity with the attitude in the United States towards politics—a means to gain or preserve political or social rights.

The SACP/ANC alliance has a different view of the ends and means of politics—to seize power. As the ANC publicly proclaimed in 1986, "All revolutions are about state power. Ours is no exception."[19] It has been a consistent theme of the ANC since the Mandela-Tambo young turks began taking control of the ANC in the 1950s. The June 1985 Kabwe Conference in Zambia reaffirmed that: "there was no reason for us to change our broad strategy, which pursues the aim of seizure of power."[20]

Politics are the determining factor in the strategic and tactical thinking of the SACP/ANC.

The basic political manifesto of the Marxist utopia planned for South Africa is the Freedom Charter. As shown earlier, the Charter's concept of a people's democracy would lead to a Leninist national democratic revolution phase which would precede the dictatorship of the proletariat. The Charter more easily prepares the way for tyranny than freedom.

Without belaboring the point, both parts of the SACP/ANC alliance have similar and complementary views on the Freedom Charter. The ANC regards it as inevitable that the Charter and its principles can only be adopted in South Africa through violent revolution. The SACP agrees that violent revolution is the only way to change in South Africa and regards the Charter as a point of departure for the revolution and that its implementation will smooth and pave the way for a communist order in South Africa.

The SACP/ANC has geared their politicizing pillar toward inducing and persuading individuals and groups or organizations, both inside and outside of South Africa, to support the revolutionary cause of the alliance. The SACP/ANC exploits and manipulates existing political, social, economic and other problems in the country to further the goals of their revolutionary campaign.

The exploitation by the revolutionaries attempts to create negative perceptions both internally and externally to South Africa with regards to the

[19] "ANC's New Years Message, 1986.

[20] ANC Press Release, Kabwe Conference, June 1985.

status quo within the country. At the same time the campaign strives to create an indisputable image that things are not going to get any better.

While trying to exacerbate conditions inside South Africa and painting a gloomy future, the SACP/ANC alliance holds out the prospect for a rosy future through adopting their program.

The SACP/ANC carries out its campaign for support by means of its propaganda organs. These include numerous publications such as *Sechaba*, *Dawn*, *Mayibuye*, *Voice of Women*, *The African Communist*, and *Umsebenzi*. Radio broadcasts over Radio Freedom from Ethiopia, Tanzania, Zambia and Angola also play an important propaganda role.

All this is part and parcel of the SACP/ANC's politicizing over the full spectrum of its revolutionary activities.

The SACP/ANC also rely quite heavily on so-called armed propaganda —acts of sabotage and terror, especially inside South Africa, to convert people to their cause and to further the ANC's strategy of armed struggle. When propaganda fails to sway potential adherents to the cause, the alliance doesn't hesitate to use terror to bludgeon them into giving their support. In fact the revolutionaries must resort to terror unless the majority of the population quickly comes to their support.

The fact that the SACP/ANC have had to rely on stepped-up terrorist acts, especially since the 1984-86 unrest in South Africa, indicates that the message being delivered by their political pillar hasn't roused the masses to support the SACP/ANC program.

The SACP/ANC terror campaign has a political context whose aims are:[21]

- To keep alive the perspective of people's revolutionary violence as the ultimate weapon for the seizure of power;
- To support and stimulate political activity and organization;
- To build an image of power especially among black people by creating the impression that the ANC can operate unhindered in South Africa, while at the same time attempting to discredit the power image of the security forces by demonstrating their "inability" to curb ANC activity;
- To intimidate the local population into participation in revolutionary activities by, for example, the assassination of police officials, councilors and state witnesses. In addition, this has the effect of discouraging assistance to the security forces;
- To create a climate of insecurity and fear, especially among whites,

[21] Stadler, *op. cit.*, pp. 15-16.

ANC Revolutionary Campaign in South Africa

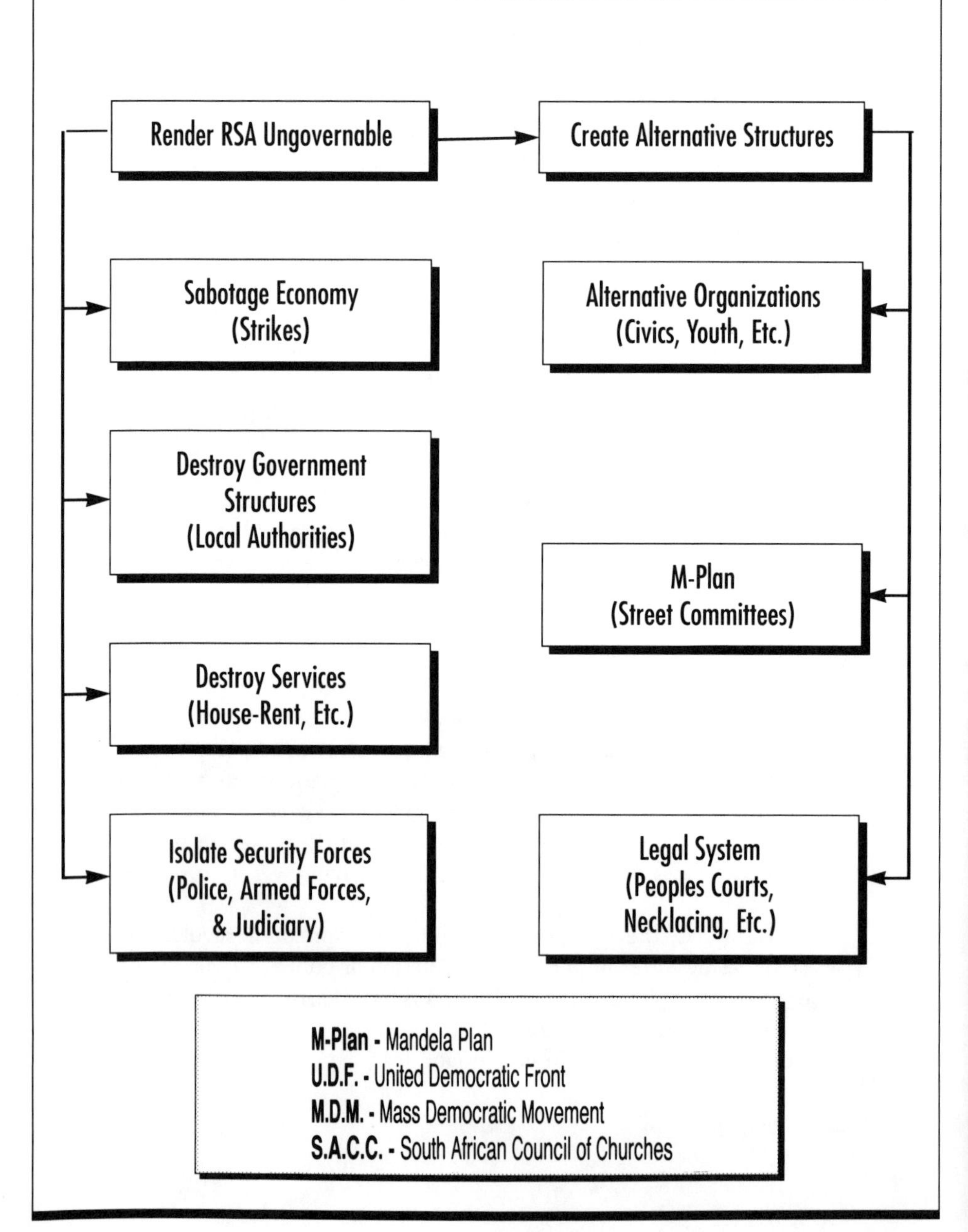

with the purpose of "convincing" them that a violent confrontation and the eventual defeat of whites in South Africa can only be prevented if black aspirations, as represented by the ANC, are accommodated in a new constitution. The ANC also feels that an attack on this "power base" will result in a weakening of the security forces;

- To promote a general militant/revolutionary climate, especially among non-whites, and to stimulate the incidence of "political violence" by means of its terror tactics;
- To keep the young radicals in the organization;
- To prove to the international community that the ANC wields real power and is the force to be reckoned with.

Greater recognition of the ANC brought about by this procedure can result in important elements in the West openly supporting the ANC—garnering the external support according to McCuen.[22]

All of this effort, the SACP/ANC hopes, will create a mass base consisting of front and mass organizations with which they can carry out their revolutionary program. We will now turn our attention to the next pillar of the SACP/ANC's revolutionary war strategy—mass mobilization of the people.

[22] See: McCuen, J.J., *The Art of Counter-Revolutionary War*, pp. 64-69.

14

SACP/ANC STRATEGY—MASS MOBILIZATION

The SACP/ANC designed the mobilization pillar of their revolutionary strategy to mobilize the population to participate in the revolutionary conflict by either persuasion or intimidation.

Since both the SACP and the ANC were banned in South Africa until February 1990, they had to operate through front groups within the country. These front groups had a key role to play in the SACP/ANC's mass mobilization schemes in South Africa.

The use of front groups by the forces of Marxism is a long established custom in their revolutionary campaign to communize the world. Front groups provide excellent seemingly legitimate screens behind which the Party is able to do its dirty work of subversion and terror.[1] The communists say, "A major specific feature of people's democracy is that the Communists and Workers parties exercise their leadership in the state not only through organs of people's power, trade unions, youth organizations, co-operatives and so on, but also through organizations like the Popular Front, which is a form of alliance of the working class, the peasantry, the urban petty bourgeoisie, and the intelligentsia. The Popular Fronts were formed because the social basis of the revolutionary movement was broad and it is necessary to unite the motive forces of the revolution and establish an alliance of the

[1] Shultz, R.H., Jr., *The Soviet Union and Revolutionary War*, Hoover Institute Press, Stanford, CA, 1989, p. 33.

working class with the peasants and other social classes and social groups coming out for a progressive society."[2]

The use of the popular front by the SACP/ANC alliance is a strategic device by them which does not compromise the alliance's basic Leninist values by their jumping in bed with some forces of populism. The SACP made this quite clear in a 1987 interview with *The Observer*: "The ANC/SACP Alliance is part of an emerging coalition of forces which have different objectives but are agreed on the immediate one of overthrowing apartheid and replacing it with a non-racial democracy based on black majority rule. The alliance must be broadened and true socialism would flow naturally in time."[3]

The SACP/ANC are no strangers to using fronts, having resorted to them long before both were banned. The Congress Alliance of the 1950s was a broad front set up and utilized by the SACP/ANC alliance to subvert the Nationalist government.

Operation MAYIBUYE and the writings of Nelson Mandela before his arrest and trial envisaged seizing power through a popular front in South Africa.

Two recent typical fronts used by the SACP/ANC alliance are the United Democratic Front (UDF) and the Mass Democratic Movement (MDM). Although the UDF was officially launched on August 21, 1983, its origins go back to 1980 when radical leftist groups, with the connivance of the SACP and ANC, decided to band together and create a so-called democratic movement based on the old Congress Alliance. The United Nations (UN), in the guise of its Special Committee Against Apartheid, encouraged the formation of the front.

From its beginnings the UDF advocated a socialist regime in South Africa. How would the UDF replace the existing limited free enterprise system in South Africa? It would establish a socialist one-party state by means of a mass revolution—the same thing the SACP/ANC alliance had been preaching for years. The SACP welcomed the birth of the UDF in its publication, *The African Communist*: "The development of a broad front of popular resistance has taken a significant step forward with the launching of the United Democratic Front."[4]

The drive to formally establish the UDF got a boost in 1983 from the

[2] *What is Revolution*, Progress Press, Moscow, 1986.

[3] *The Observer*, March 1, 1987.

[4] *The African Communist* No. 96.

popular opposition to the National Government's proposed new constitution, which established a parliament composed of three houses—one each for whites, coloureds and Indians, but none for blacks.[5]

After its formal inauguration, Albertina Sisulu, wife of then jailed ANC stalwart, Walter Sisulu, and Archie Gumede, a former high ANC official co-chaired the UDF. From the beginning, the ANC presence was strongly felt in the UDF. Of the seventy members of the national and regional committees elected in 1985, thirty-six were ex-SACP/ANC or South African Congress of Trade Union (SACTU) members. It is open to speculation whether these ex-members, in point of fact ever, left the ANC as nothing they've said or done indicates any ideological change of heart on their part.

Oliver Tambo had nothing but high praise for the UDF: ". . . the ANC was pleased, to say the least, when the United Democratic Front was formed in South Africa. The UDF, that outstanding example of political maturity of our people, is a product of the years that our country's forces of progress have spent. . . ."[6]

The UDF claims that over 700 to 800 different groups in South Africa are members of its loose-knit coalition. On closer examination many of these are small local groups formed to take action on local issues, such as education and housing. Many of the groups have overlapping membership and the UDF's claim to have two million members must be taken with a pinch of salt.

One doesn't walk into the local UDF office and join up. If you try you are told to join an existing organization that already is affiliated with the UDF. If you are a white left-leaning university student you are steered to the National Union of South African Students (NUSAS). As the largest white UDF affiliate, the student group enables the UDF to use university facilities to propagate the ANC's socialist agenda.

NUSAS' baptism of fire for the UDF was its involvement in the UDF-sponsored 1983 petition drive opposing the government's new constitutional proposals. Unfortunately for the student group, their petition drive came to a screeching halt when someone discovered that copies of the petition lists were finding their way into the offices of the ANC to be used as

[5] Radu, M., "The African National Congress: Cadres and Credo", *Problems of Communism*, Washington, D.C., July-August 1987, p. 13.

[6] Tambo, O., "Storm Over South Africa", *World Marxist Review*, January 1986, p. 88; see also: *Documents of Second National Consultative Conference of the ANC*, Zambia, 16-23 June 1985.

possible recruiting lists by the terrorists.[7]

Other student groups in the black and coloured universities fulfill similar roles within the UDF.

The student groups are a valuable asset for the SACP/ANC alliance, working through the UDF. Many of the "comrades"[8], who imposed a reign of terror over the black townships, were recruited from black student groups and formed the cutting edge of the ANC's campaign to make the townships ungovernable. (This mirrored the Viet Cong terror campaign in 1960 in which 10,000 village chiefs of the 16,000 village hamlets in South Vietnam were murdered.)

These student groups serve as valuable recruiting agents for the revolutionary cause. Olivia Forsyth, a South African policewoman, infiltrated first the NUSAS, then other similar organizations, eventually ending up in the high echelons of the ANC itself. She points out the value of these organizations and their recruits to the SACP/ANC alliance: "The main reason organizations like the ANC and South African Communist Party rely on such recruits is that the university environment provides much of the groundwork for recruitment attempt. I refer more specifically to the left wing academics who apply academic pressure on the students as well as the radical student organizations which recruit them and provide both ideological and organizational training. After groundwork, and by the time a student has been through, for instance, an English-speaking university or through student organizations, the ANC or SACP can be fairly sure the student has been prepared for a future revolutionary role. It means that if they have been right the way 'through the ranks', then they will support the revolutionary overthrow of the South African government; they will support the ANC and its methods of trying to bring this about. They will be prepared to undertake any number of missions, with any number of risks, to achieve these objectives. . . .

"There are various phases which an organization like this takes students through. The first is to use the guilt. The second is to provide them with an answer for those guilt feelings, for instance an alternative history of South Africa. What they do is say to students: this is the history which you have been

[7] Parker, A., "ANC surrogates: NUSAS and the UDF connection", *Aida Parker Newsletter*, No. 127, Johannesburg, 1989, p. 13.

[8] The "comrades" were the bands of students and youths who enforced the ANC's reign of terror during the period of township unrest in the 1980's in South Africa. They were largely drawn from the Congress of South African Students (COSAS).

given in your Christian National education for the past five years, now we want you to hear the real history of South Africa. They then provide the students with a history which is basically the history of the ANC. The emphasis is entirely on the ANC, although they don't openly support the ANC. If the student accepts that alternative uncritically, he is going to be drawn very quickly into an ANC way of thinking and at least tacit support for the ANC.

"Not every student who joins an organization like this ends up supporting the armed struggle. Most students join these organizations because they don't believe in apartheid; that is a perfectly legal and legitimate reason to join a political organization. But the objective amongst the hard-core leadership is to take as many students as possible through a calculated programme in which they end up supporting the armed struggle."[9]

The UDF uses other organizations as fronts for the ANC in a manner similar to the student groups.

Non-blacks, especially Indians, figure prominently in the UDF, which has caused some resentment by the more nationalist-minded black members, especially members of the Pan African Congress (PAC).

The UDF's present evolution appears to reflect the mid-1950s development within the ANC but with a nucleus of better-organized, better-trained, and politically-astute non-black members playing a disproportionate role behind the scenes compared to what their numbers suggest. Today, unlike the 1950s, domestic organizations like the UDF are a more natural playground for non-blacks who enjoy greater freedom of movement and access to liberal or "progressive" circles, political, religious and social, than blacks.[10]

The UDF's political agenda is almost parallel to the ANC's. It includes the declared intention of making South Africa "ungovernable". This is to be done by a strategy of violence against the persons and property of those opposing their political agenda. During the riots and unrest that swept the black townships in South Africa from September 1984 onwards, there have been repeated examples of lynchings and "necklacings" of anti-ANC political opponents by mobs whipped into frenzy by UDF orators. Necklacing is a brutal form of terror where an auto tire filled with gasoline is placed over the victim's head and set on fire resulting in a gruesome violent death by burning.

[9] "Forsyth interview", *Aida Parker Newsletter, op. cit.,* pp. 34-35.

[10] Radu, M., *Problems of Communism*, p. 15.

The hard-core controlling leadership of the UDF has acted as "the internal wing of the ANC".[11] In spite of the UDF's claim to oppose violence, the UDF has never lifted a finger or raised its voice in opposition to the gruesome murder of ANC political opponents nor did it deplore the widespread destruction of property during the unrest.[12]

The UDF and its affiliates have repeatedly denied that they have any links with the ANC. But statements by the ANC and the SACP suggest otherwise. In their 1987 New Years message in *Sechaba,* the ANC boasted, ". . . We have also succeeded to create mass democratic organizations representative of these active and conscious masses, ranging from street committees to COSATU, the UDF, the NECC and their affiliates and other democratic formations".[13] The SACP/ANC Alliance was even more blunt, stating in *The African Communist*, "The years of painstaking work by the party and the ANC are showing results. There is the continued tremendous growth of internal organized opposition, exemplified by among other events, the momentous gathering in Cape Town during last month which launched the UDF."[14]

The ANC made it clear at its Kabwe conference in 1985 just how important a mass organization, such as the UDF, was to further its revolutionary aims.

As one of the conference documents stated, "The key to our further advance is organization. . . . We need a strong organization of revolutionaries because without it, it will be impossible to raise the struggle to greater heights in a planned and systematic fashion. . . ."[15]

It is within this mass movement that the ANC terrorists will operate. ". . . The people are engaged in active struggle as a conscious revolutionary force and accept the ANC as their vanguard movement. They are organized in mass democratic organizations. . . . What is missing is a strong underground ANC presence as well as a large contingent of units of *Umkhonto we Sizwe*.

"We must correct this weakness in a determined and systematic manner

[11] Parker, A., "Marxism on SA Campuses", *The Aida Parker Newsletter*, Johannesburg, No. 127, 1989, p. 15.

[12] *Ibid.*

[13] *Sechaba*, April 1987.

[14] *The African Communist*, No. 96.

[15] "Need for a Strong Revolutionary Organization", *Documents of the Second Consultative Conference of the African National Conference*, Kabwe Conference, Zambia, June 16-23, 1985, p. 34.

because it is within these mass revolutionary bases that we will succeed to root our army. It is the risen masses in these areas who have to be organized into larger formations of *Umkhonto we Sizwe*, turned into organized groups of combatants, and who have to replenish and swell our military ranks. . . ."[16]

The UDF was important because it could "mobilize the masses of our people into action and to draw them into mass organizational formations."[17] But equally important to the ANC, the UDF would "ensure that these masses adhere to a common political platform",[18] which happens to be the ANC's.

And, lastly, the ANC could use the people forming under the umbrella of the UDF as a ". . . political army of revolution, under one command, focusing on the central question of all revolutions, whether peaceful or violent, the question of state power."[19]

The ANC has been, and still is, obsessed with the question of state power, and they are determined to seize it.

McCuen stresses, "To the revolutionaries, mobilization of the masses requires more than mere persuasion, it requires intimidation and, most important, organization."[20]

Echoing McCuen, the ANC stressed, "The key to our further advance is organization. . . . We need a strong organization of revolutionaries because without it, it will be impossible to raise the struggle to greater heights in a planned and systematic fashion. Without such a strong revolutionary organization, we cannot take advantage of the uprisings . . . which are a reality of the mass offensive of our people."[21]

The UDF fits the ANC's criteria for a revolutionary organization to a tee. It pushed the ANC agenda; it recruited new cadres to provide a larger manpower pool for the ANC and, in general, created chaos which is such fertile soil for the growth of Marxism's malignancy.

The UDF wasn't above participating in the ANC's so-called armed struggle. Radu points out, "UDF members have been implicated in the 'necklacing' of supporters of anti-ANC organizations such as Inkatha and Azanian People's Organization (AZAPO) in attempts to discredit or

[16] Documents, Kabwe conference, pp. 34-35.

[17] Kawbe documents, p. 31.

[18] Kabwe documents, p. 31.

[19] *Ibid.*

[20] McCuen, J., *The Art of Counter-Revolutionary War*, Stackpole Books, Harrisburg, PA., 1966, p. 55.

[21] Kabwe documents, p. 34.

intimidate the leaders of the newly founded United Christian Conciliation Party . . . AZAPO, Inkatha, and local vigilante groups of moderate Blacks have all begun to resist UDF-sponsored intimidation and violence openly and forcefully."[22]

The UDF, to this day, is still involved in the violence with Inkatha in Natal, especially near Pietermaritzburg. Well over 3,000 deaths have occurred since 1987 in UDF-Inkatha clashes.

But the UDF's days were numbered as the South African government soon fought back. In 1986, the government declared the UDF an "affected organization". This prohibited the UDF from receiving all foreign overseas funding, which had provided the group with almost all of its financial resources. It was a serious blow to the UDF and was followed by an even harder blow—it was banned by the government in June 1986 as part of its nationwide State of Emergency proclamation.

These measures severely crippled the UDF and its usefulness to the ANC lessened as a result. Although the UDF appeared dead after its banning, it wasn't forgotten by the ANC. The SACP/ANC campaign of "Mass Action for People's Power" which launched a new mobilization of the masses' Defiance Campaign resuscitated the UDF in 1989.

"Drawing on and continuing that experience (the Defiance Campaign of the 1950s), and developing on the heroic actions of church leaders and other patriots last year, our approach must be one of militant mass defiance," said the ANC.[23]

During a June 5-7, 1989 meeting in Lusaka, Zambia, the vampire of the UDF rose from its coffin to once again stalk the highways and byways of South Africa. A delegation of about thirty people, mainly officials of the banned UDF and the Marxist-leaning black Congress of South African Trade Unions (COSATU) met with the SACP/ANC alliance in Lusaka. A discussion on strategy ensued and out of it the "Mass Democratic Movement" (MDM) was born. It was the old UDF with a new face-lift.

The MDM was the new SACP/ANC front from 1989 until South African State President de Klerk unbanned both groups in February 1990. The MDM's own writings make this clear. For example, in "Discussion Papers for the Conference for a Democratic Future" (CDF) held December 9, 1989 in Johannesburg, the MDM repeated the same old tired cliches that have permeated the sayings of the SACP/ANC for years. On the subject of negotiations, for example, the MDM repeats the SACP/ANC party line:

[22] Radu, M., *op. cit.,* pp.14-15.

[23] Stadler, *op. cit.,* p. 18.

"The kind of negotiations we consider consistent with our strategy of armed seizure of power are not those the commercial media are speculating about. . . . We are not engaged in a struggle whose objective is merely to generate sufficient pressure to bring the other side to the negotiating table. . . ."[24]

The task of the MDM, as they see it, "is to deepen the isolation of the regime, maximize unity against it and weaken its ability to resist the struggle for a democratic and non-racial South Africa."[25] The term "non-racial South Africa" is lifted entirely from the Freedom Charter.

"The MDM displays growing unity in both ideology and political programmes, as trade unions (COSATU), political formations (UDF) . . . adopt the Freedom Charter and define their political aims in terms of it."[26] As pointed out earlier, the Freedom Charter is a cleverly worded blueprint for a future socialist South Africa.

As a mass mobilizing agent the MDM's specific agenda is identical to the ANC's:

"a. The broadening and consolidation of the MDM: drawing more forces into our ranks and influencing and leading those outside the MDM;

"b. Uniting all the forces for change led by the MDM in campaigns around specific issues;

"c. Keeping the strategic initiative firmly in the hands of the MDM and taking advantage of the regimes political and economic crisis;

"d. Dividing the ruling bloc by fragmenting the National Party's social base, drawing forces away from its organ and influence, thus weakening and isolating the most dangerous and reactionary core;

"e. Isolating the regime from international support and mounting international pressure on it;

"f. Ultimately outlining and shaping a political path that ensures maximum unity on the side of the democratic movement so that the democratic movement can determine both the terrain and terms of struggle;

"g. Ensuring that UDF and COSATU lead the mass contingent of the coalition".[27]

[24] "Discussion Papers for the Conference for a Democratic Future, Issued by: MDM", n.d., pp. 4-5.

[25] Discussion Papers, Phambili Collective, p. 2.

[26] *Ibid.*

[27] *Ibid.*

The MDM is a prime example of a front group following the classic Marxist-Leninist pattern. The MDM admits it: "Mass action makes our organizations strong. By picking up issues facing our members we are able to draw many people into action against oppression. Through mass actions we are able to register victories and it is in this way that more people join our organizations. . . ."[28]

The SACP/ANC have effectively geared the mass mobilization pillar of their strategy to advance their subversive revolutionary program in South Africa.

[28] *Ibid.*

15

THE ARMED STRUGGLE—THE ANC'S GRAND DELUSION

The third pillar of the ANC's revolutionary strategy against the South African government is the armed struggle. It is the shining jewel, crowning the ANC's efforts to topple the semi-capitalist system and seize power in South Africa. Unlike the Culinane diamond that came from the bowels of the earth in South Africa, the ANC's jewel is imported and made of glass.

Since its initial banning on April 8, 1961, when the ANC decided to tread the path of violence to gain its ends, until today, its literature is constantly extolling the armed struggle. As such, it has created its own mythology, at least in the eyes of the ANC, its supporters and the naive, that numerous bands of guerrillas are roaming about the countryside waging battles against the South African security forces. Reality is a different matter altogether.

In June 1961, the ANC established its military wing, *Umkhonto we Sizwe*, and the ANC began planning its revolutionary terror path to power. On December 16, 1961, the ANC carried out numerous acts of sabotage throughout the country, consisting mostly of blowing up pylons supporting electrical transmission lines. That day also marked the appearance of placards on walls and poles in the black townships announcing the ANC's armed revolutionary "struggle for freedom and democracy."

To carry out the revolution the ANC was following the plan they termed "Operation MAYIBUYE", which has been detailed earlier in this book. MAYIBUYE envisioned both guerrilla activity as well as mobile warfare and the possibility of outside military intervention.

Castro's recent triumph in Cuba had influenced Mandela and the other ANC planners of MAYIBUYE. "As in Cuba, the general uprising must be sparked off by organized and well-prepared guerrilla operations during the course of which the masses of the people will be drawn in and armed,"[1] was the idea behind the ANC's plan.

The plan never got off the ground as most of the plotters and would-be leaders were either arrested, tried and sent to prison, or had fled the country. Though MAYIBUYE may have been a bust on its first go, the ANC still uses it as the basis of some of its activities. This is more predominant in the organizational dimension of ANC activities, especially the formation of revolutionary cells.

After the emasculation of the ANC as a result of security force activities culminating in the Rivonia treason trial, ANC activity had entered a period of the doldrums. Its "guerrilla war" consisted of minor isolated acts of sabotage.

Attempting to breathe new life into its revolution, the ANC held a conference in Morogoro, Tanzania in 1969—described in greater detail earlier. The ANC reconfirmed its commitment to violence and drew up plans to carry out its threat to seize power by means of a people's war.

Nevertheless, their efforts of trying to conduct guerrilla warfare inside South Africa were dismal failures. For example, between October 1976 and December 1984, 185 personnel from SOG—the ANC's elite three-man Special Operations Group terrorist units—were captured or killed. This effectively meant that the ANC had lost 249 cadres on 262 missions, a massive attrition rate for the ANC.

As a result militants inside South Africa had grown weary of waiting for the ANC guerrillas to come and liberate them and were now turning to their own devices in order to confront the South African government. They began to flock behind the banner of the Black Consciousness Movement of Steve Biko, described earlier.

The Soweto riots in 1976 caught the ANC unprepared and flooded their external facilities with thousands of youths clamoring for guns and eager to join the ANC's revolutionary struggle. How best to utilize this opportunity was a paramount question yet to be answered within the hierarchy of the SACP/ANC alliance as the 1970s were drawing to a close.

The ANC needed a strategic re-evaluation of its revolutionary campaign to impose a socialist state in South Africa. Hastening the need for this ANC soul-searching were indications that the Soviet Union was reviewing its

[1] Stadler, H., "The Revolutionary Campaign Against RSA", *op. cit.* p. 7.

support for the ANC in the light of its failure to exploit the opportunity in South Africa which the Soweto riots had presented them.[2]

The ANC looked to the Far East for guidance. In 1978, Oliver Tambo led a delegation to Hanoi where they conducted exhaustive research into the methods used by North Vietnam in its revolutionary struggle against the French and South Vietnam. Their observations convinced them that, although they had been correct in deciding to wage a people's war, in order for it to be successful, they had to first organize and mobilize the people.

The ANC delegation returned to Lusaka and decided to launch a three-year, or longer if circumstances required, program aimed at organizing and mobilizing the masses before they would be in a position to launch their "people's war".

"By people's war," said the SACP/ANC alliance, "we mean a war in which a liberation army becomes rooted amongst the people who progressively participate actively in the armed struggle both politically and militarily, including the possibility of engaging in partial or general insurrection . . . such a struggle will lead inevitably to a revolutionary situation in which our plan and aim must be the seizure of power through a general insurrection (or whatever other ways might present themselves)."[3]

According to the SACP/ANC's scheme, existing political, social, economic and other problems inside South Africa would be converted into revolutionary situations through a process of manipulation or coercion, or what the SACP/ANC term armed propaganda: "In the *Communist Manifesto,* Marx and Engels declared that the ends of communists 'can be attained only by the forcible overthrow of all existing social conditions.' Force, in their view, involved the whole range of forms which working class struggle takes: mass demonstrations, general strikes, boycotts and armed uprisings. . . ."[4]

These various activities form an orchestrated whole whose goal is to advance the SACP/ANC's agenda towards its ultimate seizure of power.

The SACP/ANC's main stress is on the armed struggle. "Our armed struggle," they say, "has to rely, above all, on the people in active struggle. The working class, in particular, possesses vast possibilities to take the war to the

[2] This emerged after the capture and interrogation of KGB Major Alex Koslov by South African Counter Intelligence in 1979. He revealed that the KGB was concerned with the ANC's failure to exploit the situation in Soweto during and after the riots.

[3] *The African Communist*, No. 84, First Quarter, 1986, p. 32.

[4] Mtungwa, M.K., "The Road of Struggle That Leads to Freedom", *The African Communist*, No. 81, Fourth Quarter, 1981, p. 69.

ANC Peoples War Strategy
Liberated Zones-Alternative Structures

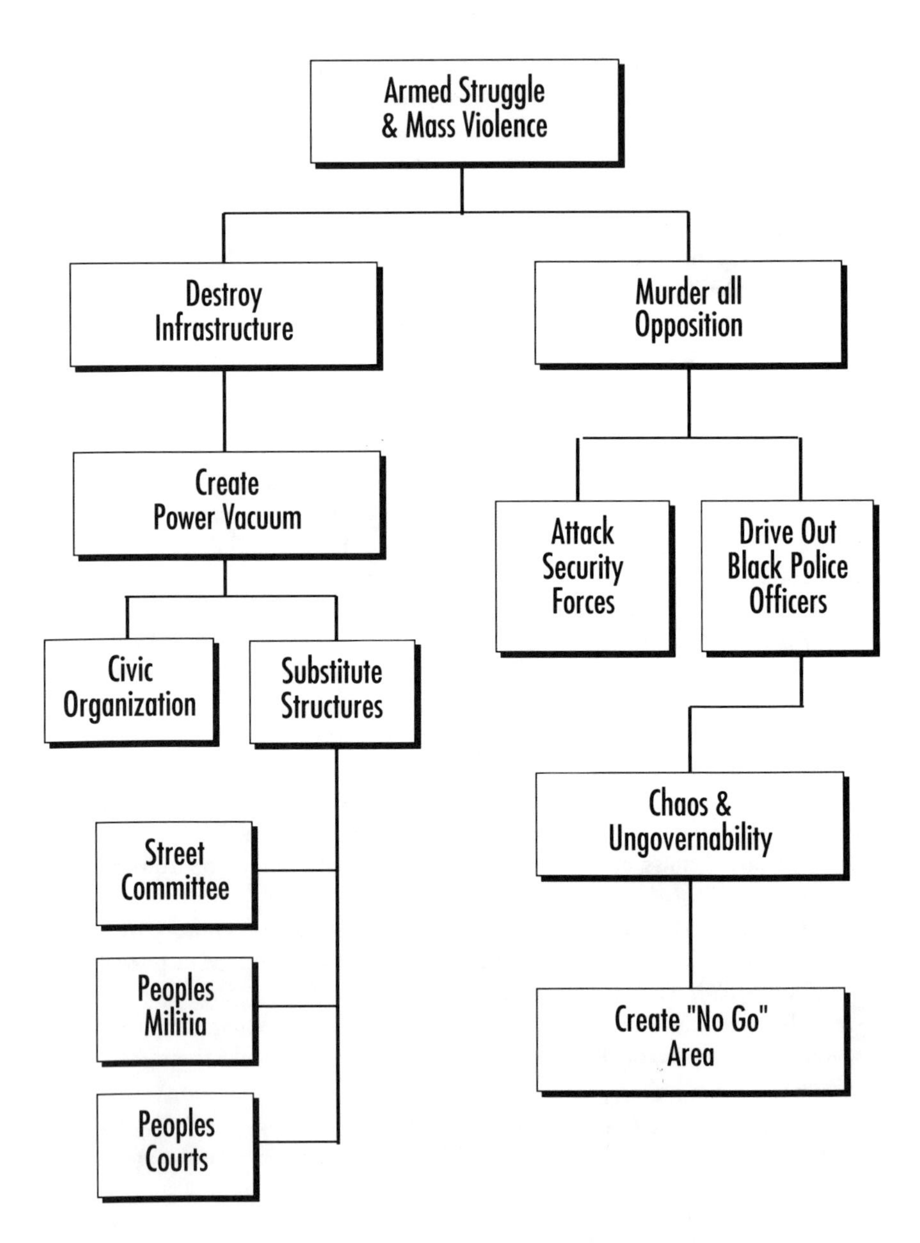

Formation of a Liberated Zone / "No Go" Area

nerve centers of apartheid colonialism. In mass action, the people create the conditions in which the armed struggle can be grounded. . . ."[5]

Future operations of the SACP/ANC must be oriented towards establishing base areas inside South Africa in order to insure the survival of their terrorists who infiltrate from bases outside the country. They looked at the black townships as the best possible site for these areas. However, they recognized that they had to have or create certain conditions and build organizations inside the country to make that strategy work.

The opportunity came during the South African government's new constitutional proposals which would set up a new Tricameral national parliament and other reforms creating new local black governing units in the black townships. The ANC rightly identified these new local black governing units as threatening to their revolutionary program and credibility. They had to be neutralized. (For more details see the chapters on the United Democratic Front and the township unrest elsewhere in this book.)

The main vehicle which the ANC has relied on to carry out its so-called armed struggle is its terrorist wing, *Umkhonto we Sizwe*. Established in 1961 by Nelson Mandela and Joe Slovo, *Umkhonto* is thoroughly controlled by the SACP and is structured along classic Marxist revolutionary lines—a duality where a military arm is always accompanied by a political arm.

The top structure is intertwined with that of the ANC's top echelon, again along classic Marxist lines. Political commissars from the political structure operate alongside military operators from the top down to the cadres in the field.

Overall control of *Umkhonto,* theoretically, starts with the alleged democratic ANC national conference. However, since there have only been two fully representative congresses convened in the last thirty years—the third is scheduled in December 1990—it is difficult to find much democracy in the national conference.

The next tier of the structure is the ANC's National Executive Committee (NEC) a majority of whom are also members of the SACP, followed by the National Working Committee (NWC) which administers the day-to-day activities of the ANC, and then the Political Military Council (PMC).

The PMC is the most important executive body of the ANC. It consists of representatives of *Umkhonto we Sizwe*, the intelligence and security branch and the political and labor wings of the ANC.

The Chairman of the PMC is Oliver Tambo. The vice-chairmen are

[5] *Umsebenzi*, March 1989, p. 10.

ANC Secretary-General Alfred Nzo, also a member of the SACP and ANC Treasurer-General Thomas Nkobi, a SACP member, SACP Secretary General Joe Slovo and John Nkadimeng, Secretary-General of the South African Congress of Trade Unions (SACTU). A powerful figure on the PMC is Josiah Jele, a SACP member, who is executive secretary. Other members include Chris Hani, Joe Modise, Ronnie Kasrils, Steve Tshwete, Jacob Zuma, Mac Maharaj (all known SACP members), and Sizekele Sigxashe, Joe Nhlankia and Mlungisi Mywayi.

The PMC includes the ANC's top military and political strategists headed by the military commander of *Umkhonto we Sizwe*, Joe Modise and the political commissar, Chris Hani. Both are hard-core Stalinist communists.

Modise, a protege of his deputy Joe Slovo, works closely with his white mentor. Slovo, along with Nelson Mandela and others, was one of the founding fathers of *Umkhonto*. He was the man responsible for most of the planning of the ANC's terror deeds carried out inside South Africa. Slovo is regarded as the ANC's top military strategist and was also head of the military intelligence section of *Umkhonto we Sizwe*, the ordnance section, training and the special operations sections. In other words, Slovo was deeply involved in the crucial areas of the ANC's military wing. Given his position as general secretary of the SACP and the presence of numerous communists in the PMC, it is difficult to deny the control and influence the communists have in the ANC's military wing.

Hani is one of the leaders of the emerging new batch of young turks that are lurking in the wings, itching to grasp the reins of power from the old guard—the Tambos, Nzos and Mandelas. He is in charge of political indoctrination of the ANC terrorists, a job which as a militant committed Marxist he pursues with gusto.

After the Rivonia raid, Hani fled South Africa and settled in Lusaka, Zambia where he became the ANC's administrative secretary in 1965. He then started his rapid rise up the ANC's ladder, became a member of the ANC revolutionary council in 1973, and moved up the following year to become its secretary.

The ANC sent him to Lesotho to become head of the ANC's activity in that country from which he directed terrorist infiltration into South Africa. His ANC activity got him deported from Lesotho in 1982 and he returned to ANC headquarters in Lusaka where he was soon made political commissar of the ANC.

The intelligence, ordnance and training sections' functions are self-explanatory and need not be detailed here. The special operations section functions as an ANC "hit squad", responsible for the deaths of several ANC opponents, defectors and other members or supporters suspected of political or security violations within the ANC. One of the most famous assassinations carried out by the special operations section hit squads was of Bartholomew Hlapane and his wife.

Hlapane, a former member of the ANC's National Executive Committee and of the Central Committee of the SACP, had testified before the Denton U.S. Senate Subcommittee on Security and Terrorism, where he had given a first-hand account of the terror activities of the SACP-controlled ANC.[6] For this sin, the ANC killed him and his wife and crippled their daughter for life.

From their headquarters in Lusaka, the PMC and *Umkhonto we Sizwe* chain of command extends down to the regional political military committees (RPMCs). Operating with the RPMCs are the ever-present regional political commissars and intelligence personnel.

The RPMCs are the practical coordinators of *Umkhonto* activity in a given area. They control the activities of the various demarcated "machineries" e.g. the Transvaal Rural Military Machinery. Each machinery has a complex structure which includes a commander, a commissar, various chiefs of staff and logistic and security officers. The RPMCs also control the Area Political Military Committees (APMCs). [For more details, see the chart on *Umkhonto we Sizwe*.]

The RPMCs all have sub-sections controlling command structures, infiltration, intelligence, transport routes, as well as propaganda funds, communications and front organizations. The practical functioning of the *Umkhonto* hierarchy is based on a control system whereby the military commands are given by the central *Umkhonto* headquarters and are then channeled down through the regional command structure to the operational teams.

Terrorist recruits were trained, until recently, in various African countries including Angola. The 1988 Tripartite Agreement between Angola, Cuba and South Africa caused the ANC to be booted out of Angola. Zambia is also anxious to rid itself of the ANC terrorists, although allowing the ANC to keep its headquarters there prior to its return to South Africa. Other African countries that allowed the ANC training facilities were Algeria, Botswana, Ethiopia, Libya and Uganda. (Although unconfirmed, there are indications that the ANC was also given training by Irish

[6] See: "Soviet, East German and Cuban Involvement in Fomenting Terrorism in Southern Africa", *Report of the Chairman of the Subcommittee on Security and Terrorism, Committee on the Judiciary, United States Senate*, 97th Congress, 2nd Session, November 1982.

Republican Army [IRA] and Palestine Liberation Organization [PLO] instructors.) ANC terrorists were also trained in Cuba, East Germany and the Soviet Union.

After obtaining their terrorist training they were, theoretically, assigned to the regional PMCs. In actuality, most of them languished in ANC camps in Zambia or Tanzania, now that the ANC camps have been shut down in Angola. (In 1984, there was a revolt by some ANC cadres in Angola because they were ordered to fight Jonas Savimbi's UNITA guerrillas in Angola instead of returning to fight in South Africa.)

Many recruits, as evidenced from court transcripts of those caught and tried in South Africa, are recruited on the basis of false promises by the ANC. Most of the promises are in the form of scholarships awarded to youths either to complete certain subjects for qualification for a high school certificate, or for advanced educational training outside the country.

The potential scholarship recipient is usually told to go to Swaziland for transportation to his "school". From Swaziland he was sent to Mozambique and from there to the Caculama ANC training camp in Angola. Here, instead of the promised academic subjects, he was given courses in sabotage, explosive training and the other fine arts of terrorism. The recruits were then told that they had to first win the revolution before they could finish their education.

After completing their training they were assigned to *Umkhonto we Sizwe* units or sent to Soviet Bloc countries for more advanced terrorist training.

If any of the recruits became recalcitrant over the fraudulent manner in which they were enlisted they were dealt with very severely. The most common form of discipline was to exile protestors to ANC penal camps. A number of these were established in Tanzania, Angola and Zambia. Here the dissidents were subjected to "re-education" in camps noted for their squalid living conditions, poor food and brutal treatment.[7] The most important was the "Quatro Camp" in Angola. Olivia Forsyth was kept here. A group of recent ANC detainees returned to South Africa were all kept in this camp. They were mostly kept in underground dungeons in the most appalling of circumstances. All were accused of being South African spies. Some of their former comrades were executed without trial by the ANC.

Here is how the ANC would launch a typical revolutionary terrorist mission from abroad into South Africa.

[7] See: *Africa Confidential*, Vol. 31, No. 1, January 12, 1990, p. 4; and Vol. 31, No. 4, February 23, 1990, p. 4.

Infiltration Routes of Communist-Backed ANC Terrorists in Southern Africa

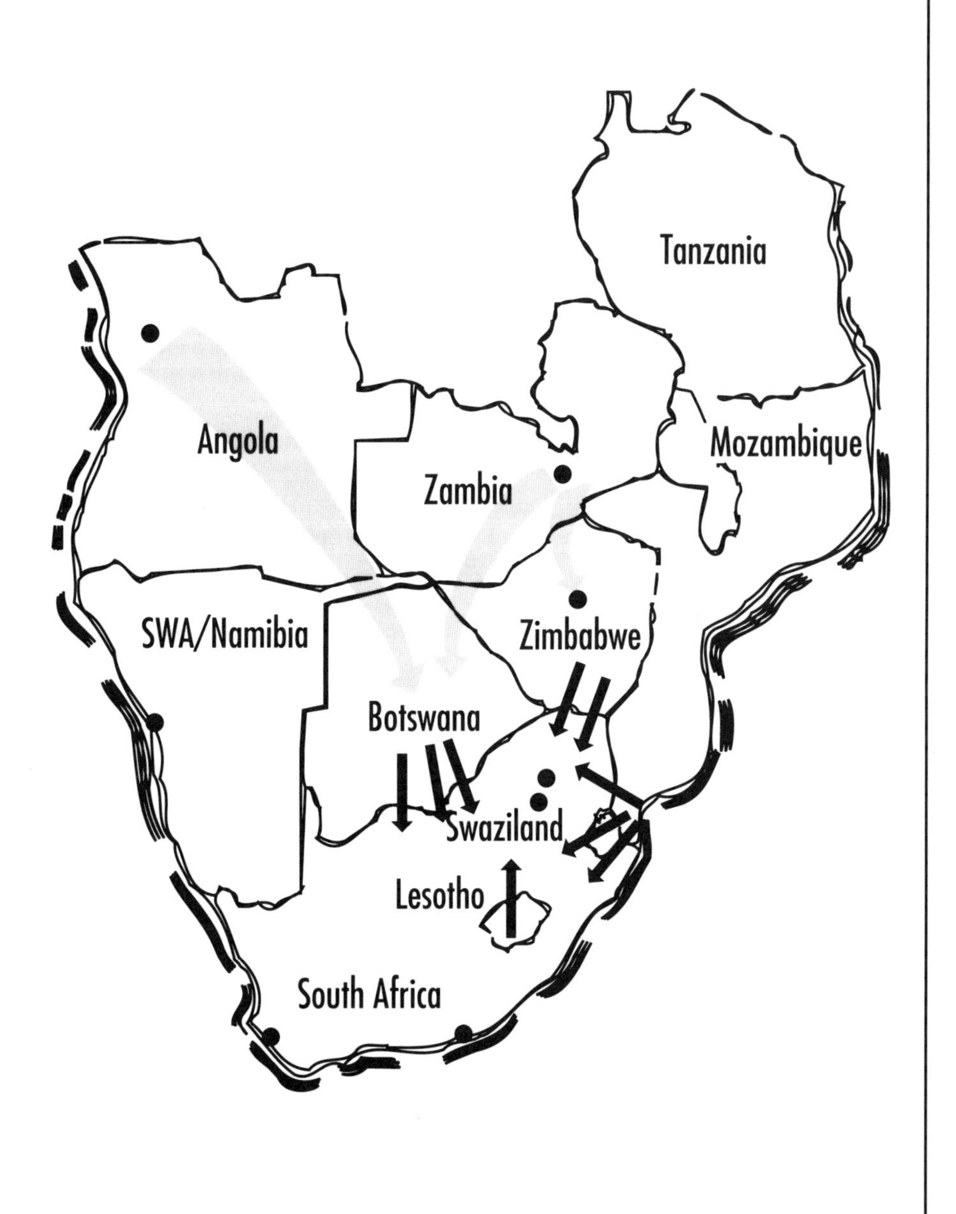

The NEC of the ANC would, for example, decide to launch a rural guerrilla war campaign in the Northern Transvaal region of South Africa. Specifically, it would target the area bordering Botswana and Zimbabwe. The ANC's purpose would be four-fold: 1.) to take the war to the white South African farming community in the area; 2.) to either recruit or chase the local blacks out of the area; 3.) to wreck the local economy; and, 4.) to give grist for their propaganda mills, both inside South Africa and for the foreign media, showing they are actively pursuing the armed struggle inside the country.

The national PMC in Lusaka would study the feasibility of the NEC's mission. The PMC would examine the situation in the targeted area and adjust its pursuit of the mission accordingly.

The operational area designated by the NEC is the South African Soutspansberg Military Area (SMA) in the Northern Transvaal District of South Africa. It is a thinly populated area made up of farms growing cotton, vegetables or game. The largest town is Messina, the administrative center. Messina also contains copper mines and is the northern terminal of the rail and road transportation net that crosses the Beit Bridge over the Limpopo River into Zimbabwe. (This busy route is the key trade route for Zimbabwe's trade with the outside world. This fact is a bitter pill for Zimbabwe's Marxist leader Robert Mugabe to swallow.) DeBeers is opening a diamond mine about sixty miles west of Messina which will greatly boost the local economy.

Fifty percent of the farms are unoccupied as they are used as game farms. They are only used during the hunting season and are owned by absentee owners who live elsewhere in South Africa.

As a result the ANC often uses the area as an infiltration route to get its terrorists to the industrial heartland centered in Johannesburg. Thus, at first glance, the targeted area would appear to be a prime area for engaging in rural guerrilla war. Unfortunately for the ANC, their efforts have been for naught due to three countermeasures of the South Africans.

The first is a physical barrier consisting of a wire-screened fence that, in addition, carries five wires conducting a lethal dose of electricity, that runs along the border.

Secondly, South African army units regularly patrol the border. When ANC spoor is picked up and/or reported by the locals, the army units pursue the terrorists until they either capture or kill them.

Third, the local farmers and their most reliable workers have been organized into a local commando. (The commandos are similar to our militia. They are South Africa's citizens-in-arms who can be mobilized at any time.[8]

[8] For a more detailed look at the South African commando system see: Steenkamp, W., "The

The men were issued the army's R-1 assault rifle while the women were issued Uzi submachine guns. The military provided each farmer-commando with a radio and they maintained regular daily check-ins with the SMA command center at Messina. The government also provided the farmers with assistance, both financial, material and technical, to strengthen and fortify their farms with anti-rocket grenade screens, high walls and other reinforced concrete defensive structures for their farms.

In addition, the SMA command has a reaction force, 907 company, on twenty-four-hour standby ready to respond to any ANC incursion in the area. Using the mine-proof South African Police Casspir vehicle, that proved its worth in South West Africa/Namibia, to follow up any ANC spoor, the reaction force has made ANC activity in the area an extremely perilous venture for the would-be terrorists.

As a result the ANC's options are limited to infiltrating terrorists through the area, minor hit and run attacks on farms or, their most common action, planting landmines on dirt roads. Thus the ANC's armed struggle in the Northern Transvaal is almost entirely limited to planting landmines that target mostly the civilians in the area. A typical indiscriminate ANC terror mission, which we will now describe, will revolve around that type of terrorist action.

The ANC's national PMC in Lusaka will task the mission to the ANC's regional PMC in Harare, Zimbabwe.

The higher *Umkhonto* command may give the regional PMC in Harare the latitude to decide on the specific target area. If so, the RPMC will assign the mission to the area PMC. Depending upon where the target is in the Northern Transvaal, the area PMC involved will be either the western area located at Bulawayo or the eastern area at Masvingo. For the sake of illustration, let's assume our typical mission will be carried out under the control of the western area PMC at Bulawayo, from where, in actual fact, the ANC directs most activity in the SMA.

The western area PMC will run the operation in four phases: reconnaissance or recce, logistical, external operation and the exfiltration phase.

During the recce phase, the ANC will send a team to scout the prospective target. The team will take pictures or, more likely, make a sketch of the target. They will also select both infiltration and exfiltration routes.

This phase is usually a quick in, quick out as strangers loitering in the

Commandos of South Africa", in: Norval, M., *The Militia in 20th Century America*, Gun Owners Foundation, Fairfax, VA, 1985, pp. 127-142.

area come quickly to the attention of the security forces. After completing its recce, the team returns to headquarters (Bulawayo) and makes its report to the area PMC.

Using the information supplied by the recce team, the headquarters plans the terrorist mission and selects the weapons to be used. The area PMC then initiates the logistic phase. Using a different group of ANC cadres from those that made up the recce team, the weapons and other material selected, such as rations, are delivered to a collaborator, or to a cache designated for the mission. Some of the collaborators are members of the Zimbabwe police—the ANC terrorists actually stay in the local Zimbabwean police base. (For example, in late 1989 there were six ANC terrorists at the Sengwe Zimbabwe Police base.[9] Other caches and safe-houses storing weapons, food and equipment for the ANC were at the Tuli police station and the Limpopo store.[10]) After the logistic group has delivered the weapons and equipment for the mission to the collaborator or cache, they return to Bulawayo. The next phase, the external operation, is ready to begin.

The terrorists tasked for the mission will go to the cache, collect their weapons, cross the border and plant their mines. After planting their mines, the terrorists will move back across the border by a different route than the one they used on entering and will return to Bulawayo.

The terrorists that do the actual mine-planting operation may not be the ones that did the recce. In most instances, there is at least one member of the recce team with the operational team. Or, the whole recce team can also do the operation at a later date. It all depends upon the area PMC headquarters, the availability of trained manpower, etc. Normally the whole recce team does not do the subsequent operation.

This sounds good on paper, but in real life the ANC seldom live up to their dreamy operational plans. In actual fact, most ANC operations were flops. Lines on organizational charts mean little as the ANC command has no control as soon as their cadres cross the border. Sometimes they throw their weapons away, don't do the assigned mine laying but return, after a decent interval, and lie to their commanders. Some don't even bother to go back at all. In actuality, the ANC cannot control their terrorists if and when they get inside South Africa.

For a while, as a result of the mid-1980s unrest in the black townships, the ANC would get recruits from South African townships and take them to neighboring countries, predominantly Botswana, for a quick two to three day

[9] Author's intelligence briefing, Messina, December, 1989.

[10] *Ibid.*

crash course on becoming a terrorist. This was nothing more than quick, elementary training in the use of firearms, hand grenades and limpet mines.

After their training in a safe house, usually in Gaberone, Botswana, they were sent on terrorist missions back into South Africa. South African security force raids on ANC safe houses in Gaberone, after 1985, put a damper on this kind of ANC activity,[11] although it didn't totally eliminate it.

These raids reinforced the diplomatic and economic pressures applied by South Africa on those states that allowed the ANC bases from which to launch terrorist attacks against targets inside South Africa.

This policy bore fruits, as noted by *Africa Confidential*: "Pretoria's victories included the Nkomati Accord, neutralizing Mozambique; and the 20 January 1986 coup in Lesotho, putting in a pro-Pretoria government. This involved the expulsion of a formidable *(it was actually more troublesome than formidable—ed.)* ANC regional intelligence unit which had cultivated good contacts in Lesotho's National Security Service. Some remaining ANC cadres were arrested. Others were murdered and abducted acting on information from ANC defectors. . . ."[12]

The ANC also infiltrated its terrorists into the black townships where they recruited trainees and gave them an even more rudimentary quick course than that given in the safe houses in Gaberone. The locally recruited terrorists were shown how to plant bombs, how to make Molotov cocktails out of gasoline and how to decipher coded messages. In addition to recruiting and training local black youths into becoming terrorists, they organized mass acts of violence such as mob attacks on opponents, killing opponents by means of the infamous necklacing method, tossing Molotov cocktails at policemen's houses and stone throwing incidents at *Umkhonto we Sizwe* selected targets such as trains, buses, police vehicles, schools and administrative offices in the black townships. These locally recruited and trained terrorists, however, were nothing more than cannon-fodder. They didn't last long and often their first mission was their last.

In terms of actual practice the ANC's armed struggle has been a dismal failure. Breytenbach lists the reasons: 1.) the waging of a protracted and costly guerrilla war—involving the front line states and the surrogate forces of international powers—was unlikely to dislodge the South African government; 2.) no analysis with any comparative depth has been able to

[11] For more details, see: Chapter 11, "The Guns of Gaberone", in: Norval, M., *Red Star Over Southern Africa* , Selous Foundation Press, Washington, D.C., 1988, pp. 119-130.

[12] *Africa Confidential,* January 20, 1989, p. 7.

suggest that successful revolution is even remotely possible in South Africa; 3.) the success of diplomatic and economic pressure on front line states by Pretoria; 4.) backlash on the ANC's involvement in the township uprising of 1984-86; 5.) the recent cautionary attitude of the SACP toward the armed struggle; and, 6.) the ANC's downgrading of the armed struggle.[13]

So dismal has been the ANC's armed struggle that it has been reduced to planting limpet mines in the waste baskets of Wimpey's, a popular fast food hamburger chain in South Africa patronized by all races. Thus the ANC's loudly proclaimed armed struggle has been reduced to acts of random wanton terror against innocent civilians, most of them black.

How can a group which professes to stand for democracy, as the ANC claims it does, choose violence to bring it about as the ANC has done? Violence and democracy are not synonymous. But the ANC has, it appears, come to believe its own rhetoric. Even Nelson Mandela seems reluctant to give up the armed seizure of power.[14] Can the ANC, therefore, abandon violence? Steeped as it is in the Marxist-Leninist ideology of revolution it seems doubtful. The ANC ". . . cannot and will not renounce violence as an important strategy towards attaining political power. . . ."[15] because, "a violence-free ANC will soon be forgotten by all."[16] The ANC also can't renounce violence because if they did they would lose the support of the young radicals who would shift to their rivals, the Pan African Congress (PAC).

Statements by ANC officials give credence to such observations. Pallo Jordan, a non-military influential member of the ANC's National Executive Committee said, "We have always said that the notion of the ANC unilaterally abandoning the armed struggle is out of the question."[17] Thabo Mbeki, leader of the so-called moderate faction in the ANC echoes Jordon's statement: ". . . the ANC will never lay down arms unilaterally. . . ."[18]

[13] Breytenbach, W.J., *The ANC: Future Prognosis*, No. 4, July 1989, Political Series, Socio-Political Environment, Institute For Futures Research, University of Stellenbosh.

[14] See: "Transcript of Mandela's Speech at Cape Town City Hall: 'Africa It Is Ours!' ", *The New York Times*, February 12, 1990; "Hailing South Africa's Communists" *The Washington Post*, February 13, 1990.

[15] Cilliers, J.K., *Strategic Review*, Institute for Strategic Studies, University of Pretoria, Pretoria, 1988, p. 2.

[16] Muller, P., *Rapport*, September 18, 1988.

[17] Ottaway, D., "South Africa's Mandela Credits Resistance Forces, Sanctions for Changes", *The Washington Post*, February 4, 1990.

[18] Mbeki, T., "The Rebel's Answer to Pretoria", *The New York Times*, February 4, 1990.

Nelson Mandela told an April 4, 1990 rally in Umtata, Transkei: "The ANC will not discard any of its present methods and strategies. Only successful negotiations can convince us to end the armed struggle."[19]

It is important to point out that none of the elements of the ANC's organizational structures are democratically elected. The entire organization operates on the committee principle—office-bearing does not entail electoral accountability. Accountability is to the organization, and not to its members. Criteria for recruitment and advancement in the organs of the ANC are therefore based on selection, nomination or appointment, not election. This characteristic of its control process is swept under the rug by its proponents and apologists in South Africa and elsewhere. Even though statements by the ANC seem to be advocating democracy, the prevailing political culture within the ANC is Marxist through and through.[20]

The unbanning of the ANC has put the organization on the spot with its continued advocacy of the armed struggle. With events in other parts of the world suggesting the crumbling of the Marxist empire by peaceful democratic means, the ANC's strident advocacy of violence puts it running against the prevailing political winds sweeping the globe.

Breytenbach's listing makes sense, in an intellectual way, and points to the painful dilemma the ANC now finds itself as to the failure of its armed struggle.

Williamson is more blunt: "The morale of the organization is lower than ever before. Their deep depression is partly a reaction to the false euphoria of 1984 and 1985 when, as in 1961 and 1976, 'liberation' was considered to be imminent. The resilience, ingenuity and resources of the South African government and its security forces have again proved superior to the military and political strategy of the ANC. . . . The organization that could once boast of its ability to sabotage a nuclear power station, of ungovernability in liberated zones and of the imminent collapse of the South African state is now reduced to malicious blows against ordinary innocent people. . . . The ANC-SACP alliance has proved over 27 years to be the most incompetent and least successful Soviet-backed revolutionary organization *(sic)* in the world. Nowhere else has a revolutionary group supported by the Soviets been so decisively battered time and again and put back to square one."[21]

[19] Transcript, Mandela speech, April, 4, 1990, Umtata, Transkei.

[20] *Africa Confidential*, Vol. 31, No. 1, January 12, 1990, pp. 1-4.

[21] Williamson, C., "ANC Clandestine Operations" in: *Challenge: Southern Africa within the African Revolutionary Context*, p. 291.

Targets of Terror in South Africa

1988

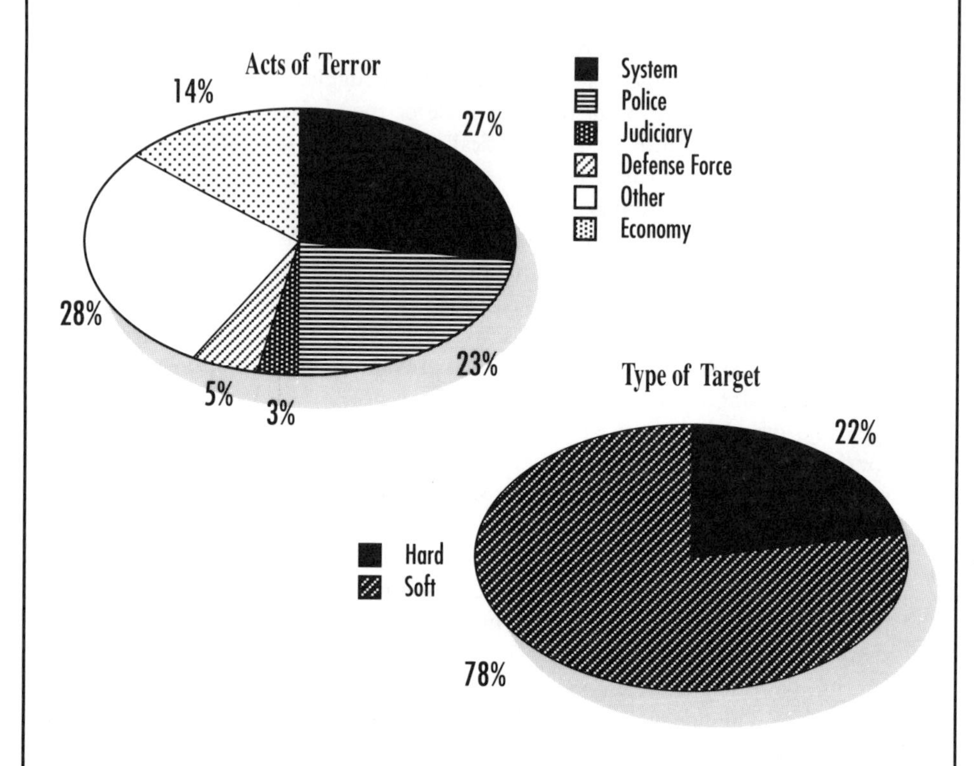

Target Analysis

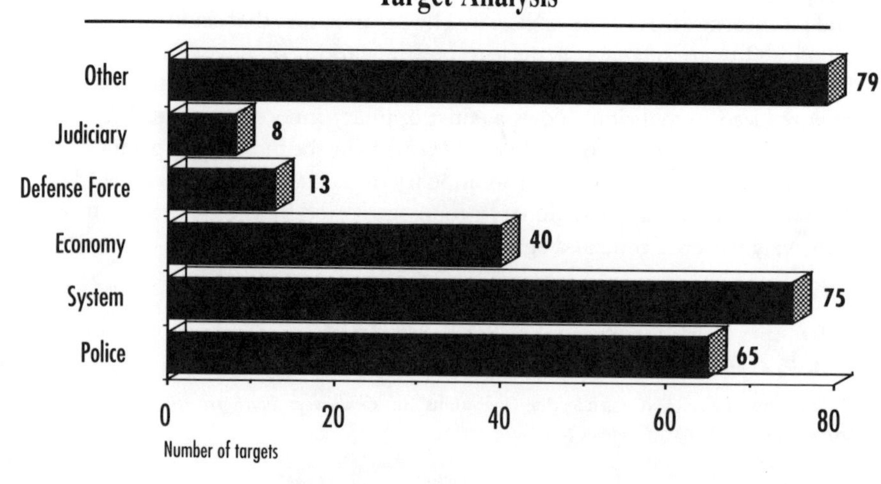

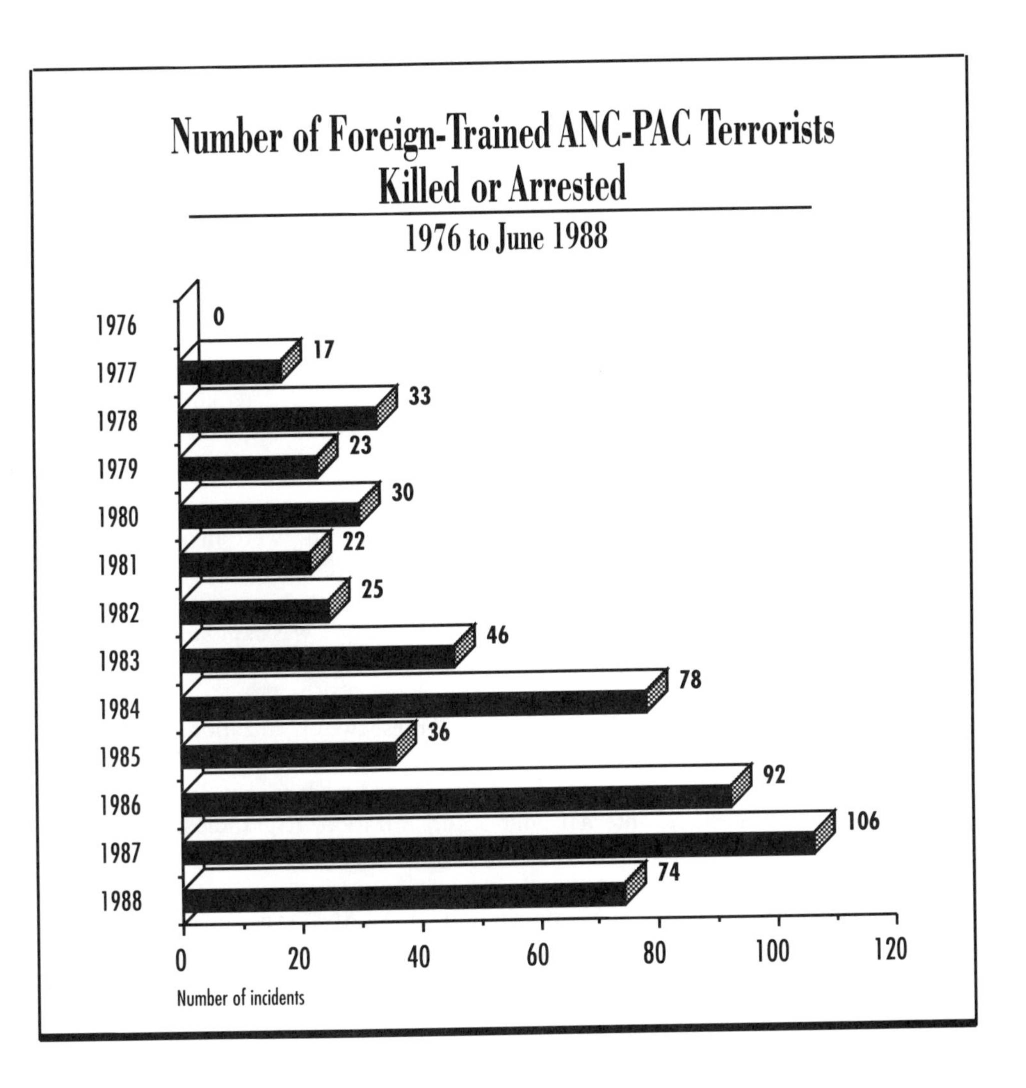
Number of Foreign-Trained ANC-PAC Terrorists
Killed or Arrested
1976 to June 1988
1976
1977
1978
1979
1980
1981
1982
1983
1984
1985
1986
1987
1988
0
17
33
23
30
22
25
46
78
36
92
106
74
0
20
40
60
80
100
120
Number of incidents

Williamson wrote these words in 1989 before the unbanning of the ANC and the release from prison of Nelson Mandela and his fellow Rivonia prison mates. As a result of those actions morale in the ANC has decidedly improved. However, as Williamson's observation makes clear, the ANC is ill-suited to handle setbacks and if things don't go well for them in the future, based on their past, it is reasonable to assume that their incompetence will return with a vengeance.

It is clear the ANC has failed in its attempt to seize power by means of armed conflict in South Africa. The implementation of the "foco" strategy from the 1960s to the middle of the 1970s brought nothing but failure for the ANC. The first trained terrorists began infiltrating into South Africa through then Rhodesia in August 1967. Their infiltration peaked in 1973 as they were neutralized by South African security forces almost as soon as they arrived inside the country.

The ANC tried to rationalize their lack of success by terming the period 1961 to 1976 as a preparatory phase in their revolutionary campaign. It was idle talk, however, because it was an era of failure. Not only were all terrorists who infiltrated into South Africa arrested, but the ANC also lost contact with what was going on inside South Africa.

The vacuum caused internally by the ANC failures was exploited by the Black Consciousness groups, namely the South African Students Organization (SASO) and the Black People's Convention (BPC). The 1976 unrest, which can be credited mostly to the actions of these two organizations instead of the ANC, brought about an increase in the activities of the SACP/ANC alliance. The ANC initiated armed propaganda and made renewed efforts to build up its moribund internal political organization. It grandiosely proclaimed it was launching its "people's war" based on its four pillars strategy.

This strategy gained some momentum for the ANC, especially after the formation of the United Democratic Front (UDF) in 1983. After the outbreak of unrest in September 1984 in South Africa, the SACP/ANC propaganda took on a euphoric tone that tried to create the perception that the South African government was on the verge of collapse and it was only a question of time before a total transfer of power would come about. During the 1985-86 period ANC propaganda boasted that it would be running South Africa from the Union Building in Pretoria by December 1986. Joe Slovo also believed the same thing.

The declaration of the State of Emergency in South Africa in 1986 changed the ANC's mood to gloom. The South African security forces succeeded in checking and rolling back the ANC's revolutionary advance. At the Arusha Conference in December 1987, the ANC itself acknowledged that its "people's war" strategy had failed.

To add to the ANC's misery, the dawning of the Gorbachev era has compounded the ANC's problems. The dominant partner in the alliance, the SACP, never imagined the extent to which the *glasnost* and *perestroika* in the Soviet Union would bring Moscow and Washington together. The Soviets, starved for cash and busy trying to keep the lid on the boiling pot of nationalism and freedom in their homeland and to hold on to their influence in their former Eastern European vassal states, want to resolve regional conflicts, such as those engaged in by the SACP/ANC alliance, by political means. This does not strengthen the position of the "armed struggle" proponents in the ANC by any means.

However, they haven't given up and are in an entrenched position within the ANC to continue with their campaign of terror and violence.

Organizational Chart of ANC

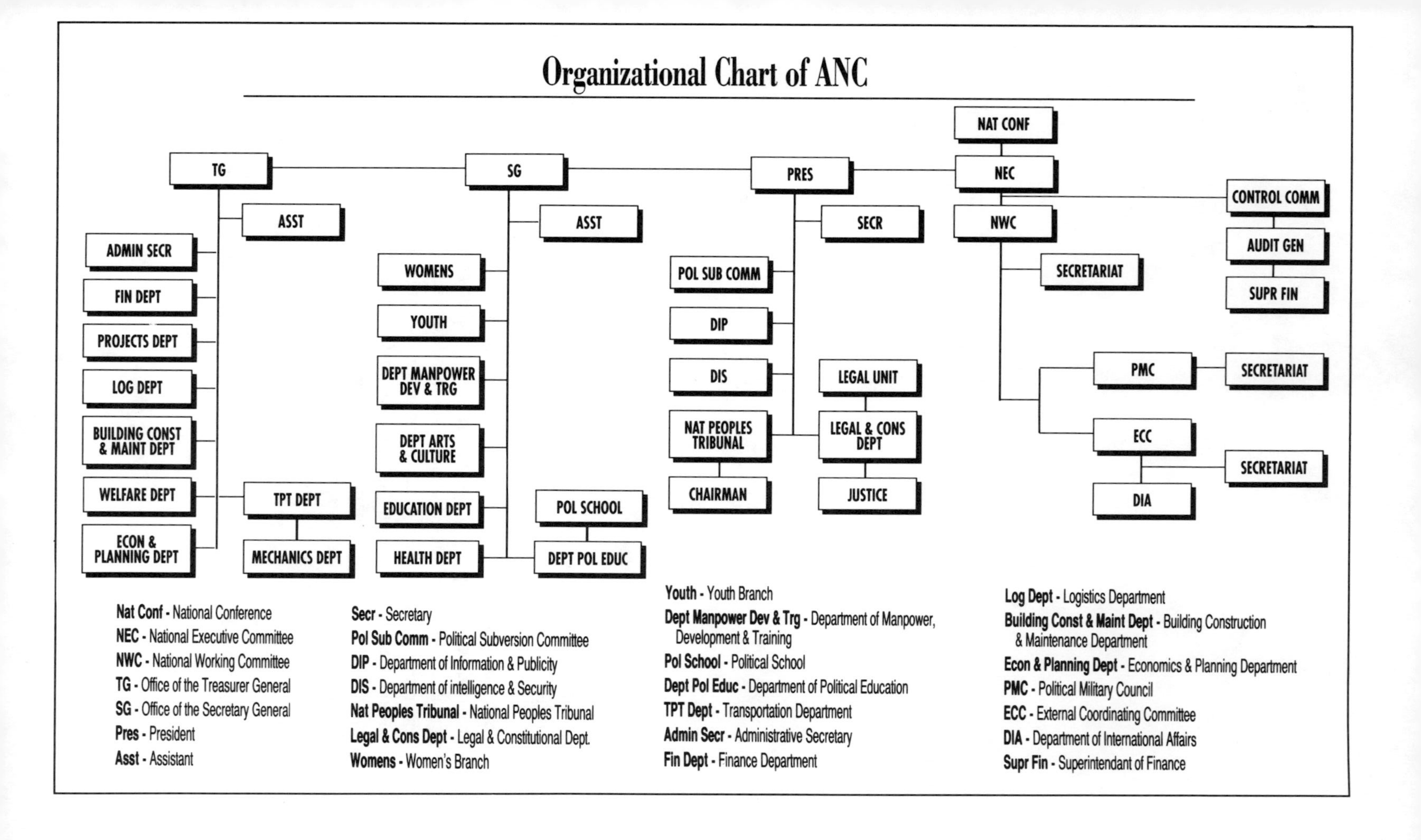

Nat Conf - National Conference
NEC - National Executive Committee
NWC - National Working Committee
TG - Office of the Treasurer General
SG - Office of the Secretary General
Pres - President
Asst - Assistant

Secr - Secretary
Pol Sub Comm - Political Subversion Committee
DIP - Department of Information & Publicity
DIS - Department of intelligence & Security
Nat Peoples Tribunal - National Peoples Tribunal
Legal & Cons Dept - Legal & Constitutional Dept.
Womens - Women's Branch

Youth - Youth Branch
Dept Manpower Dev & Trg - Department of Manpower, Development & Training
Pol School - Political School
Dept Pol Educ - Department of Political Education
TPT Dept - Transportation Department
Admin Secr - Administrative Secretary
Fin Dept - Finance Department

Log Dept - Logistics Department
Building Const & Maint Dept - Building Construction & Maintenance Department
Econ & Planning Dept - Economics & Planning Department
PMC - Political Military Council
ECC - External Coordinating Committee
DIA - Department of International Affairs
Supr Fin - Superintendant of Finance

16

THE ANC's REVOLUTIONARY ORGANIZATION

Before discussing the fourth pillar of the ANC's revolutionary strategy—the international isolation of South Africa—it is worthwhile to examine the organization created by the ANC to carry out its program of terror and intimidation.

The ANC is a tightly controlled revolutionary organization whose tentacles extend into South Africa from the safety of their bases many hundreds of miles away. The ANC is controlled by its National Executive Committee (NEC), made up of thirty-five members, the majority of whom are also members of the SACP. The NEC, like most corporate political entities, is broken down into committees that oversee the day-to-day operations of the ANC and, prepare policy matters under their control for final approval by the whole NEC.

The most important committee is the National Working Committee (NWC). The NWC coordinates the efforts and work of the various committees and organs of the ANC. It functions as a clearing house passing information gathered throughout the ANC up the pipeline to the appropriate decision making body within the ANC and passing instructions down from the NEC.

The NEC also oversees the office of the president of the ANC. Besides the office of president, the most important groups coordinated by the NEC are the Political Military Council (PMC) and the External Coordinating Committee (ECC).

Of the two the most important is the Political Military Council. This group is responsible for the conduct of the ANC's terrorist war inside South Africa.

The PMC directs and controls *Umkhonto we Sizwe* through its regional and area PMCs. When the ANC headquarters in Lusaka, through the national PMC, decides to mount an operation, they will task whatever regional PMC is in charge of the area in which the target is located. The area PMC will provide the equipment, logistical support and the personnel for the actual terrorist act, unless otherwise directed by higher authorities—either the regional or national PMC.

As the name implies, the PMC has a political as well as military component. The political headquarters oversees the political aspects of the ANC's so-called people's war. It provides input on the political and propaganda significance of potential targets of terrorist acts under consideration by the ANC.

Just as important to the ANC is the task of maintaining the ideological purity and zeal of its cadres. This, too, is the job of the political side of the PMC. The personnel of the political headquarters within each level of the PMCs are, in effect, the political commissars of the ANC. Each ANC regional and area PMC, therefore, has its own political commissars. In this manner the ANC keeps a tight rein from top to bottom and makes sure that everybody toes the party line. It is a system quite familiar to students of the Soviet military system with its political commissars from top to bottom throughout the Soviet defense force.

Under the office of president of the ANC's direct control are the political subcommittee, the department of information and publicity (DIP); the department of intelligence and security; the National People's Tribunal; and the Legal and Constitutional department.

The office of president, in his capacity as head of the Political Military Council (PMC), also exercises organizational input and control over the military wing. We will examine the PMC in more detail later in the chapter.

The ANC president is also titular head of the External Coordinating Committee (ECC). The two most important entities in the ECC are the office of secretariat and the department of international affairs (DIA). By virtue of the fact that the secretariat oversees the day-to-day administrative affairs of the ECC, the head of that office has tremendous clout within the higher corridors of power in the ANC.

The political subcommittee handles and coordinates political matters for the office of president. These matters can then, in theory, be passed up the chain of command from the president to the NEC, and, if important enough, to the National Conference of the whole ANC. However, since national conferences are few and far between, important decisions normally are taken by the NEC.

The department of information and publicity is the ANC's propaganda organ. It issues press releases, ANC policy statements and oversees the various ANC publications that disseminate the ANC's message to their cadres and the rest of the world.

The department of intelligence and security collates and analyzes the intelligence data collected by ANC intelligence units within the ANC. It functions as the strategic level of the ANC intelligence network and passes its assessments up the chain of command or sends them to other organs, mainly the military wing, if it feels the information is necessary for any terrorist activity being planned by any ANC unit under the control of the PMC.

The office of security's main function is to prevent penetration by agents of the South African government. Given the number of successful agents Pretoria has had and still has inside the ANC, its security branch isn't that great.

Another of its functions, as it is with any Marxist organization, is to keep an eye on its own cadres to make sure they are toeing the current party line. Given the widespread discontent among ANC cadres,[1] the security branch has its hands full keeping an eye on its own disgruntled terrorists.

The National People's Tribunal is the ANC's court where "treasonable" or recalcitrant ANC members are brought to get ANC-style justice. As might be expected, the tribunal is nothing more than a kangaroo court that makes a mockery of justice.

The Legal and Constitutional office has two basic functions. The more important one as far as the day-to-day operations of the ANC is concerned is its function as prosecutor. This is the office that draws up the charges and prosecutes the individual ANC cadres who have angered somebody within the ANC or have committed some crime that offends the sensibilities of the ANC. The constitutional function is limited even though the ANC makes a big show of advocating a so-called democracy based on the Freedom Charter. There is no doubt this department assisted Dr. Pallo Jordan in his project, financed by Sweden, to draw up a proposed ANC constitution for a post-apartheid South Africa.

The office of secretary-general is a very important office of the ANC.

[1] See: "Crackdown Hits Hani's Men", *Africa Confidential*, Vol. 30, No. 18, September 8, 1989, pp. 3-4.

This becomes evident when one examines the departments that are under its control. The secretary-general can influence ANC policy through his various departments, especially three: manpower development and training, education and, probably most important of all, the political education department. His viewpoint, as expressed and carried out by these three, can either keep the ANC on its ideological course, or change it in another direction. It is for this reason that the post of secretary general is an extremely important one in communist parties. It is no less important in the ANC.

The youth department is the key to the long-term prospects of the ANC. Considerable effort is devoted by the ANC, as well as by all Marxist organizations, to the training and indoctrination of the youth.

The office of treasurer-general is more than just the ANC's bookkeeping department. The office also has charge of the daily operation of the ANC's physical plant, such as its training camps, etc. The office also, through its economic and planning department, provides estimates as to how much money the ANC is likely to get, how much is available for current or future projects, etc. The office keeps the president, and through him, the NEC, advised as to the fiscal health of the organization, the state of its camps, offices, and vehicles. In short, the treasurer-general's office has budgetary as well as management functions in order to make sense of the ANC's far-flung facilities.

In general, the ANC has received about a third of its funds from the Scandinavian countries, a third from the Soviet Union and its East Bloc surrogates—primarily East Germany (whose secret police, the *Stasi*, provided counterfeit rands),[2] and the balance from the United Nations,[3] World Council of Churches,[4] other religious groups, and some Western governments, including the United States. The ANC used the Scandinavian funds for expenditures in the Frontline States,[5] the World Council of Church funds in the ANC's rear bases,[6] and the counterfeit South African currency inside South Africa.

Africa Confidential said, "ANC sources also report the use of forged

[2] "South Africa: Money", *Africa Confidential*, Vol. 31, No. 12, June 15, 1990, p. 8.

[3] See, for example: "Proposed Programme Budget For The Biennium 1990-1991" General Assembly, Official Records: Forty-Fourth Session, Supplement No. 6 (A/44/6/Rev. 1), "Section 3. Political affairs and decolonization", pp. 7-9 & 24-27.

[4] Lefever, E. W., *Amsterdam to Nairobi: The World Council of Churches and the Third World*, Ethics and Public Policy Center, Washington, D.C., 1979, p. 92.

[5] *Africa Confidential, op. cit.*

[6] *Ibid.*

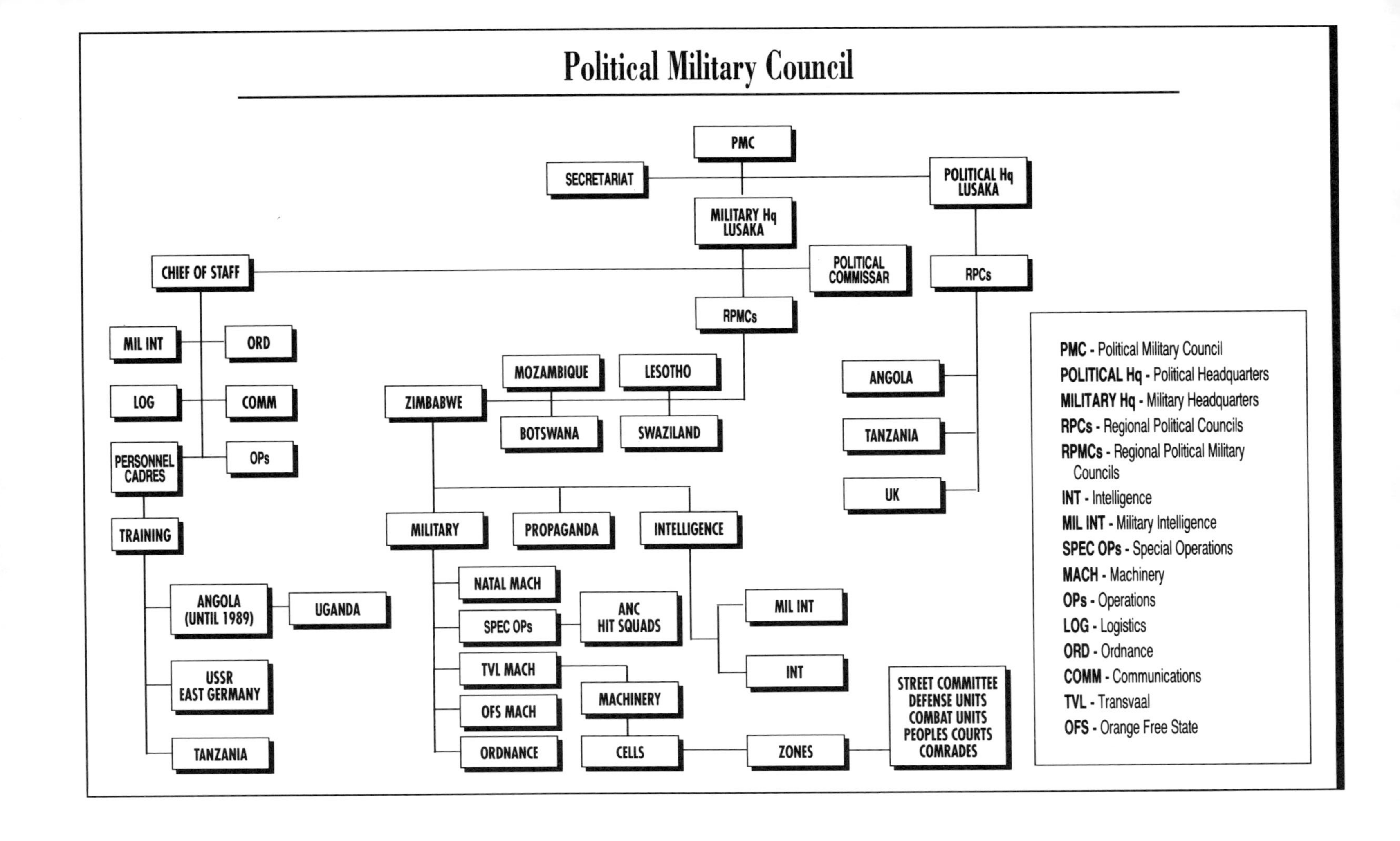
Political Military Council
PMC
SECRETARIAT
POLITICAL Hq LUSAKA
MILITARY Hq LUSAKA
POLITICAL COMMISSAR
RPCs
CHIEF OF STAFF
RPMCs
MIL INT
ORD
LOG
COMM
PERSONNEL CADRES
OPs
TRAINING
MOZAMBIQUE
LESOTHO
ZIMBABWE
BOTSWANA
SWAZILAND
ANGOLA
TANZANIA
UK
MILITARY
PROPAGANDA
INTELLIGENCE
NATAL MACH
SPEC OPs
ANC HIT SQUADS
TVL MACH
MACHINERY
OFS MACH
ORDNANCE
CELLS
ZONES
MIL INT
INT
STREET COMMITTEE
DEFENSE UNITS
COMBAT UNITS
PEOPLES COURTS
COMRADES
ANGOLA (UNTIL 1989)
UGANDA
USSR EAST GERMANY
TANZANIA
PMC - Political Military Council
POLITICAL Hq - Political Headquarters
MILITARY Hq - Military Headquarters
RPCs - Regional Political Councils
RPMCs - Regional Political Military Councils
INT - Intelligence
MIL INT - Military Intelligence
SPEC OPs - Special Operations
MACH - Machinery
OPs - Operations
LOG - Logistics
ORD - Ordnance
COMM - Communications
TVL - Transvaal
OFS - Orange Free State

United States dollars of Cuban origin, although these were of a lower standard than the East German rands."[7]

As mentioned earlier, the PMC has a dual command structure with both a military and political wing. It is a top-down structure that is efficient for giving orders, but does not have much leeway to get feed-back from the lower levels.

At the top level under the PMC are the headquarters, political as well as military, which are both located in Lusaka, Zambia.

The next level down are the regional political military councils (RPMCs) located in Angola, Tanzania, Great Britain, Swaziland, Mozambique, Lesotho, Botswana and Zimbabwe. Each RPMC has under it three main departments: intelligence, propaganda and military. It is the RPMCs that plan and oversee most of the terrorist activity inside South Africa, acting on general instructions from the national PMC. The location of the target in South Africa largely determines which RPMC will be in charge of the prospective operation.

The military wing of each RPMC has under it the special operations, ordnance and the local terrorist machine groups in its area of operations. For example, the RPMC located in Swaziland is responsible for ANC terrorist activity in Natal and part of the Eastern Transvaal.

Depending upon the target location, the RPMC will task the appropriate area PMC (APMC) to carry out the terrorist mission. The APMC will select the terrorists and weapons and provide logistic support for their operation. If they exist inside South Africa, the APMC may use the local terrorist machine in the target area to do the terrorist deed.

The ANC military machine in, for example, the Transvaal, is broken down further into ANC cells within the black townships in South Africa. Each cell is responsible for ANC terrorist activity within a designated zone within the township. The zone is further broken down into street committees where terrorists are responsible for ANC terror and intimidation deeds on their designated street or streets; so-called self-defense units whose main job is to back up ANC intimidation measures and provide muscle to force the people in the zones to attend rallies, funerals or other agit-propaganda measures decreed by the ANC. Each zone is supposed to establish people's courts to further terrorize the residents in their zones by meting out ANC justice—beatings, fines and even death in some gruesome manner such as necklacing; and the formation of the "comrades"—young street thugs that

[7] *Ibid.*

serve as intimidators and enforcers. They constitute the bottom of the barrel of the ANC cannon fodder.

The purpose of the machinery organization is two-fold: first, by its acts of terror and intimidation to render the area ungovernable and thus discredit the government; and, second, to provide an alternative structure to that of the governing authorities so that the ANC can rule the area.

The ANC structure does not make any provision for democracy, in spite of ANC bombast. It is always the same people who make the decisions in the ANC—even on who is to be "elected" to the higher echelons of power within the ANC. It is a nomination and awarding process, there are no free elections of officials by the ANC members.

That, in a nutshell, is the organizational layout of the ANC and of its political military council. It may look impressive on neat organizational charts, but to rely on the charts may give one a false reading on just how effective the terrorist group is. As is clear throughout this book, it looks better on paper than its actual performance on the ground indicates.

17

ARMED STRUGGLE BEHIND AN ORGANIZATIONAL FACE

The February 1990 unbanning of the African National Congress (ANC) and the South African Communist Party (SACP) has called into question the role of the armed struggle in the political situation in South Africa. There are factions, in both groups, who not only want to continue the armed struggle, but to escalate it and target whites.

It seems a bit ironic that a group professing to be liberating its black brothers from white oppression nevertheless directs most of its violence against those it is supposed to be liberating. Its call to shift its targeting from the oppressed to the oppressor somehow has a hollow ring to it. Such a course of action suggests the motives of the ANC are not as altruistic as it would have one believe, as discussed elsewhere.

Others in the ANC, however, want to travel a different road to power—through the political process involving negotiations. This difference of opinion is tied in with the power struggle within the ANC over who will eventually take over from the Tambo-Mandela old guard. Given the interlocking relationships between the ANC and the SACP, what happens in one organization has its effects on the other. This is especially true regarding the question of the importance of the armed struggle vis-a-vis negotiations.

Africa Confidential points out, "The most divisive issues within the ANC—the role of the armed struggle in particular—divide the SACP as much as they do the ANC as a whole. While the party line has been to restrict the armed struggle to attacks on military targets and to refrain from hitting soft targets, it is deeply ambivalent on the question of eventual negotiations with the government in Pretoria. While this might be tactically desirable, it would entail the unbanning of the ANC and would probably weaken the party's grip over the organization since it would abolish the need for secrecy."[1]

The struggle centers around two men, both leading lights in the ANC and SACP—Thabo Mbeki and Chris Hani.

Mbeki, a brilliant Marxist theoretician, is the leader of the ANC faction favoring negotiations. As a member of the SACP, he is able to push his position for negotiations within the Party, which is basically Stalinist in its view.

A Stellenbosch University publication notes that: "Mbeki remains the SACP's leading dissident. Scion of a top ANC family and the organization's most skillful politician, he has the ear of Oliver Tambo. He has been instrumental in managing the ANC's public image and has contributed mightily to putting the organization on the diplomatic map. He himself hardly hides his distaste for party work but finds it useful to keep his place in the politbureau. He takes care never to breach the SACP disciplinary code. He is too important to expel from the party."[2]

Mbeki's position has been enhanced by the current political climate within South Africa. His skillful political and diplomatic maneuvers for the ANC had the blessings of Oliver Tambo, whose international reputation protects him from the long knives and purges endemic to the ANC and similar Marxist organizations. Such is his reputation that even the series of strokes he suffered has not reduced his prestige in the ANC. This has also helped Mbeki.

One of Mbeki's initiatives was to expand relations between the ANC and white liberals and church groups in South Africa. SACP/ANC hard liners look upon both of these groups with disfavor.

More helpful to the negotiators was the study, financed by Sweden, done by Mbeki and Dr. Pallo Jordan. This study, titled *Post-Apartheid South Africa*, advocated far-reaching constitutional proposals designed to, and which did,

[1] *Africa Confidential*, August 26, 1990, quoted in: Breytenbach, W.J.,

[2] From *Africa Confidential*, August 26, 1988, as quoted in Breytenbach, W.J., *The ANC: Future Prognosis*, Institute for Futures Research, Stellenbosch University, Stellenbosch, RSA, 1989, p. 27.

attract attention in the West. They were a cleverly designed mixed bag of proposals and not a total socialist commitment to nationalization of the South African economy. As such, SACP/ANC hard liners looked on them as a sell-out.

These proposals increased pressure on the hard liners to abandon their insistence on escalating the armed struggle. The more terrorist bombs explode in South Africa, the more support they lose from the white liberals and the international media. Terrorism, finally, has rightfully acquired a bad international image.

How can an organization claiming to be working for democracy do it by bombing their way to a democratic society, especially in today's climate of negotiation? Any rational person can readily see that terrorist acts and democracy mix as well as oil and water. Yet, that is the situation the ANC currently finds itself in-—to bomb or not to bomb, is the ANC's big question.

Given the current world-wide political climate against solving differences by violence, the fact that such a question is still being seriously discussed shows the depth of strength within the SACP/ANC alliance for the continuation of the violent armed struggle. Even Nelson Mandela, elevated to near sainthood by the international media upon his release from prison, has refused to renounce the armed struggle.

The tenacity of the armed struggle position has been due to the successful power grab in the ANC by Chris Hani. Hani, a hard line Marxist-Leninist, consolidated his power within the strongest group in the ANC—its military wing. Hani has the support of thousands of youthful ANC cadres who left South Africa to join the struggle. These militants have been languishing in ANC training camps outside South Africa and are growing impatient to go back and fight. They are looking for Hani to lead them back to the promised land.

When Hani became chief of staff of *Umkhonto we Sizwe* in 1987 he move quickly to consolidate his power. He had his protege, Steve Tshwete, named in his place as political commissar. Breytenbach points out in his study of a future South Africa that: "This stunned insiders who knew that Tshwete had previously been designated ANC representative in Zimbabwe. Tshwete, who had only recently come out of South Africa, is an impressive thinker, but had undergone a mere two-month training course in East Germany in 1986 and was not qualified to be number three in *Umkhonto we Sizwe*."[3] So

[3] *Africa Confidential*, August 12, 1988, as quoted in Breytenbach, *op. cit.*, p. 26.

successful were Hani's efforts that his supporters occupy six of the eight *Umkhonto* high command positions.

Hani was ready to challenge the leadership of the SACP/ANC alliance.

Breytenbach's report continues: "The calculated challenge to the leadership of the African National Congress (ANC) and the South African Communist Party (SACP) by the ANC's brightest rising star, Chris Hani, seems to have succeeded. Hani, technically number two in the ANC's armed wing *Umkhonto we Sizwe*, is now arguably the most powerful person in the ANC.

"In making his challenge, Hani, reportedly a member of the SACP politbureau, has taken on the hierarchies of both organizations. Whereas observers have generally thought that the principal tension in the ANC is between members and non-members of the SACP, recent events show the deepest division to be on the role of violence, with the younger militants agreeing with Hani that attacks on white civilian targets should be the next target.

"Hani threw down a challenge to the leadership with a series of newspaper interviews in June which he gave in tandem with the then *Umkhonto* political commissar and number three Steve Tshwete, a close ally. . . . The two spoke on the record about the ANC's need to take the war in South Africa into white areas. Subsequent bomb attacks on soft targets—notably a white sports ground—seemed to emphasize the seriousness of this remark. ANC President Oliver Tambo dissociated himself from Hani and Tshwete's remarks, saying they were not ANC policy. The ANC has not claimed responsibility for the Ellis Park rugby stadium bomb or other attacks on soft targets."[4]

Tambo and the NEC have reiterated the ANC's long established principle that military action must be subordinated to the political policy of the ANC. *Africa Confidential* points out, ". . . In other words there are to be no attacks on soft civilian targets. But since then there have been further bomb attacks on white civilian targets—presumably the work of *Umkhonto* —which appears to reflect the views of Hani and his supporters. . . ."[5]

Hani's position on the armed struggle was given intellectual backing within the ANC by an article in the September 1988 issue of *Sechaba* by Ronnie Kasrils, a Hani supporter and a founding father of *Umkhonto we Sizwe*. Kasrils' article, "The Revolutionary Army", lays out the justification for the use of force even during a process of negotiations. It undergirds the

[4] Breytenbach, W.J., *op. cit.*, pp. 29-30.

[5] *Africa Confidential*, August 12, 1990, as quoted in Breytenbach, W.J., *op. cit.*, p. 26.

ANC hard liners' position on the armed struggle. Given the ANC's reluctance to renounce the armed struggle, its influence goes beyond the hard liners. As such, we will examine in detail Kasrils' argument in *Sechaba*.

In an attempt to counter the growing influence of the so-called Mbeki moderates within the councils of the ANC leadership, Hani ally Ronnie Kasrils took their case for the armed struggle to the ANC cadres. By using the pages of *Sechaba*, the ANC's official journal, Kasrils was bypassing the leadership and pleading his case directly to the members of the ANC. He was very clever with his arguments.

His solution was to hide elements of the armed struggle behind the facade of forming mass movements and other underground revolutionary organizations inside South Africa, a long cherished ANC goal.

Kasrils tried to disarm the moderates by seemingly admitting that the ANC's policy of armed struggle had been a failure. In Kasril's words, "The fact that we proclaimed our armed struggle on December 16, 1961, and that it is still at an extremely low stage of development, must force us to examine the problem areas frankly and critically."[6]

The failure of the ANC to take advantage of the unrest in the townships during 1984-86 demonstrated the abject failure of the armed struggle path to power. If ever conditions were ripe for the advancement of the ANC's cause it was during that tumultuous period of unrest in the townships. Yet the tactics of terror and intimidation by means of necklacings, people's kangaroo courts and repression by the ANC's "comrades"—militant young thugs functioning as ANC enforcers—failed dismally to advance the revolutionary plans of the ANC.

Kasrils' analysis in *Sechaba* tried to soften and gloss over the stark reality of the ANC's failure as too little, too late. ". . . Yet, despite the tremendous upsurge of mass resistance over the past three years, we were not able to take full advantage of the favorable conditions that materialized. We were unable to deploy sufficient forces at home; our cadres still found big problems in basing themselves amongst our people; our underground failed to grow sufficiently, and our people were left to face the enemy and his vigilantes with sticks and stones. As a result, the incredible mass resistance and the strikes were not sufficiently reinforced by armed struggle."[7]

Kasrils then asked the question heretofore unmentionable within the ANC: ". . . is it possible that we are incorrect in believing that armed struggle

[6] Kasrils, R., "The Revolutionary Army", *Sechaba*, March 1988, p. 3.

[7] Kasrils, p. 4.

is the way forward?"[8] This question must have sent a warming shiver of hopeful anticipation up and down the spines of the moderates as they read those words. The feelings would soon depart.

Using standard Marxist analysis and rhetoric, Kasrils began his sermon of revolutionary redemption for the ANC cadres. He claimed that the unrest in the townships showed that revolutionary conditions existed inside South Africa but the ANC, through organizational weakness, had been unable to capitalize on them.

These revolutionary conditions still exist inside South Africa, Kasrils claimed, but success will depend on the subjective conditions within the country—"the mood of the masses, their confidence in the revolutionary movement, and its organizational ability to lead them out of the current impasse to the seizure of power."[9]

"When we speak of subjective conditions", Kasrils emphasized, "we are referring to the presence of revolutionary organizations and their ability to organize and lead the masses in all forms of struggle—armed struggle included. . . ."[10]

The ANC moderates could be pardoned if they were getting suspicious feelings that Kasrils was setting them up with his confessional tone to take a tumble.

Organization inside South Africa is the key to success was Kasrils' message, not striped-pants negotiators, his unsaid message. Still holding out the olive branch, he points out that organization will benefit both the political and military aspects of the ANC's revolutionary program.

The failure of the ANC to capitalize on the recent unrest showed the almost total lack of ANC organization inside the country. This was the ANC's Achilles' heel and it was, in Kasrils' opinion, the prime job of the ANC to rectify the situation. There appeared to be general agreement within the ANC as to its task, yet nothing seemed to be getting done. An obviously frustrated Kasrils commented, ". . . We have had endless discussions and meetings about how it should be done. . . . We appear to agree in meetings but differ in practice. . . ."[11]

There shouldn't be such confusion, Kasrils maintained, because there aren't that many ways to seize power. What is needed is unity of purpose among the ANC, a clear jab at the Mbeki faction. "For, unless we have a clear

[8] Kasrils, p. 4.

[9] Kasrils, p. 4.

[10] Kasrils, p. 4.

[11] Kasrils, p. 4.

vision on how power is to be seized, we cannot effectively address the question of what type of organs are required for such a task. We cannot effectively address the subjective tasks."[12]

The ANC must decide how it is going to seize power and plan carefully on ways to implement its decisions. This plan, Kasrils stresses, must be clear to everyone in the ANC both as to its ultimate goal and what every individual's task will be to attain that goal. And who will play the key role in carrying out this new plan? It will not be the negotiators of the ANC, but Hani, Kasrils and company. "Central to the creation of the subjective factor is *Umkhonto we Sizwe*. For to achieve our goal—seizure of political power through our strategy of revolutionary armed struggle—it is necessary to create a revolutionary army."[13]

Such an organization is an obvious necessity, claims Kasrils, because it is the South African security forces—the South African Defense Force (SADF) and the South African Police (SAP)—that stand in the way. Obviously they can only be countered and overcome by force.

Therefore, the proposed counterforce—Kasrils' revolutionary army—has to be developed, organized, armed and trained inside South Africa. Logic dictates that *Umkhonto we Sizwe*, not talking politicians, will be the nucleus of Kasrils' future underground revolutionary army, a fact he is not shy in pointing out to his fellow cadres: ". . . It has to be extended and developed to embrace all potential revolutionary forces."[14]

The creation of such a force would enable the ANC to work inside the country and would eliminate a problem that has plagued the ANC for years: "A revolutionary army must be composed and structured in such a way that it can be situated among the masses. *The problem facing us is that the bulk of our army is recruited and trained outside the country, and remains there.*" [Emphasis added-ed.][15]

Such an admission by Kasrils, whether he likes it or not, casts doubt on the ANC's claim of massive support inside South Africa. If such massive support existed there would be little problem recruiting ANC terrorists inside South Africa instead of out of the country, as Kasrils' admission tellingly points out.

In spite of this fact, Kasrils claims his revolutionary army would get ANC military forces inside South Africa but by what means he is strangely

[12] Kasrils, p. 5.

[13] Kasrils, p. 5.

[14] Kasrils, p. 5.

[15] Kasrils, p. 5.

silent. Nevertheless, if his army got inside South Africa, by some as yet unmentioned means, it would be able to merge with the ANC's front groups and bring about the downfall of the South African government.

The revolutionary army would be composed of three elements, each reflecting different levels of political and military missions, requiring different organizational structures. Central to each element, however, are the trained cadres of *Umkhonto we Sizwe*. Thus, the military wing of the ANC would be the dominant factor as Hani and Kasrils lay out their scenario.

The three elements are: 1.) Guerrilla units which will operate in the rural areas of South Africa; 2.) Underground urban fighting groups whose function is to carry out acts of sabotage, terrorism and assassinations in urban areas of South Africa; and, 3.) Self-defense units which would develop as security elements for ANC front organizations, or to police and control, with acts of terror and intimidation, the black townships in South Africa. It is essential that these so-called self-defense units be firmly controlled by the ANC so that they don't become a potential opposing force. In order to insure this, "trained cadres of *Umkhonto we Sizwe* must merge into these people's self-defense units and lead them."[16]

By organizing his revolutionary army, with its three elements, inside South Africa, Kasrils was blending classic guerrilla war theory of Mao Tse-tung, Lenin and others, with the urban guerrilla war theory of Carlos Marighela. Such a move, if successful, would have the crucial effect of establishing ANC bases inside South Africa. This would enable the ANC to recruit and train cadres from the local population. This situation, Kasrils prophesied, ". . . will enable us to root the armed struggle amongst our people within our country. This will enable us to arm our people and realistically prepare and plan for the armed seizure of power."[17]

In addition, Kasrils envisioned the creation of this revolutionary army as having a snowballing effect towards achieving the ANC's ultimate goal. As the struggle develops inside South Africa, more and more activists will be reached and drawn into the fight until, finally, they are numerous enough, and armed well enough, to neutralize and eventually overcome the South African security forces.

The ANC, at one time, had a small underground inside South Africa. But the arrests and Rivonia trial had rolled it up. This left the ANC without an effective underground organization inside the country.

This was a serious setback because *Umkhonto we Sizwe* cadres receiving

[16] Kasrils, p. 5.

[17] Kasrils, p. 6.

guerrilla training abroad could not be received back in South Africa by the underground which would hide them, feed them and provide a network within which they could operate. "The underground would have carried out the all-essential political tasks of organizing the masses, developing illegal means of propaganda, engaging in all-round vanguard activity. The underground would have been the backbone of our revolutionary forces and army, would have recruited for it and given it leadership. . . ."[18]

Bemoaning the lack of an underground and, at the same time taking a slap at past and current ANC policy, Kasrils urged the ANC to rectify the situation: ". . . The lack of such an underground at home, and the presence of a large guerrilla force outside the country, waiting to come to the defense of the people and punish the enemy, has, I feel, clouded our vision. In the most pragmatic sense, the need to deploy cadres of *Umkhonto* at home for combat work could not wait on the reconstruction of our internal underground. In the process, this has helped to create a serious imbalance between our political and military structures."[19]

More effort, Kasrils believed, should have been devoted to building an underground inside South Africa. In fact, it is this lack of effort that has cast the ANC seemingly adrift in its attempt to seize power in South Africa.

"How will power be seized?", Kasrils asks his cadres. He provides the answer while taking a well-calculated swipe at the Mbeki faction within the ANC: "We cannot say exactly, but we must have a developed strategy. Yet in our policy documents and official statements, surprisingly little guidance is given. One is left with the impression that a combination of mass struggle, strikes and armed blows will somehow create so much pressure on the regime that it will collapse, and our movement will seize power."[20]

Twisting the knife which he has driven into his opponents' backs, Kasrils snidely suggests that some of his colleagues think that such a scenario might come about through some forum of negotiations. Nonsense, claims Kasrils, it will be his revolutionary army that will guarantee the success of the ANC's program. ". . . The revolutionary army is not only the organ for building up the revolutionary forces and for seizing power; it also becomes the organ for defending and guaranteeing the revolution. *If power came prematurely, through some negotiated formula imposed by circumstances beyond our control, and we had no revolutionary army at our disposal, we would find our people cheated of real power.*[Emphasis added-ed.] So

[18] Kasrils, p. 7.

[19] Kasrils, p. 7.

[20] Kasrils, p. 8.

whatever way we look at it, the creation of a revolutionary army is our most crucial task."[21]

The revolutionary army would thus become the ANC's vehicle for more than the seizure of power. It would be the instrument for controlling the population. It would do this by the usual Marxist-Leninist method of eliminating opponents and, eventually, the moderates within the SACP/ ANC alliance. The army would also solidify control inside South Africa by means of militarizing the society—a process that has taken place in all successful Marxist revolutions in the world. Kasrils' warning that an internal negotiated settlement, without the presence of his revolutionary army, may be fatal to the ANC drives that point home. Without that force the ANC would lack the necessary instrument for controlling the people. Or, in the alternative, it would have no vehicle to rectify what Kasrils blithely terms "our people cheated of real power." In short, the ANC would have no way of seizing power in an armed coup without the presence of its revolutionary army in South Africa.

His warning to the ANC is clear: you cannot abandon the formation of the ANC's revolutionary army unless you are abandoning the ANC's goal of seizing power in South Africa. The two are linked inseparably together. Kasrils' article in *Sechaba* not only makes that clear, but lays out the theoretical guidelines for the militant Hani faction within the ANC. That his scheme clearly follows a Marxist-Leninist plan for a revolutionary seizure of power shouldn't surprise anyone.

Kasrils and Hani also tossed out a scrap or two to woo the doubting in the Mbeki faction. If the ANC devoted its attention to Kasrils' proposal a purposeful underground revolutionary organization could be set up in a relatively short period of time. (Kasrils estimated in as little as five years.) Might not this give the negotiators some breathing space to either try to achieve their goals or to buy the time necessary for Kasrils' scheme to be developed?

One should never forget that Marxists have time and again used the negotiation process to buy time for them to either regroup, sort out differences within their movement, dupe their adversaries or use it as a cover for implementing new tactical maneuvers.

To paraphrase the old saying about the Trojan War (Beware of Greeks bearing gifts): beware of Marxist-Leninists coming to the negotiation table.

The SACP's program reinforces the validity of this paraphrase. "Whatever prospects may arise in the future for a negotiated transition, they must not be

[21] Kasrils, p. 9.

allowed to infect the purpose and content of our present strategic approaches. *We are not engaged in a struggle whose objective is merely to generate pressure to bring the other side to the negotiating table. . . .*"[Emphasis added—ed.][22]

What is the ultimate object of the SACP's struggle? Quite simply a reiteration of Kasrils' theme: ". . . its sights must be clearly set on the perspectives of a seizure of power."[23]

How does the SACP plan on getting its stated goal? Again, it endorses the concept spelled out by Kasrils for the ANC. ". . . The seizure of power will only be assured if the revolutionary movement has already effectively prepared the necessary political and organizational forces with the capacity to launch an offensive for the seizure of power at the right moment."[24]

When will that moment occur? It will come when a combination of forces and crisis led by the revolutionary force creates the opportunity for, as the SACP aptly puts it, the insurrectionary breakthrough. This is all to be created by the work of the revolutionary movement which will cause ". . . all-round mass action, led by a well-organized underground, and international pressure are the keys to the build-up for the seizure of power. . . ."[25]

With at least the tacit approval of the ANC, Hani and the hard liners tried to escalate the armed struggle in 1988 as part of the SACP/ANC's campaign to disrupt the October municipal elections in South Africa. This was done by removing the ANC's facade of observing so-called humanitarian considerations in its terrorist war by openly targeting civilians for attacks.

Official South African statistics showed an increase in violence: there were almost 300 terrorist attacks in 1988, compared with 230 in 1986, and 50 in 1984. The attacks in 1988, however, peaked prior to the October 26th elections.

The escalation hurt the ANC. Over 200 *Umkhonto* cadres were arrested and many ANC networks, especially in the Western Cape, were destroyed by diligent police work.

As with most terrorist acts, the targets were not the military or police but "soft" targets such as restaurants and shops. The lack of an effective internal network in South Africa reduced the effectiveness of the ANC's terrorist activities, as *Africa Confidential* shows: ". . . Many attacks were carried out by *Umkhonto* cadres hurriedly trained in South Africa itself, reflecting the difficulty the ANC was having . . . in maintaining a conveyor-belt for the transmission of trained fighters from Angolan bases to the forward operational areas.

[22] "On Prospects of a Negotiated Transfer of Power", *Umsebenzi*, March 1989, p. 12.

[23] *Ibid.*

[24] *Umsebenzi, op. cit.* p. 11.

[25] *Ibid.*

"Even before the departure from Angola, the ANC had the capacity only for relatively small-scale sabotage but not for mass guerrilla warfare. Individual attacks on soft targets, as advocated by Hani, have symbolic value but are politically damaging. . . ."[26]

It is interesting to note that Oliver Tambo, considered by many observers to be among the so-called moderate faction of the ANC,[27] hasn't renounced violence. This is evidenced by his message of support to the 7th Congress of the South African Communist Party. In his message, Tambo spoke warmly of the SACP/ANC alliance. "As never before we need to move arm-in-arm, shoulder-to-shoulder, with all our allies, friends and supporters. Within our own movement we need to close ranks now as never before and wage intensive struggle with reinforced vigour, including the intensification of our armed struggle. . . ."[28]

"Our message to the 7th Congress, therefore, is: let us consolidate and strengthen the alliance and advance in concert. Let us remain vigilant and watch out for those forces who never leave the boardrooms where they studiously plot our own undoing. Our victories are many and significant. But now more than ever we need to defend them in order to secure our offensive and ensure our advance to the victory of our revolution. We wish your 7th Congress every success."[29]

Since then, Tambo has suffered a series of strokes so we may never know which is the real Tambo—the so-called moderate or the hard-line advocate of violence.

Even in today's new open climate in South Africa, old ANC habits are not fading away. Nelson Mandela has been released from jail and has resumed his political activity. He has, however, refused to renounce the ANC's armed struggle, thus tacitly endorsing violence. The grisly torture-murders of ANC political rivals and "class enemies" have resumed.

This process of eliminating "stooges and puppets" was described by the leader of the negotiating faction, Thabo Mbeki, as "cleansing the waters in which the fish (guerrillas) must swim."[30] Such words lay to rest his carefully cultivated posture as a moderate and demonstrate how deeply the ANC is committed to violence in their revolutionary assault in South Africa.

[26] *Africa Confidential*, Vol. 30., No. 2, January 20, 1989, p. 6.

[27] See: *Africa Confidential*, August 25, 1989, pp. 1-2.

[28] *Umsebenzi*, March 1989, p. 13.

[29] *Ibid.*

[30] Clifford-Vaughan, F.M., "Terrorist Activities of the African National Congress", *Conservative Review*, Vol. 1, No. 1, February 1990, p. 17.

Kasrils' *Sechaba* article has obviously had its effect in furthering the cause of violence within the ANC.

18

The FOURTH PILLAR —INTERNATIONAL ISOLATION

Any rational analysis of revolutionary wars shows, that from the revolutionaries' point of view, securing outside support for their cause is a vital and fundamental principle of their strategy.[1] The SACP/ANC alliance was no different as their fourth pillar of their revolutionary strategy, international isolation of South Africa, depended upon outside support.

The SACP/ANC alliance has received outside support in spades. As mentioned earlier, it has gotten massive amounts of Soviet bloc aid. It is also the beneficiary of vast amounts of financial, political, and propaganda support from the socialist international community, the Organization of African Unity (OAU) and the anti-Western Third World in general.

The United Nations has taken the ANC under its wing, given it money, facilities and a world platform for its propaganda efforts. The ANC even gets money from the free world in the form of direct subsidies from countries such as Sweden, its largest financier outside the Soviet bloc, and other Scandinavian countries. Religious organizations such as the National Council of Churches and the World Council of Churches give it direct cash donations. To give the Devil his due, one must point out that there is no way these donating organizations can control how the ANC uses the money. It could have been granted for humanitarian purposes, but used for terror. The ANC uses these

[1] Tse-tung, M., "On the Tactics of Fighting Japanese Imperialism", *Selected Works*, Vol. I, International Publishers, New York, 1954, p. 173; see also; McCuen, J., *The Art of Counter-Revolutionary War*, p. 65.

donations to help fund its war of terror on innocents inside South Africa.

Angolan assistance has included material, training and base facilities as well as actual physical protection of ANC camps and bases by soldiers of the People's Republic of Angola. This is no longer being rendered to the ANC as it has been forced out of Angola as part of the Tripartite Agreement of 1988 between Angola, Cuba and South Africa.

Without outside help, the ANC would have been long ago consigned to the dustbin of history. Instead, it stands the possibility to gain solely through the efforts of its international friends that which it has utterly failed to attain with its armed struggle—political power in South Africa.

The Soviet bloc and the international terrorist network have provided the instructors and training facilities to the ANC cadres in order for them to become proficient in the use of their Soviet-supplied weapons. As we have seen, the SACP/ANC's attempt to incorporate their terrorist training into successful action designed to overthrow the South African government has been a dismal failure.

The outside support given to the SACP/ANC alliance was not limited to doling out money, military hardware and instruction on the baser arts of terrorism. By far the most valuable help rendered to the alliance lay in other areas. It was a well-coordinated drive to isolate South Africa from the rest of the world.

South Africa's isolation covers four general areas: diplomatic, economic, military and socio-cultural.

South Africa officially maintains diplomatic mission with only twenty-three other states. This means that only about thirteen percent of all nations have diplomatic representation in South Africa. Malawi is the only internationally recognized Black African state to recognize it and no country from the communist bloc has formal diplomatic ties with the government.

South Africa is not a member of any of the major sub-global political organizations such as the British Commonwealth, the Organization of African Unity (OAU) or the Non-Aligned Movement.

In contrast, the ANC maintains an unofficial diplomatic mission in thirty-three countries throughout the world. Only four countries, however, have granted it diplomatic status—East Germany, India, Kenya and the Soviet Union.

Nevertheless, the ANC has a visible presence throughout the world. The key centers for ANC diplomatic activity are: 1.) London—the ANC's most important diplomatic center, with its links to the British Anti-Apartheid Movement, the British Communist Party and the Commonwealth Office; 2.) Scandinavia, especially Sweden, is most congenial to the ANC,

ANC International Offices & Chief Representatives

(as of June 30, 1988)

Country	City	Chief Representative
1. Algeria	Algiers	Godfrey Motsepe
2. Angola	Luanda	Uriah Mokeba
3. Australia	Sydney	Dan Cindi
4. Benelux Countries	Brussels	Ted Pekane
5. Cuba	Havana	Stanley Manana
6. Denmark	Copenhagen	Aaron Mnisi
7. Egypt	Cairo	Nyako Mahlatsi (aka Capt Lerole)
8. Ethiopia	Addis Ababa	Godfrey Motsepe
9. West Germany	Bonn	Tony Seedat
10. Finland	Helsinki	Max Moabi
11. France	Paris	Solly Smith (acting)
12. Great Britain/Ireland	London	Mendi Msimang
13. East Germany *	Berlin	Bernard Molewa
14. Ghana	Accra	Simon Mhlauze
15. Hungary	Budapest	Gideon Vakala (aka Dhingala)
16. India *	New Delhi	Moosa Moolla (aka Mosie)
17. Italy/Greece	Rome	Bennie Nato De Bryun
18. Japan	Tokyo	Joe Matsila (aka Jerry)
19. Canada	Toronto	Yussuf Saloojee
20. Kenya *	Nairobi	Thami Sindelo
21. Madagascar	Tananarive	Teddy Life Montsoe
22. Mozambique	Maputo	Kingsley Xuma
23. Netherlands	Amsterdam	Mbonga Masepule
24. Nigeria	Lagos	ZW Nkondo (aka Victor Matlou)
25. Norway	Oslo	Raymond Mokoena
26. Senegal	Dakar	Ahmed Qono
27. Sweden	Stockholm	Billy Modise
28. Tanzania	Dar es Salaam	Graham Morodi
29. United Nations	New York	Lindowe Mabuza (aka Eddy Funde)
30. USSR *	Moscow	Simon Makana
31. Venezuela	Caracas	Unknown
32. Zambia	Lusaka	Maxwell Mlangeni
33. Zimbabwe	Harare	Stanley Mabizela

*** Full Diplomatic Recognition**

although somewhat unhappy with the ANC's proclivity for terrorist bombings; 3.) Washington is becoming more important in the eyes of the ANC due to its activity in the sanctions campaign against South Africa and to its position as the West's premier superpower. The ANC is greatly assisted in Washington by the ultra-leftist TransAfrica movement; 4.) Moscow has long been, and still continues to be, the ANC's Mecca. Relations with the Kremlin are still solid and will continue well into the future[2]; 5.) Harare is important to the ANC because of its proximity to South Africa and the unflinching support from Zimbabwe's Marxist leader, Robert Mugabe; and, 6.) Tanzania, which has long been a home to ANC cadres from the late 1950s. It has trained and assisted the terrorist group for years and still houses ANC camps on its territory. Tanzania is also important to the ANC because of its great influence in the OAU's liberation committee. This committee orchestrates the campaigns of public support for the ANC throughout Black Africa.

If the South African government's diplomatic endeavors were able to match the scope and effectiveness of the ANC's and its supporters, they would get a far better hearing within the world community.

A good indication of South Africa's isolation from the world community is the number of agreements signed between it and other countries. These agreements between states cover a multitude of areas: trade, boundaries, monetary affairs, fishing rights, overflight rights, postal and communication matters, military assistance and so forth. In South Africa's case the picture is very gloomy.[3] South Africa has long been the target of economic trade sanctions and boycotts. "Already in the early 1960's, the UN General Assembly began passing resolutions calling for trade sanctions against the Republic. Several other inter-governmental organizations (IGO), including the Commonwealth, OAU, Non-aligned Movement and the European Community, have since joined the sanctions offensive. So too have independent states, notably the United States. Today, at least 100 countries officially restrict trade with South Africa and up to 90 percent of the Republic's merchandise exports is affected by politically motivated restrictions abroad."[4]

In 1985, in the wake of growing Congressional pressure for more severe

[2] See: "Radio Moscow", April 10, 1990.

[3] Geldenhuys, D.J., "The International Isolation of South Africa", *Strategic Review For Southern Africa*, Vol. XI, No. 2, Institute for Strategic Studies, University of Pretoria, Pretoria, November 1989, p. 45.

[4] Geldenhuys, *op. cit.*, p. 49.

restrictions, President Ronald Reagan imposed limited punitive sanctions on the South African government by Executive Order. Reagan's action didn't last long. In 1986, the Congress, looking ahead to the up-coming mid-term Congressional elections, voted a harsh sanctions measure, cryptically titled for the voters no doubt, the Comprehensive Anti-Apartheid Act of 1986 (CAAA). It was enacted into law over the veto of President Reagan. ". . . Under the CAAA, the importation into the United States of textiles, agricultural products, iron and steel, coal and uranium from South Africa was banned. Additionally, any article that is grown, produced, manufactured, marketed or otherwise exported by a parastatal organization of South Africa or Namibia was also banned. The CAAA prohibited new investment in South Africa or to organizations controlled by the South African government. It also revoked landing rights for South African Airways and the rights of U.S. owned commercial aircraft to provide service between the U.S. and South Africa. . . ."[5]

In South Africa, the effect of sanctions has been destructive to the South African economy. At present, the South African Reserve Bank estimates that more than $2 billion a year is leaving South Africa to repay foreign banks for short-term loans. It has been estimated that between two to three percent of the nation's Gross National Product (GNP) goes towards repaying outstanding loans. This is money that can't be used to expand the economy for the benefit of South Africans of all races.

The South Africans got into this trouble by the usual form of governmental mismanagement of the economy. Ever since the late 1960s South Africa has experienced rising inflation. Such a long history of inflation does not instill the confidence necessary for attracting potential long-term capital investments, as these investments would quickly be eaten up by the ravages of inflation, even without considering the question of possible political instability caused by apartheid. This rising inflation led to what Professor G.L. de Wet of the University of Pretoria termed, "the greatest fiasco in South Africa's economic history, namely the debt standstill of 1985."[6]

When the economy showed signs of recovery in mid-1983, the high level of domestic inflation tended to boost the cost of imports into South Africa.

[5] "The Release of Nelson Mandela: What Next for US/South African Relations?", House Republican Study Committee, February 20, 1990, p. 5.

[6] de Wet, G.L., "Strategic Planning and The South African Economic Situation", *Strategic Review for Southern Africa*, Vol. X, No. 2, Institute for Strategic Studies, University of Pretoria, Pretoria, November 1989, p. 24.

This caused an early fourth quarter deficit in the South African balance of payments.

The government, in the fashion typical of governments throughout the world, stuck its nose in the situation and attempted to "fine-tune" the problem away. As usual, governmental action compounded the problem as de Wet points out: "Had inflation been under control at that stage, imports would have been much lower and exports much higher. . . . In the event, the economy was in grave trouble towards the middle of 1984 and the monetary authorities deemed it necessary to raise interest rates sharply. This action succeeded in cooling down the economy and restoring a surplus on the current account, but it caused havoc amongst local investors and consumers. . . . At the same time, foreign interest rates were declining. Those faced with large debts after the sudden increase in domestic interest rates, turned abroad and in a last feverish effort to find the means to pay their debt, mainly through their banks, borrowed heavily on short term in foreign markets. This mode of borrowing increased South Africa's external debt, especially short term debt, to such proportions that when foreign banks assessed the situation at the middle of 1985, they decided that the political as well as the economic risk of lending had become too high and thus refused any further credit, including rolling over existing South African loans. The Rand consequently crashed on the foreign exchange market, aggravating the situation even further. Faced with an enormous foreign debt and possible bankruptcy of some big and important domestic institutions, the monetary authorities clamped down on the exchange rate and declared a debt standstill. Although all interest has since been paid and agreement on a rescheduling the debt repayment itself was reached, the moratorium was the last nail in the coffin and since then South Africa has found it virtually impossible to obtain significant amounts of new foreign capital."[7]

In addition South Africa has lost approximately $6 billion due to U.S. companies pulling out of the country. In 1984, seven U.S. corporations pulled out of South Africa, thirty-eight left in 1985 and forty-eight in 1986. By mid-1988, two years after CAAA was enacted, over 160 U.S. firms had left, more than one-third of the total number operating in South Africa in 1984.[8]

The stated purpose of the sanctions campaign and its twin ogre, the disinvestment campaign, was to put economic pressure on South Africa to

[7] de Wet, *op. cit.*, pp. 24-25; see also: Munro, K., "Monetary Policy and Commercial Banking", *Banking and Business in South Africa*, ed. by Stuart Jones, MacMillan Press Ltd., London, 1988, pp. 128-130.

[8] Geldenhuys, *op. cit.*, p. 50.

eliminate racially discriminatory laws and give blacks the franchise.

For the black citizens of South Africa, the effects of sanctions have been devastating. Analysts estimate that 100,000 blacks have lost jobs due to the pull-out of U.S. companies and the lack of new capital investments. Sanctions have cost 800,000 jobs since their imposition became widespread in the late 1980s. Their disastrous effects are not limited to South Africa. In Southern Africa, the side effects of sanctions have meant the loss of 1.5 to 2 million jobs in countries such as Mozambique, Zimbabwe, Botswana and Zambia. In short, everyone has suffered due to sanctions, including the very people they were supposed to help.[9]

Disinvestment has also been a disappointing strategy. According to Walter Williams, "At the urging of anti-South African activists, U.S. companies like IBM, Coca-Cola, Proctor & Gamble, and Kodak have decided to pull up stakes and leave South Africa. U.S. corporations might leave South Africa, but they are not likely to dismantle their productive assets and bring them home, as well. That means that the production units wind up being sold to South Africans—mostly white South Africans. . . . A moral dilemma also confronts the proponents of disinvestment. Church and college officials disinvest when they sell their asset portfolio holdings of companies with subsidiaries in South Africa. After the transaction has been made, the stock certificate still exists; only its ownership has been changed. The church or college no longer owns it; somebody else does. Therein lies the moral dilemma: Is it moral to cleanse your soul when—of necessity—to do so requires that you get somebody else to dirty his soul? In other words, a minister can purge the church's holdings of 'evil' IBM stock *only* by selling to somebody else that 'evil' stock."[10]

It is not in the interests of the SACP/ANC alliance to see a prosperous economy in South Africa. Its message of greed and envy, which is the root of the so-called class struggle, falls on a more receptive audience in times of chaos or economic depression than it does during periods of stability and prosperity. The SACP/ANC will do all in its power to see that chaos is the order of the day so they can better spread their poisonous message of Marxism.

Oliver Tambo, in the convoluted logic of Marxist thinking that permeates the ANC, extolled sanctions at a press conference after the ANC's Kabwe Conference in 1985. In a rambling answer to the question: "In the

[9] House Republican Study Committee, *op. cit.*, p. 6.

[10] Williams, W., *South Africa's War Against Capitalism*, Praeger, A Cato Institute Book, New York, 1989, pp. 135-136.

escalating struggle how do you see the question of sanctions?",Tambo replied: "The South African regime is illegitimate in relation to the majority of the people in South Africa. . . . So it goes back to the question of the removal, the abolishing, the destruction of the apartheid regime and hence the isolation of that regime and all the measures that constitute pressures on the regime—sanctions, disinvestment, cultural, other economic pressures and other acts isolating the regime. . . ."[11]

As the ANC and Tambo have made quite plain destroying the regime requires destroying capitalism. Thus, while Tambo's Kabwe statement isn't as short and to the point as Marie Antoinette's "let them eat cake", the message is essentially the same: let the people suffer.

The total arms embargo against South Africa enacted by the UN in 1977 was designed to and has, in some areas, deprived South Africa of access to the ultra-sophisticated modern military technology of the West. One unintended result, from the UN's point of view, was the development of a sophisticated arms industry by the South Africans.

Willem Steenkamp, military correspondent for the *Cape Times,* pointed out the beneficial side of the arms embargo to South Africa. He said, "Thanks to its combination of imported technology, locally acquired experience, inspired corner-cutting and intensive research and development, the South African arms industry has taken less than forty years to develop to such an extent that the country is now an exporter of weapons and equipment . . . the tenth largest in the world supplying no fewer than 23 different countries, many of which would not be seen dead speaking to it in any public forum such as the United Nations. . . ."[12] So big were the arms industry's sales that in 1987 foreign earnings from the export of military arms and equipment ranked just behind gold and coal.[13]

In spite of this, South Africa is still the only country against which the UN Security Council today maintains a mandatory arms embargo. Yet, as indicated above, South Africa has largely defeated the UN's efforts to the point that in 1984 the UN Security Council found it necessary to request all states not to buy arms from South Africa.

In spite of the South African arms industry, the boycott has hindered South Africa from getting advanced naval and air electronic technology

[11] "Press Conference, Lusaka, June 25th, 1985", *Documents of the Second National Consultative Conference of the African National Congress*, pp. 43-44.

[12] Steenkamp, W., "Armscor Today—Selling Arms to the Enemy", *Challenge: Southern Africa within the African Revolutionary Context*, p. 470.

[13] *Ibid.*

essential for modern conventional warfare. This has hurt, especially in the area of aircraft and anti-air missile defense technology. The arms industry can only develop this capability at a great cost unless it can gain access to the technology from foreign sources. With these exceptions, however, the South Africans have been quite successful in overcoming the UN arms embargo.

Many countries throughout the world will not permit South Africans to enter their countries, or do so only in exceptional cases or under strict limitations. This limitation on travel by South African citizens is also evident in the world's attitude towards South Africa's transportation systems. Most African states and a large number elsewhere deny South African aircraft landing and overflight rights and close their harbors to South African ships. Other states prohibit their aircraft and ships from visiting South Africa.

ANC sympathizers, their front groups and private organizations have launched campaigns to discourage visits, concerts and exhibitions in the field of art and entertainment. One of the biggest participants in this campaign is the United Nations which compiles and maintains a blacklist of artists who have performed in South Africa.

Another painful area of isolation for South Africa is in the field of sports. This is particularly irksome because the South Africans, black as well as white, are sports fanatics. The UN is also the focal point of the long-standing campaign of isolating South Africa in the field of sports competition. The UN's Special Committee against Apartheid compiles, disseminates and updates a blacklist of people who have had the courage to compete in sports events in South Africa. The British Commonwealth also has an agreement among its members prohibiting sports competition with South Africa.

Sports isolation efforts are not confined to governments. Non-governmental international sports bodies, including the International Olympic Committee, also ban South African athletes from competing in their sponsored events.

All of this meets with the approval of not only the ANC, but one of its most visible cheerleaders—the UN. The UN has taken the ANC under its wing, given it money, gifts of food, housing, health services and a platform for its propaganda efforts on the world stage. The ANC, for example, makes wide use of UN-sponsored radio propaganda broadcasts.[14]

The ANC has prospered in the UN because over the years that world body has elevated so-called national liberation movements (NLMs) to the status of sainthood. The fact that most are not saints but are thugs was

[14] Gulick, T.G., "How the UN Aids Marxist Guerrilla Groups", *The Heritage Foundation Backgrounder*, Washington, D.C., April 8, 1982, p. 2.

pointed out in September 1980 by the presidential candidate Ronald Reagan: "We live in a world in which any band of thugs clever enough to get the word 'liberation' into its name can thereupon murder school children and have its deeds considered glamorous and glorious. Terrorists are not guerrillas, or commandos, or freedom fighters. . . . They are terrorists and should be identified as such."[15] Although Reagan was referring to the Palestine Liberation Organization (PLO) in his speech, his description also fits the ANC, which has regularly proclaimed its solidarity with the PLO.[16] It is also worth noting that the U.S. government has classified the ANC as a terrorist organization.[17]

The Third World and the Soviet bloc have seized control of the UN General Assembly and, as a result, the view emerged that what really counted in freeing countries from colonial rule was not the mere fact that they were free. The true test of liberation was that the former colonies must be totally free from the influence of their former western masters. Independence was thus demanded by the Soviet bloc and their Third World Allies "not just for non-self-governing territories, but also for non-independent territories that are fully self-governing and may not wish a different status."[18] Under this UN theory, the independence of Puerto Rico was demanded even though the vast majority of Puerto Ricans don't want independence from the United States.

H.O. Schoenberg points out that, "Identifying self-determination with independent statehood and treating the latter as an urgent necessity regardless of the wishes of the people concerned inevitably affected the methods used to bring it about. Under this revolutionary approach, which delegitimized alternatives such as autonomy or partition, the UN moved from rejection of colonialism to support of its overthrow by force. The democratic process was short-circuited and the self-appointed national liberation movement took its place. . . ."[19]

[15] Reagan Bush Committee, "Address by the Honorable Ronald Reagan," B'Nai B'rith Forum, Washington, D.C., September 3, 1980, p. 12.

[16] See, for example: "Statement of Oliver Tambo to UN General Assembly, November 9, 1982," in: *Sechaba*, December 1982, p. 6.

[17] See: *Terrorist Group Profiles*, U.S. Government Printing Office, 1988, pp. 129-130.

[18] "Statement by Carl Gershman, United States Representative to the Third Committee of the 37th General Assembly of the United Nations on Item 79, Self-Determination, October 15, 1982", Press Release, USUN 83-(82) of 15 October 1982, p. 4.

[19] Schoenberg, H.O., *A Mandate For Terror: The United Nations and the PLO*, Shapoesky Publishers, Inc., N.Y., 1989, pp. 208-209.

The United Nations Charter was stood on its head by this new rationale. "Peace and security were clearly inscribed as the principle objectives of the UN Charter. These objectives required the elimination of armed conflict and the peaceful settlement of disputes. But within five years of the adoption of Resolution 1514 *[Soviet-sponsored Declaration on the Granting of Independence to Colonial Countries and Peoples passed in 1960 that gave the underpinnings to the new path the UN was now treading—ed.],* the UN was licensing violence. On December 20, 1965 in Resolution 2105(XX) the General Assembly recognized the legitimacy of national liberation movements in colonial territories, and in Resolution 2708(XXV) of 15 December 1970 and repeatedly thereafter, it sanctioned their use of 'all necessary means at their disposal' to achieve their ends. Resolution 3103(XXVIII) of 13 December 1973 delegitimized resistance to UN-approved NLMs and endorsed assistance to them. Likewise, the Assembly definition of aggression, found in Resolution 3314(XXIX) of 14 December 1974 exculpates terrorism when its perpetrators claim to be struggling for self-determination . . . by endorsing the use of 'all means' these UN resolutions not only countermanded the Charter injunction against the use of force, but moved even beyond a call to arms . . . to the legitimization of terrorism. . . . Not only were NLMs accepted in place of democratic procedures and granted immunity from the Charter injunction against the threat or use of force, but every member-state was enjoined to assist them . . . not only did the NLM mystique encourage confusion between terrorists and liberators, it also had an important side effect: political power in the Third World was increasingly determined by bullets in place of ballots . . . the limitation of the decolonization process to portions of the Third World evoked strong criticism at the time. This limitation arose out of a General decision to accept recommendations of NLMs from only two regional organizations—the Arab League and the Organization of African Unity (OAU). Since only these two regional groupings could recommend UN legitimization of NLMs, the scope of the 'colonial and alien domination' which the General Assembly authorized NLMs to fight was artificially limited to the overseas empires of Western Europe. . . ."[20]

This hypocrisy is nothing more than a system that ignores the blatant violations of the UN Charter and concentrates with a bizarre morbid obsession on one small state whose values and human rights record is far superior to those of its accusers. As the UN's meddling in the internal affairs

[20] Schoenberg, *op. cit.,* pp. 209-212.

of South Africa grossly demonstrates, national liberation movements can seemingly do no wrong.

Hypocrisy notwithstanding, the UN has been one of the prime supporters of the ANC and has played a key role in the SACP/ANC's revolutionary war strategy against South Africa. Given this, it is naive to think any future stable regime can evolve and enjoy peace and prosperity in South Africa when its legitimacy must get the UN's nod. Given the corruption and degeneracy into which the world body has fallen, they are not likely to approve any new political arrangement in South Africa that doesn't conform with the Marxist-Leninist goals of the SACP/ANC alliance.

19

REVOLUTIONARY ACTIVITY IN THE BLACK TOWNSHIPS

A four-year recession and a dropping gold price that wiped out South Africa's foreign exchange reserves had a disastrous effect upon the economy. This caused a soaring black unemployment rate. The fragile economy was dealt another blow by the refusal of foreign banks to renew South African loans. This exacerbated the black unemployment situation and created conditions for social unrest that could be exploited by the SACP/ANC alliance.

The recession and the rise of black unemployment caused a current of fear and anxiety over the future well-being of the inhabitants of the black townships. The ANC used the climate to step up its revolutionary activities which are easier to conduct during periods of crisis. In 1981, it began to implement its M-Plan, drawn up by, and named after, Nelson Mandela over twenty years earlier. The plan called for organizing the black townships along classic Marxist revolutionary lines. This would require setting up an ANC revolutionary cell on every street or on every block in the targeted township. Each cell would be commanded by a reliable ANC cadre called a steward. Seven cells would constitute a zone, under the command of a chief steward and four zones would make up a ward.

In theory each ANC revolutionary structure from top to bottom—zone, ward, street, block and cell—was supposed to have a political member, a finance member, a propaganda member and a trained *Umkhonto we Sizwe* member. It seldom happened that way.

Once the revolutionary organization envisioned by the M-Plan was in place in the township, it was supposed to serve, when the proper revolutionary conditions were present, as the foundation for a SACP/ANC-directed alternative government.

A device used by the ANC to facilitate the implementation of the M-Plan was to infiltrate and take over existing organizations inside South Africa, a classic Marxist-Leninist tactic. One of the easiest ways to do that was to infiltrate their cadres into existing community organizations, take them over and then incorporate the targeted organizations into their newly created front—the United Democratic Front (UDF). This would ensure tighter ANC control and would hide their activity behind the UDF's skirts.

With this in mind the ANC began looking at the numerous civic organizations inside South Africa to select the ones to go after.

"Civic organizations," said the ANC at its Kabwe Conference in 1985, "are locally based and are aimed at mobilizing the people within a specific area around bread and butter issues . . . they operate at the primary grassroots levels. As such they are of strategic importance in reaching and mobilizing the masses . . . they have an immense potential for galvanizing a whole community . . . many of these civic bodies have a tendency towards confining their activity to the narrow limits of specific issues and their leaders tend to inhibit their members from participating within the context of the political struggle. Their mass base, however, offers a tremendous potential for converting them into militant organizations.

"The emergence of a broad structured front during the recent period has created conditions for such bodies to link their locally based bread and butter campaigns with national political issues."[1]

The big national issue as far as the ANC was concerned was to "lead the people in raising the level of struggle to that of a people's war for the seizure of power."[2]

The stage was being set for another cycle of violence inside South Africa.

Fourteen local black town councils on the Witswatersrand (Johannesburg area) raised rents and services charges to black residents in their townships between March and September 1984.[3] This action triggered demonstrations and protests against the increases.

[1] Kabwe Conference, *op. cit.,* p. 10.

[2] Kabwe Conference, *op. cit.,* p. 1.

[3] Hough, M., "Township Revolt", *Challenge, op. cit.,* p. 392.

The ANC, through its UDF front, moved quickly to take advantage of the situation. It ordered its terrorists to eliminate all blacks who helped administer the townships. They were to kill or terrorize black councilors, civil servants, policemen and other blacks whom the ANC saw fit to call collaborators with the South African government. In short, the SACP/ANC alliance was launching a campaign to make parts of South Africa ungovernable so they could step in via the M-Plan and set up an alternative revolutionary structure. This would serve two functions for the ANC: First of all, it would enable the SACP/ANC alliance to demonstrate its strength against what were essentially soft targets. This process yields great returns as the primary targets are often the traditional authority figures in South African black society and their murder would provide the people with a vivid demonstration of what the possible consequences of resistance would be. Second, the destruction of property and infrastructure would enable the SACP/ANC to lower the standard of living in the townships to the point where the residents would have no vested interest in maintaining the status quo, and then be open to recruitment attempts into the revolutionary cause.

The terrorists carried out their instructions with a savage ferocity by beating their victims to death with clubs, or hacking them to death with knives and *pangas*, the African version of the machete, or "necklacing" them to death with burning gasoline-filled tires around their necks. The results of this terror campaign were encouraging to the ANC as many blacks in government jobs resigned, fled or simply hid out and refused to go to work.

Attempts by some of the town councils during October 1984 (Soweto for example) to discuss and attempt to settle the situation were rejected out of hand by the UDF.

By early 1985 the unrest had spread to the Eastern Cape, with youth-led rioting in Grahamstown and Port Alfred. In February 1985, the rioting and unrest had spread to the Orange Free State and by June to the Western Cape and Natal. Common to all of the riots were looting, stone-throwing, Molotov cocktail attacks and fights with the police. The unrest was spreading in the form of school boycotts, consumer boycotts of white businesses and organized worker stay-aways from their jobs. Those found buying goods from white-owned shops were forced by the SACP/ANC-directed thugs (called "comrades") to eat their soap powders or drink their cooking oil.

The SACP/ANC terrorists and intimidators were doing their brutal jobs well. Their techniques should be familiar to veterans of the Vietnam War, where the systematic assassination of village leaders had been used by the Viet Cong to destroy the administration of the Saigon government. Terror succeeds where minor officials go unprotected as the ANC was well aware, having studied the Vietnam War and Viet Cong methods with great interest.[4]

One example of this strategy of terror which was one of the more successful efforts by the SACP/ANC occurred in the township of Inkwekezi at Port Alfred in the Eastern Cape. The elected black community council collapsed in May 1985 after a series of necklacings and acts of terror against the councilors. The area effectively became ungovernable and the ANC cadres were able to conduct their revolutionary activity openly. Into the vacuum created by the collapse of the town council stepped the Port Alfred Residents Civic Organization (PARCO), a UDF affiliate. With the help of another UDF affiliate, the Congress of South African Students (COSAS), PARCO mobilized the township. It was renamed after Nelson Mandela and became a model for the SACP/ANC's People's Government. It was hailed in the media as an example of "peaceful co-existence". *The Wall Street Journal* described it as follows: "One branch of the townships network of area and street committees calls itself a 'soviet'. The 'central committee' of Nelson Mandela Township, occupies a building that was formerly home of the white-run administrative board of the black township. Blacks run the township health care clinic and day care center, the primary school and the 'peoples courts'".[5]

Behind the adulation of the media lay a harsher reality. The "people's government" regulated every facet of the black citizens' existence imposing rigid moral codes to undermine the authority of the traditional community leaders. The central committee "nationalized" all private land and appointed workers to grow food on the land which was collectively produced and distributed. (Another form of control. If you didn't do what the "people's government" told you, you weren't given any food.) This, and other collectivist schemes, gave the SACP/ANC effective control over all aspects of community life in this small "New Jerusalem" in Port Alfred which failed to survive the counter efforts of the South African government following the imposition of the State of Emergency.

This experience in socialist people's power, though a short lived phenomenon for the ANC, was a graphic demonstration of what any future ANC-run state in South Africa would look like.

The American State Department even contributed to this folly by financing "people's power" projects in Port Alfred townships. The American Consul General John Burrows paid a visit to the PARCO headquarters and

[4] See: "Building People's Forces for Combat, War and Insurrection", *Sechaba*, January, 1987.

[5] "Blacks Share Power, South African Style", *The Wall Street Journal*, May 5, 1986.

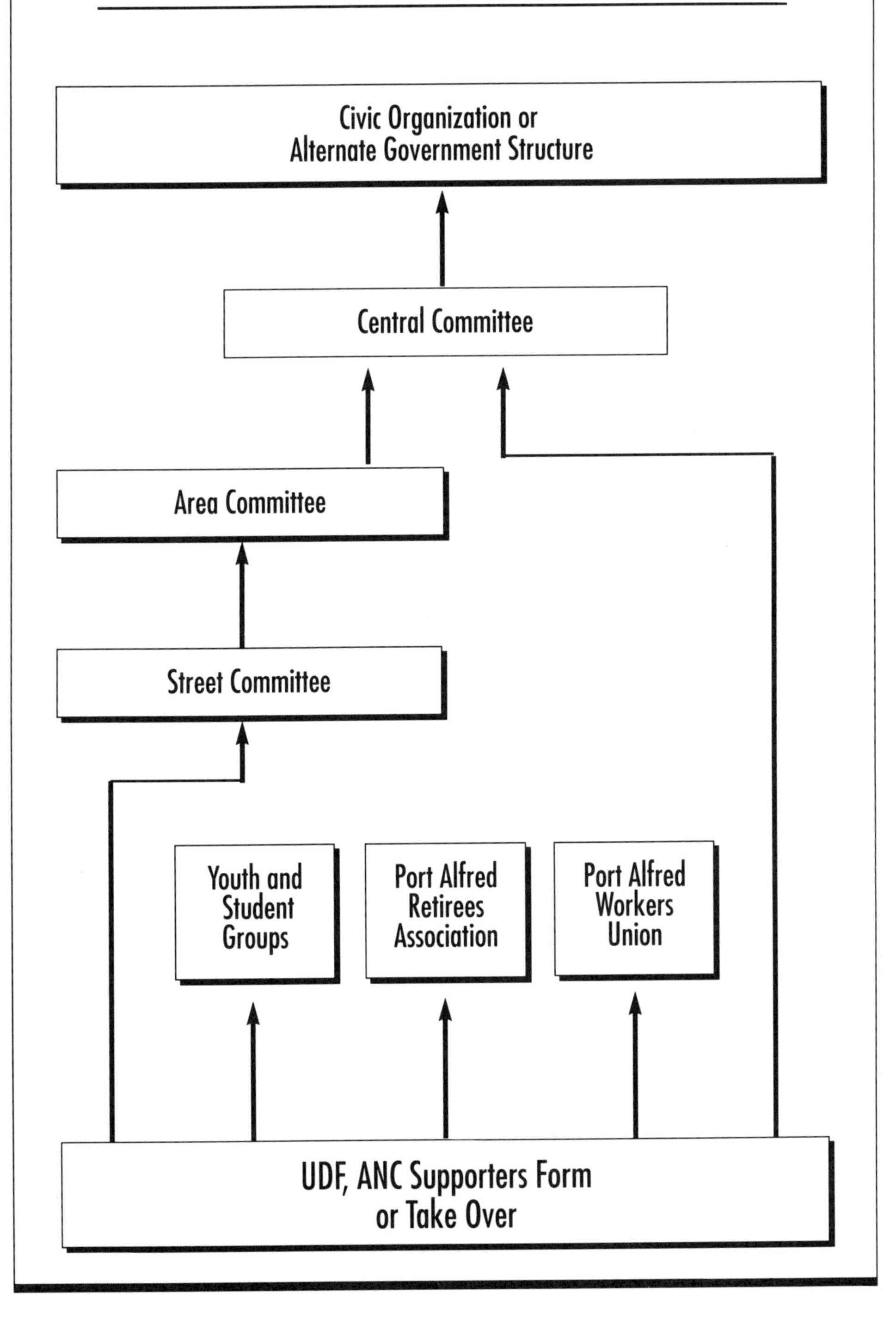
Alternate "PEOPLES GOVERNMENT"
Structures in Port Alfred
Civic Organization or
Alternate Government Structure
Central Committee
Area Committee
Street Committee
Youth and
Student
Groups
Port Alfred
Retirees
Association
Port Alfred
Workers
Union
UDF, ANC Supporters Form
or Take Over

handed over a check for a substantial, but undisclosed sum of money.[6]

A partial state of emergency was declared and police and army units began patrolling the black townships, picking up the gruesomely mutilated corpses of so-called "collaborators" condemned to death by kangaroo "People's Courts", often presided over by youths as young as twelve years old. The emergence of these so-called "courts" went hand in hand with the campaign of terror carried out by the "comrades". These "courts" were used to act against people who laid formal charges against the ANC with the South African Police and were also used to punish township residents who disregarded consumer and other boycotts called by the SACP/ANC, working through their front groups.

The SACP/ANC viewed the "people's courts" as a valuable vehicle of control and discipline in their efforts to take over the townships. Their propaganda organ *Sechaba* clearly endorsed the "courts' " barbarous acts: "Let the racist magistrates and lawyers shout their lungs out in scorn of the necklace method of punishing collaborators, let them call the people's courts kangaroo courts if they want to, but we will always reply to them by saying: when we say power to the people, we also mean the right to suppress the enemies of the people, we also mean the country's administration and control by the ordinary people. We shall not sudden be anarchists simply because we refuse to abide by the conventional legal norms generally associated with courts of law in South Africa."[7]

An incident during the unrest in 1985 in the Eastern Cape graphically illustrated many aspects of the SACP/ANC *modus operandi* in South Africa. It showed their use of terror, their use of youth as an instrument of revolution, the ethnic hostility that underlies black relationships and, not to belabor the point, what to expect in a ANC-ruled society as it refuses ". . . to abide by the conventional legal norms generally associated with courts of law in South Africa", as they put it.

The incident is taken from a murder trial involving a necklacing during the unrest. The case is: The STATE versus NDODANA MATSHOBA and fourteen others.[8]

The shocking incident begins: "One day, sometime in the third week of November 1985, an armored personnel carrier of the South African Police drew up before a house at B.A. 16 Mlungisi Township, near Queenstown in

[6] *Eastern Province Herald*, March 10, 1986.

[7] "Building People's Power" *Sechaba*, September 1986.

[8] Supreme Court of the Republic of South Africa, Queenstown Local Circuit division, Case number CC773/86, Vol. 37, pp. 3539-3542.

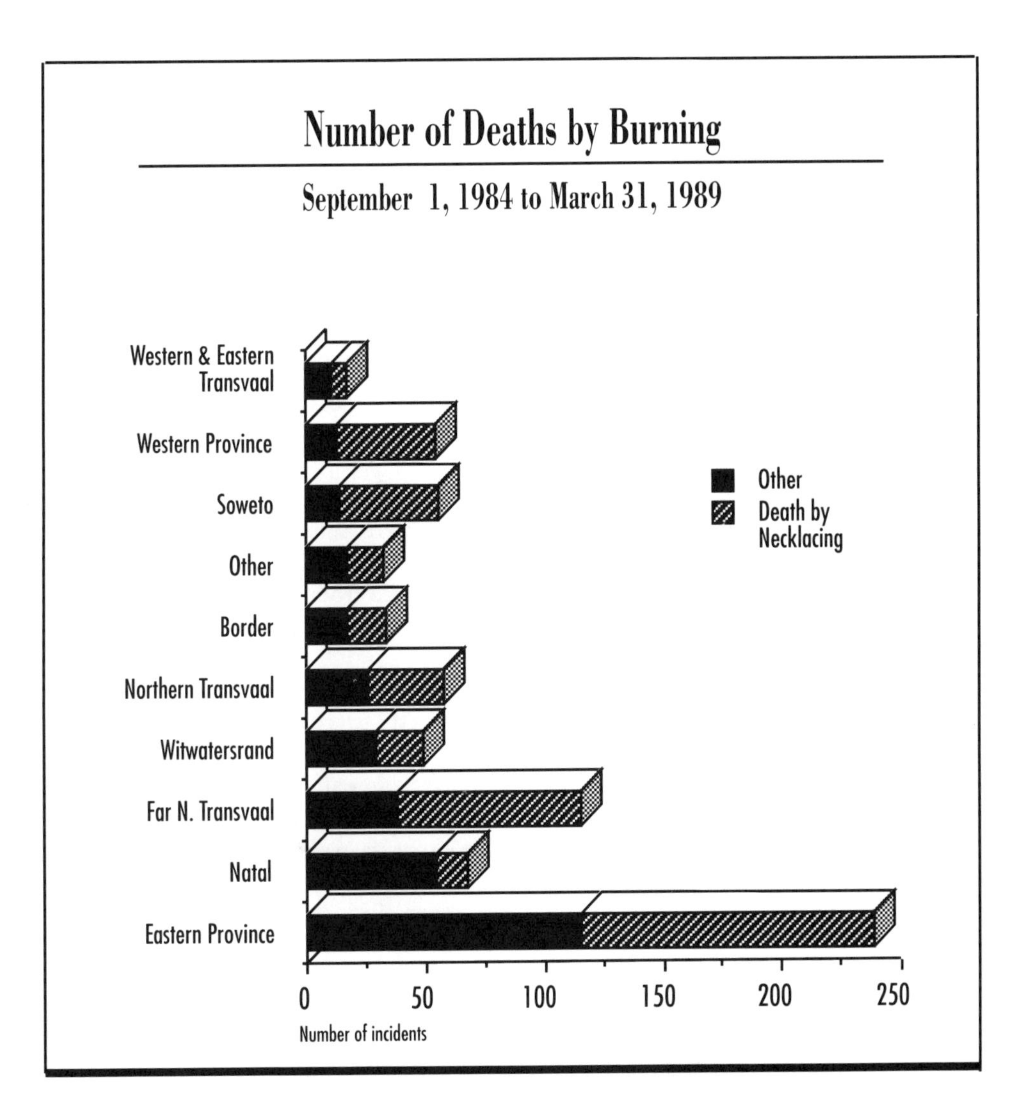
Number of Deaths by Burning
September 1, 1984 to March 31, 1989
Western & Eastern Transvaal
Western Province
Soweto
Other
Border
Northern Transvaal
Witwatersrand
Far N. Transvaal
Natal
Eastern Province
Other
Death by Necklacing
0
50
100
150
200
250
Number of incidents

the Eastern Cape. Two black policemen alighted, entered the house and asked the lady of the house, Mrs. Mercy Zamela, whether her 19-year-old daughter, Balise, was home.

"As they were speaking, Balise appeared. The policemen explained that they had been sent from the local police station to tell her to come to the station to claim her watch which had been left there some time before when Balise had been detained. They offered the girl a lift, but Balise turned it down saying that she would walk down to the station later.

"Mlungisi was, at this time, experiencing a period of unrest. The 'Comrades' were active, 'Street Committees' had been organized, and homes of policemen living in Mlungisi burnt down to force the policemen out. The local beer hall had also been burnt down. Boycott of all white-owned shops had been ordered by the 'Street Committees', as well as a crack-down on drinking and drunkenness. Enforcement of these 'Street Committee' decrees was the responsibility of 'Marshals' selected from amongst the ranks of the 'Comrades'. . . .

"To help cope with the situation, extra police had been drafted into the district. These police reinforcements, however, were Zulus, while the people of Mlungisi were Xhosas. The latter immediately dubbed the Zulu policemen 'Inkathas', a term of abuse to most Xhosas, derived from the name given to the ruling political/cultural movement of the self-governing Zulu state, KwaZulu.

"In a situation as tense as the one which prevailed in Mlungisi Township at that time, the simplest Acts might precipitate disaster; and so it turned out for the Zamela family. For this innocuous visit to the house at B.A. 16 was soon to have tragic consequences: a whispering campaign began, spreading the rumor that Balise Zamela, her younger sister Nosipho, and Balise's girlfriends, the two cousins Nana and Pixie Nojekwa, were sleeping with the 'Inkathas'.

"On the afternoon of Sunday 8 December 1985, the day after a large township funeral . . . Balise, Nana and Pixie were intercepted, as they left a friend's house, by three young men of the township. . . . They took the girls to house B.A. 21, Mlungisi, the residence of Ndodana Matshoba, who was awaiting them on their arrival.

"The three girls were interrogated about their rumored relationship with the Zulu policemen. They all denied any such involvement. . . . At this point the young men forming this 'People's Court' decided that they needed to broaden their 'enquiry' to include some of the girls' friends. Until these friends could be rounded up, the three girls were released.

"Later that afternoon, the three girls, together with Nosipho, Balise's sister—an unmarried mother with a 3-year-old daughter—and yet another couple of girls were summoned by the members of the 'People's Court', to attend a session. There were some thirteen young men present. The main focus of the enquiry soon centered on the youngest of the girls, Nosipho Zamela.

"One of the new 'witnesses', . . . , claimed that she had seen Nosipho being assisted into a police armored personnel carrier by an 'Inkatha'. Nosipho vehemently denied it; Balise supported her sister. Nevertheless, the 'People's Court' . . . decided to discipline the accused girls, Nosipho, Balise and Nana.

"Various suggestions were put forward: to whip them or burn their feet with plastic were popular options. In the end, they decided it would be best to make an example of one person only, in order to warn the rest never to have anything to do with the 'Inkathas' again. The chosen victim was Nosipho. She was taken from the 'People's Court' by a group which . . . included most of the 'Court'. One young man, Ndodana Matshoba, was left in charge of the remaining prisoners, Balise, Nana and Pixie.

"Nosipho was taken to some public toilets near her home, and outside these, she was whipped by members of the 'People's Court'. To escape further beating, she appears to have confessed to having entertained the 'Inkathas'. Nosipho was then frog-marched around the township to point out fellow 'offenders', sustaining further beatings on the way.

"At some time during the course of these proceedings, it was decided to 'necklace' her. Petrol and tires were obtained, Nosipho being made to roll a tire herself to her place of execution. . . . There the tire she had rolled to the spot was placed around her neck, doused in petrol, and set alight. Her killers danced around the stinking burning heap (it was dark by this time) singing. They scattered only when they heard the approach of a police vehicle. . . .

"A police patrol, investigating reports of a disturbance, discovered Nosipho's body shortly after 8:00 pm on Sunday evening. Her body lay in the street, her head resting on a 5-liter oil can. A smoldering tire lay on top of her hideously mutilated body which was charred beyond recognition. It took two fire extinguishers from the Casspir APC to douse the fire. The body was identified on the 11th of December.

"As a result of police investigations, Balise, Nana and Pixie were taken into protective custody. Their testimony and that of numerous other witnesses, led to the arrest of fifteen young men charged with crimes relating to the 'trial' of Nosipho Zamela. . . .

"Why, one is entitled to ask, was Nosipho given the necklace by the young judges who conducted the 'People's Court'? What purpose was served by her gruesome death, the agony of her friends, the misery and anxiety of her family and the ophaning of her baby daughter? Did she give her life in order to further some high-sounding political cause, for the freedom of her people, because she was betraying her people?

"Was Nosipho a police stooge?

"No, as it turns out she did not die for any of these reasons. She died because, as one of their tormentors, Soniwabe Kwaza, explained at his trial some months later: '. . . we grew up with the idea that it would not be in order for us to mix with the Zulus because our customs and traditions are not the same. . . . The fact that the policeman was a Zulu was important, because it would have transgressed the custom that we do not associate with Zulus. . . . When we (the 'People's Court') discussed this matter, *we approached it from the angle that she was having a love affair with a Zulu. We did not approach it from the angle that she was having a love affair with a policeman. . . . What was more serious was that she was having a love affair with a Zulu.*" [emphasis added—ed.][9]

The ANC was also ordering its cadres to use the revolutionary block committee to collect rents and fees normally collected by the government, to shanghai recruits for guerrilla training and to set up an alternative curriculum to replace that in the boycotted schools. Again, Vietnam veterans can be excused for having a feeling of *deja vu.*

Former *Newsweek* correspondent Holger Jenson described the chaos, "A small war was fought in Alexandra, outside Johannesburg, in which police were fired on with AK-47 rifles and had Russian hand-grenades thrown at them. More significantly, again like the Viet Cong, the ANC guerrillas forced black civilians to help them by digging trenches in the ground as 'tank traps' for troop carriers and armored cars used by the South African security forces. Similar battles were fought in other black townships elsewhere in Natal Province near Durban, in the Eastern Cape round Port Elizabeth and Cape Town, the seat of Parliament.

"By early 1986 more than 1,200 had been killed, most of them blacks, more than five hundred homes belonging to black policemen had been firebombed and the government had to move black members of the security forces and their families into fortified housing complexes to protect them. P.W. Botha, in fact, conceded in a rare interview with the editor of the *Washington Times* that 14 percent of the black townships were effectively beyond government control. . . ."[10]

[9] Roux, Helene, *How Revolutionaries Use Children*, pp. 2-5.

[10] Jenson, H., *Challenge, op. cit.*, p. 300.

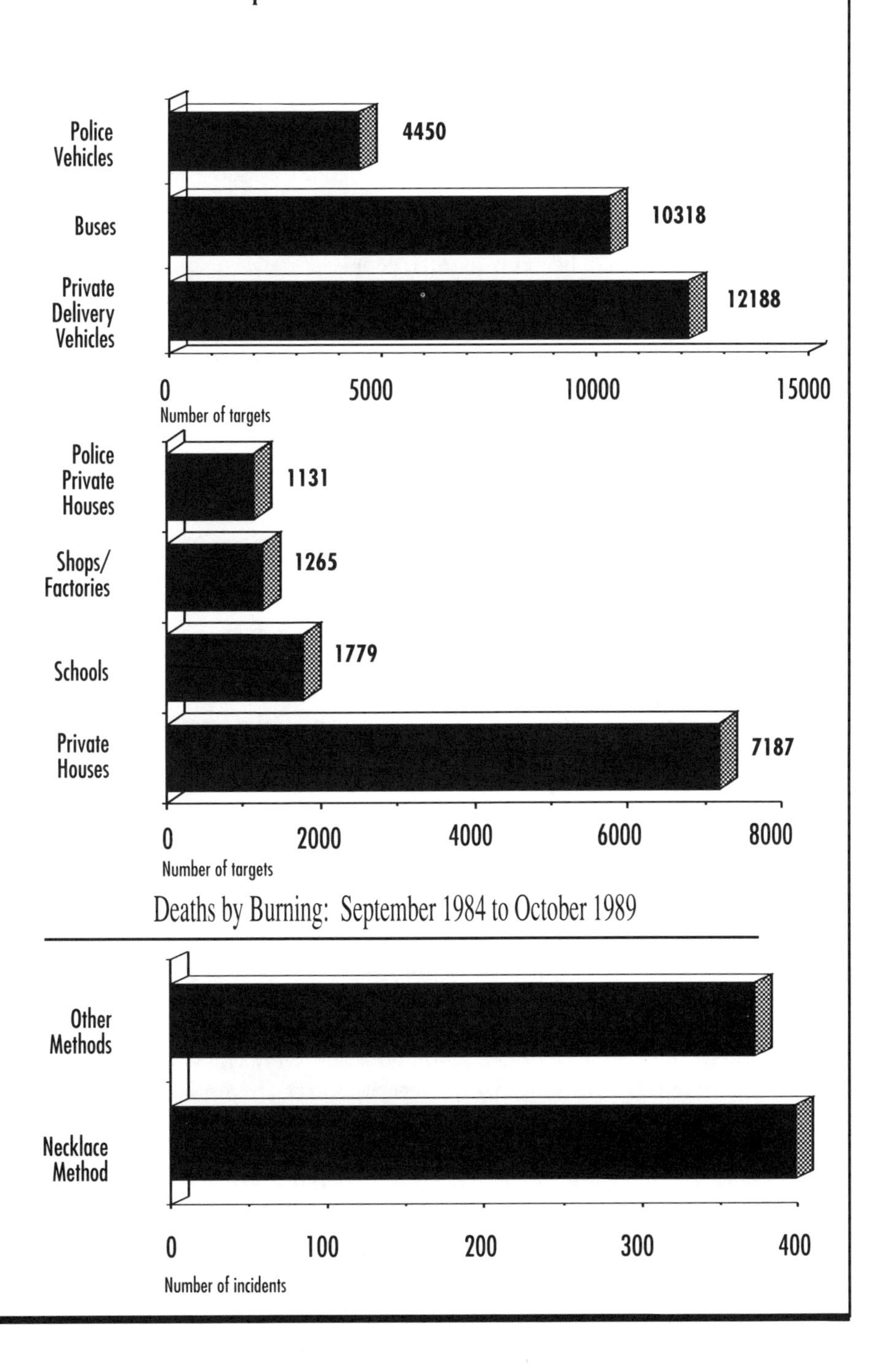

Destruction Caused by The ANC in South Africa
September 1984 to October 1989
Police
Vehicles
4450
Buses
10318
Private
Delivery
Vehicles
12188
0
5000
10000
15000
Number of targets
Police
Private
Houses
1131
Shops/
Factories
1265
Schools
1779
Private
Houses
7187
0
2000
4000
6000
8000
Number of targets
Deaths by Burning: September 1984 to October 1989
Other
Methods
Necklace
Method
0
100
200
300
400
Number of incidents

The ANC riot-leaders were well organized as the head of the South African riot police noted: "The type of riots perpetrated by the rioters in South Africa is unique in the sense that similar action is encountered nowhere else in the world. The riots are characterized by so-called hit and run techniques. Rioters and their leaders seldom act as one group. They would rather divide into twenty small groups to strike at targets, and instigate riots, by for instance setting fires to shops, beer halls and community halls at various locations. They also murder people and overturn and set vehicles alight. As soon as they have committed their acts, they withdraw, only to congregate again elsewhere, a considerable distance away, commit similar crimes. . . . Another problem faced by the SA Police is the composition of the crowds. Usually the agitators appear among or behind the crowd to incite the people. In the ensuing tumult innocent bystanders get involved, and should the police eventually act, these innocents are the first to be hit, while the culprits get away. . . . The effectiveness of the SA Police action forces the rioters to disperse quickly at the slightest possibility of a direct confrontation with the police. This of course seriously hampers arrest or linking arrested rioters to a particular riot situation. . . . It should be borne in mind that the young black adults of today were youths during the 1976 riots. They are therefore 'experienced' in organizing and executing riots. The older members of the black community are prepared to negotiate for peace, while the younger members form the militant wing of the rioters. They are not interested in negotiations, but only in instigating the so-called 'revolution'. . . . Riots are no longer spontaneous and unplanned actions by a mutinous mob, but are skillfully planned in advance to be executed in a well-organized manner."[11]

The circumstances involved in the vast majority of the unrest related deaths shows the mark of deliberate terror tactics by the murderers.

Between September 1984 and October 1989, 399 people died as a result of the gruesome "necklace" method of execution. An additional 372 were burnt to death in their homes or after gasoline had been poured over them and they were torched to death.

Ninety-two percent of the people who died during the unrest were murdered by the SACP/ANC revolutionaries. Only eight percent of those killed were terrorists killed by the security forces attempting to protect the lives and property of the innocents.[12]

[11] Wandrag, A. J., "Political Unrest—A Police View", *ISSUP Strategic Review*, Institute for Strategic Studies, University of Pretoria, Pretoria, October 1985, pp. 8-9.

[12] Groenewald, P.H., "Counter-Revolutionary Action in South Africa; 1984-1989", *American*

Killing people was not the only weapon in the ANC's bag of tricks during the unrest. Their revolutionary activities caused immense damage to property. To give an idea of the extent, between September 1984 and October 1989, 12,188 private delivery vehicles, 10, 318 buses and 4,450 police vehicles were extensively damaged or destroyed.[13]

During the same period 7,187 private homes—the vast majority belonging to blacks, 1,779 schools—overwhelmingly in black areas, 1,265 shops and factories, and 1,131 homes belonging to black policemen were damaged or destroyed.[14]

The SACP/ANC-directed violence during the unrest caused more damage in South Africa than any other event in the country's history, including the Boer War (1899-1902).[15]

These figures show the SACP/ANC's attitude is to destroy the country in order to save it. Only in the minds of demented nihilists does this make any sense.

All was not bleak, however, as a backlash against the SACP/ANC-directed violence was detected in the townships. A South African official pointed out that, "An encouraging backlash against the forces of anarchy and lawlessness can be detected in most areas where inhabitants have suffered because of unrest and lawlessness during recent times. Indeed, the combined military and police crime prevention exercise carried out at Sebokeng and elsewhere during 1984, while attracting the predictable international backlash at the United Nations and elsewhere, met with a different type of criticism by some of the residents who had suffered at the hands of criminal elements; they wanted to know why such an exercise had not been carried out sooner. It is a well-known fact that black members of the Force also play a vital role in quelling the political unrest."[16]

Others black residents began to fight back. During May 1986, vigilante groups were formed in the squatter community of Crossroads near the Cape Town international airport. These vigilantes began attacking the ANC "comrades". The vigilantes were quite successful at Crossroads and the activities of the "comrades" were severely curtailed. In personal visits to Crossroads in 1988 and 1989 there were visible signs that most of Crossroads

Review, Vol. 10, 2nd Quarter, 1990, Institute for American Studies, Rand Afrikaans University, Johannesburg, pp. 17-18.

[13] Groenewald, *op. cit.*, p. 18.

[14] *Ibid.*

[15] *Ibid.*

[16] *Ibid*, p. 15.

Destruction Caused by The ANC in South Africa

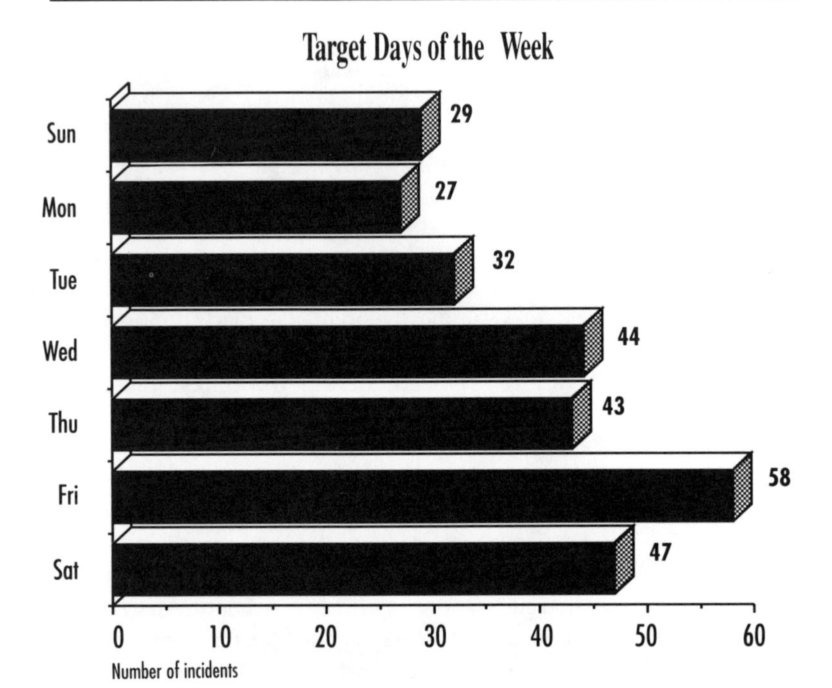

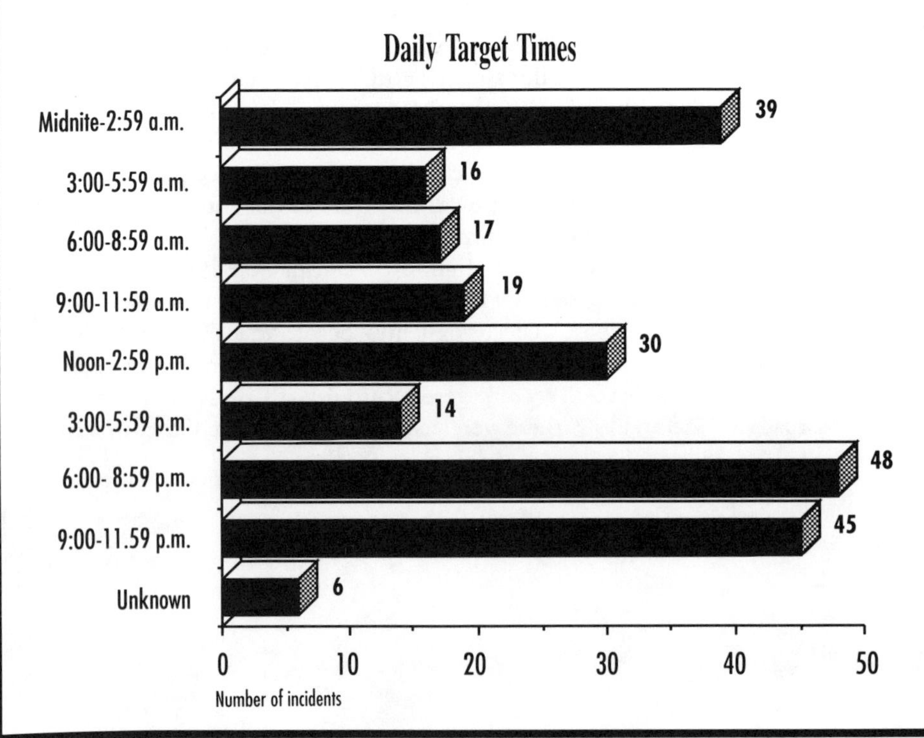

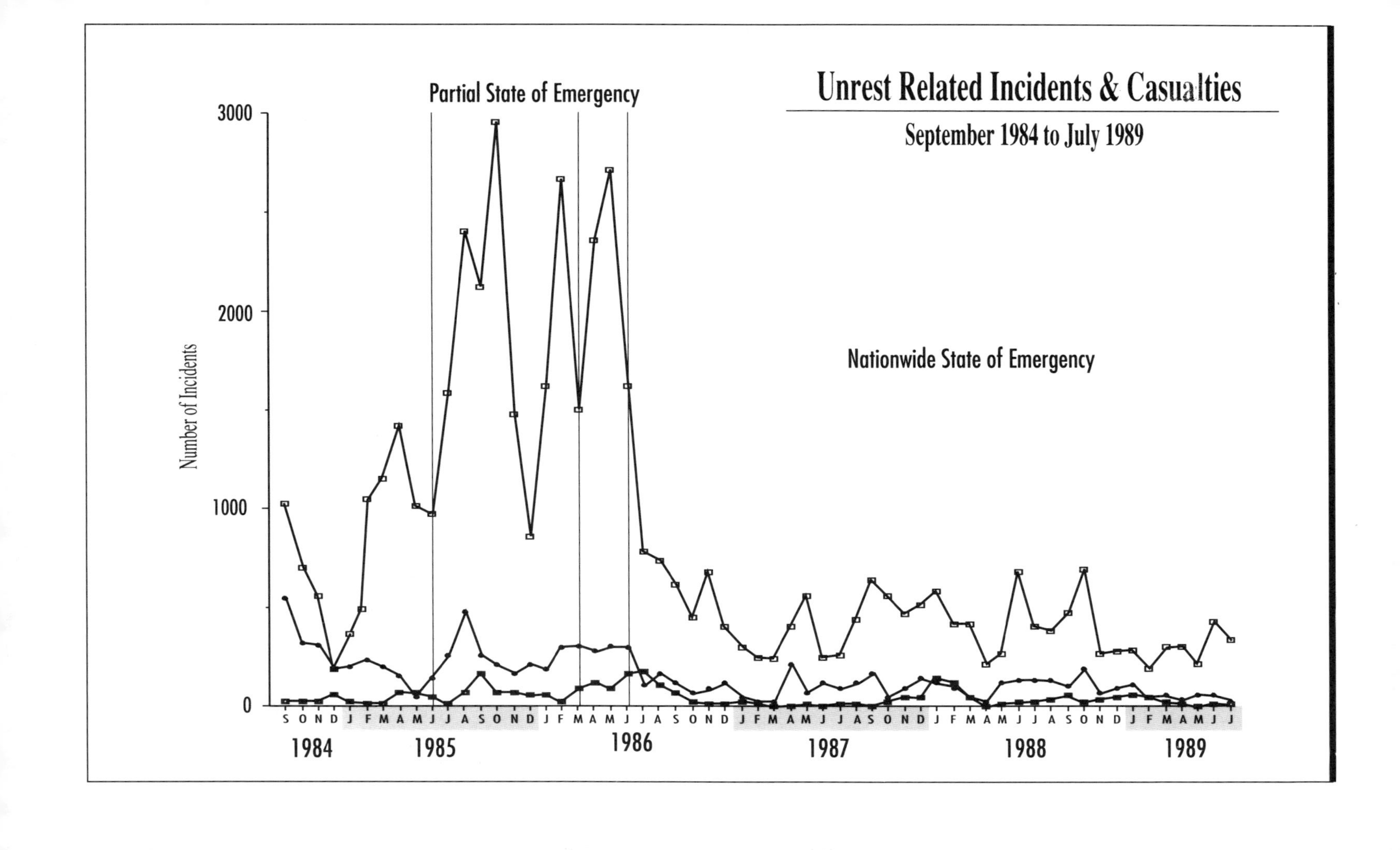
Unrest Related Incidents & Casualties
September 1984 to July 1989
Partial State of Emergency
Nationwide State of Emergency
Number of Incidents
3000
2000
1000
0
S O N D J F M A M J J A S O N D J F M A M J J A S O N D J F M A M J J A S O N D J F M A M J J A S O N D J F M A M J J
1984
1985
1986
1987
1988
1989

was sick and tired of the ANC and its allies. There were numerous anti-ANC and UDF graffiti and others telling Bishop Desmond Tutu to "go to hell". There were, however, still sections of Crossroads—mostly where the new arrivals would set up their shanties—that were under the influence of the "comrades" and the situation is extremely fluid and could deteriorate to the benefit of the SACP/ANC alliance.

Similar vigilante groups sprang up in other black townships in South Africa including Mamelodi, outside of Pretoria. This activity considered along with the effects of the State of Emergency regulations showed the ANC's efforts to take over the black townships was running into serious trouble.

Actually, the ANC realized that it lacked the resources at the time to seize power in the townships. The Kabwe Conference report on Cadre Policy makes that clear: "More particularly we directed our attention to the question whether the people's committees should attempt to assume the functions of an administrative organ which caters for the daily needs of the residents or whether they should concentrate on their political roles as representatives of the people.

"We concluded as follows:

"a. In the absence of an early seizure of power those committees would not be able to sustain or finance any of the basic requirements of municipal government for any length of time.

"b. In these circumstances any attempt to hold but the promise of a permanent alternative administration would be frustrated and would therefore lead to a discrediting of the people's committees. . . ."[17]

The admission by the ANC tries to put a good face on their very real failure to advance their revolutionary program. As McCuen points out, a successful revolution will organize an area in such a manner that it will isolate it from the government and eventually pass under the control of the revolutionaries. "The revolutionaries organize a front governing body elected ostensibly by popular suffrage. They set up women's committees, youth groups, farmer's associations, legal societies, worker's councils—something to commit, propagandize, and supervise everybody. Local self-defense forces and guerrilla groups are maintained to police the area, keep the people in line, and support the regional units. Every government, political, military, social organization has its controlling revolutionary cells, which function as a part of the central political network."[18]

[17] Kabwe document, *op. cit.*, p. 19.

[18] McCuen, J., *The Art of Counter-Revolutionary War, op. cit.*, pp. 34-35.

The UDF, the "comrades" and *Umkhonto we Sizwe* terrorists in the townships during the unrest were all trying to do the things McCuen was describing—carrying out basic revolutionary war doctrine. That they failed was due to security force action buttressed by the regulations issued under the State of Emergency and the fact that the ANC didn't have as much support in the townships as it thought it had. The State of Emergency regulations allowed the ringleaders of the various SACP/ANC front groups to be scooped up and detained by the police. Without their leaders, the effectiveness of the front groups quickly plummeted.

A high South African police official said, "As a result of the state of emergency since 1986, the South African security forces succeeded in checking the revolutionary advance in the RSA to a large extent. Not only were literally hundreds of 'alternative structures' and 'people's courts' eradicated but statistics also show that the almost 15,000 incidents of unrest in 1986 declined to 5,000 in 1987. At the Arusha conference in December 1987 the ANC itself acknowledged that the 'people's war' strategy had failed."[19]

Graphically demonstrating that failure was the ANC's 1987 "Christmas against apartheid campaign" which was an attempt to plant bombs, to initiate nationwide work stay-aways by black workers, to start consumer boycotts and to reactivate the street committees in the townships. All failed.

Other recent failures were its inability to stir up new rent boycotts, the spark that touched off the 1984 unrest, in spite of rent increases in the townships.

In its annual message in January 1988, the ANC began to admit it had not been able to transform the unrest into insurrection. It blamed its failure on the emergency restrictions on its front organizations and on the arrest of its regional and national leaders.[20]

These setbacks indicate a growing weariness with the ANC's emphasis on a violent seizure of power especially in view of the obvious accelerating reform program launched by the South African government. By steadily holding to its Marxist revolutionary formula for seizing power by violent revolutionary means, the ANC risks being overtaken and being left in the dust by the political reform process underway in South Africa.

The unrest period from 1984 to 1986 was a golden opportunity for the

[19] Stadler, *op. cit.*, p. 26.

[20] See: "Message to the People of South Africa from the National Executive Committee," African National Congress, January 8, 1988.

ANC to advance its revolutionary cause inside South Africa. That it failed was largely due to its own incompetence and to the effectiveness of the South African counterinsurgency measures.

20

THE UNREST—SOUTH AFRICA'S RESPONSE

Faced with the unrest in the townships the South African government had to decide upon a course of action.

Fortunately for the South Africans they were not strangers to Marxist-style insurgencies. Their involvement in South West Africa/Namibia had exposed them to the necessity and means of countering an insurgency. They could profit from that experience and wouldn't have to "re-invent the wheel" to deal with the SACP/ANC revolutionary terrorist war in the Republic.

While that part of the South African army stationed in South West Africa/Namibia was developing into a skilled counterinsurgency force, the bulk of the army and the rest of the Defense Force—the Air Force and Navy—were doctrinarily geared to counter a conventional war threat to the Republic. This was the least likely military threat facing South Africa.

To cope with the unrest and all of its ramifications the South Africans had to analyze and decide just what exactly they were facing in the unrest situation. The unrest situation could be described as a low intensity conflict, as the current lexicon of the U.S. national security community terms it. One thing for sure, the unrest situation in South Africa was not the result of hordes of invaders pouring across the borders in Soviet-supplied tanks and armored personnel carriers bent on conquering South Africa. In short, it was not a conventional war situation by any stretch of the imagination. The South Africans were involved in a revolutionary war and measures to counter it had to be thoroughly thought out and then put into practice.

South Africa, like most countries including the United States, had developed its governmental security structures, policies and bureaucracies to fight a conventional war not a revolutionary one.

"The purpose of a conventional war is very clear," said Groenewald, "the occupation of the enemy's territory."[1] This usually involves destroying the enemy's armed forces which protect his territory. The military effort to accomplish that becomes the prime focus of the government's efforts. This means the other elements of the state—the political and economic bureaucracies—devote their energies to support the war effort instead of their normal functions within the governmental infrastructure.

When the war ends and peace breaks out the focus of governmental energy shifts from waging war to the creation and maintaining of its nation's prosperity. This allows the political and economic functions of the state infrastructure to displace the military in importance and priority of effort. Thus public administration in most states is either geared for a state of war or state of peace.

In a revolutionary war the objective of the struggle is to impose a new regime on the society by means of a protracted conflict as Richard Shultz, Jr. demonstrates: "Revolutionary warfare strategists combine unconventional military tactics with political and ideological structure."[2] Crucial to the success of the revolutionary is the support of the people. In a twist of irony, the success or failure of a democratic regime also rests on its support of the people—the consent of the governed. Differences soon make their presence felt.

In a democratic society, political wars are fought and won with voting power, nothing else. The democratic process allows any individual to develop a political vision for the future, convey this vision to the people and create a political organization with the aim of participating in an election. With that election the people can either accept this vision or reject it.

The revolutionary, especially the Marxist variety, professes to support the democratic process but in reality uses it to subvert the regime and replace it with a totalitarian dictatorship, as noted in greater detail elsewhere in this work.

The revolutionary, in order to succeed, still needs the support of the population but instead of allowing his vision of the future to compete in the

[1] Groenewald, P.H., "Counter-revolutionary Action in South Africa: 1984-1990", *American Review*, Vol. 10, 2nd Quarter 1990, Institute for American Studies, Rand Afrikaans University, Johannesburg, p. 19.

[2] Shultz, R.H., Jr., *Soviet Union and Revolutionary Warfare, op. cit.*, p. 3.

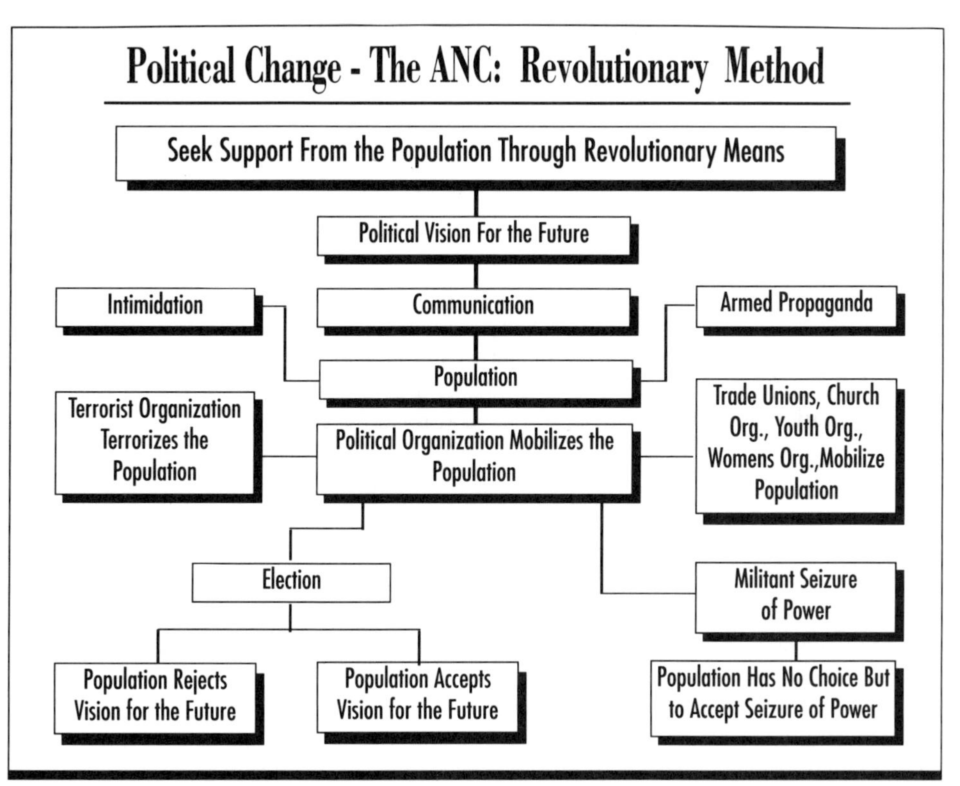

Political Change - The ANC: Revolutionary Method
Seek Support From the Population Through Revolutionary Means
Political Vision For the Future
Intimidation
Communication
Armed Propaganda
Population
Terrorist Organization Terrorizes the Population
Political Organization Mobilizes the Population
Trade Unions, Church Org., Youth Org., Womens Org.,Mobilize Population
Election
Militant Seizure of Power
Population Rejects Vision for the Future
Population Accepts Vision for the Future
Population Has No Choice But to Accept Seizure of Power

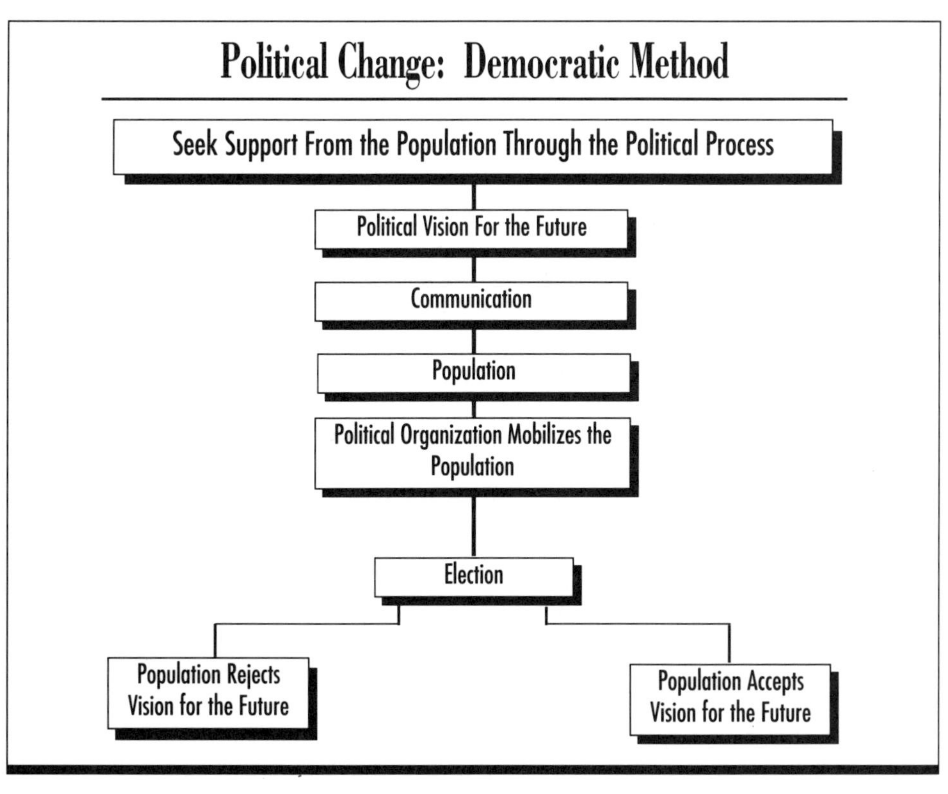

Political Change: Democratic Method
Seek Support From the Population Through the Political Process
Political Vision For the Future
Communication
Population
Political Organization Mobilizes the Population
Election
Population Rejects Vision for the Future
Population Accepts Vision for the Future

market place of ideas, he resorts to force—intimidation, armed propaganda and subversive organization.

Intimidation uses terror tactics to coerce the people into following the revolutionary program.

Armed propaganda uses modern communication to create a sense of chaos and incompetence within the existing society while portraying the revolutionaries in as positive an image as possible.

In order to exploit modern mass media, especially television, revolutionaries commit deeds of violence primarily for purposes of propaganda and not with the aim of destroying military or police targets.

There have been reports where the ANC, through its UDF front, staged gruesome necklacings specifically for the media.[3] In these cases the media become nothing more than voyeuristic vultures and accomplices to murder, not alleged defenders of "the public's right to know", as they keep on reminding us.

Organization is used in a democratic process to mobilize its supporters to give it a greater voice and say within the market place of ideas. This is central to a free and democratic society.

The revolutionary, however, as demonstrated elsewhere in this work, subverts and politicizes organizations across the total spectrum of human activity, by exercising central control, solely to advance the revolutionary political agenda. The aim of these actions is not to participate, but to seize political power, as the ANC's own statements constantly proclaim. The people have no say in this revolutionary process but are mere cannon fodder to be used according to the dictates of the revolutionary leaders.

The South Africans were facing a revolutionary war with a state defense and security apparatus that was geared to fight a conventional war. Obviously, a change of plans was necessary in order for it to cope with the SACP/ANC alliance's revolutionary assault.

Since fighting a revolutionary war involves roughly twenty percent military and eighty percent political activity, the conventional approach to war is an inappropriate model to follow. Furthermore, the high proportion of political versus military involvement in counterinsurgency activities meant that governmental organs other than the military would have to play a key role in the South African effort against the SACP/ANC alliance. To insure

[3] On March 21, 1985, Benjamin Kinikini, a local Town Councilor in the Eastern Cape, and his sons were hacked to death with knives, doused with gasoline, and set afire while a Dutch television crew filmed the incident. The entire event lasted twenty-five minutes while UDF participants, who incited the killings, gave the Marxist power salute and intensified their violent performance for the benefit of the tv crew.

that government action was not running willy-nilly all over the landscape and working at cross purposes required an overall coordinating mechanism.

The existing coordination structure, the Cabinet, was not sufficient for the task that lay ahead.

The South African Cabinet, like most parliamentary cabinets throughout the world, runs on a committee system. The Cabinet was broken down into a series of committees structured for the specific task of running the governmental departments under its control. This means that every element of the power base of the government functioned separately and was controlled by its Cabinet Committee. In the South African context of countering the SACP/ANC revolutionary war, this consisted of a committee overseeing security affairs (the State Security Council); a committee for constitutional affairs; a committee for economic affairs and one for social affairs.

This arrangement fell into two general categories—a security and a general welfare group.

The security group consisted of the military, police and national intelligence agencies. The rest fell into the welfare group.

Government bureaucracies everywhere are notorious for expanding their power and protecting their turf, usually as their first order of business. Getting all to work together on a common policy is not the easiest task in the world and can be likened to the mythical labors of Hercules. Although the task is difficult, it is not impossible, especially when the stakes are high.

To overcome this bureaucratic problem the South Africans, in 1986, set up an umbrella group, the Joint Management Committee (JMC), to plan, coordinate, and manage South Africa's counterinsurgency efforts against the SACP/ANC alliance. The JMC concept was classic McCuen counter-revolutionary war doctrine. "Counter-revolutionary warfare requires the use of military, political, psychological, economic, and organizational action from the village to the national level. These actions must be carefully co-ordinated in unified doctrine and plans to achieve specific objectives. Each unified plan must be backed up by detailed plans of civic action, political operations, economic operations, security, military operations, etc., which co-ordinate all available resources to achieve the required objectives. A unified plan obviously requires at each level a centralized intelligence, planning and control group and some individual who is responsible for ensuring co-ordination and for the success or failure of operations. Unified planning, centralized control, and a single point of responsibility are the very minimum for a unity of effort which will offer success against a unified revolutionary movement. . . . Unity of effort, however, is extremely difficult to achieve because it represents the fusion of civil and military functions to fight battles which have primarily political objectives. Usually, faced with traditional separation of civil and military power, the civilian administration and the military command tend to expand their own peacetime operations, co-ordinating only as necessary to avoid conflicts or obvious duplication. . . . Although the soldier and administrator should continue to operate generally within their own spheres of competence, their functions must be fused toward achieving the common objective of winning the war. . . . Unity of effort can be achieved by a single commander, as the French advocate. Unity of effort can be achieved by a committee, under civilian leadership, as the British advocate. Both systems have worked, and this is the imperative. They must work, for failure of the governing authorities to achieve unity of effort is one of the shortest roads to defeat. . . ."[4]

The first task of the JMC at the national level was to evaluate the whole situation in South Africa from a revolutionary war model. The study took the following questions into consideration: 1) what type of war was South Africa involved in? 2) who organizes the unrest and what is the enemy's strategy? 3) how did the implementation of the SACP/ANC strategy differ from the normal democratic process? and, 4) what should the counter-strategy be?

Their study turned up some surprising facts. It was discovered that almost all of the incidents (ninety percent) occurred in only thirty-six out of the more than 700 black towns in South Africa. This was a startling fact and the JMC wanted to know the reason why.

After further research the study group discovered that five fundamental reasons existed for the unrest—unsound and weak local authorities, unemployment (between forty and eighty percent), poor housing, insufficient education, and inadequate medical services.

All the revolutionaries had to do was to exploit these problems in order to further their revolutionary campaign. The proof of their effort was the violence in the townships, described earlier.

It was a phony campaign by the SACP/ANC. They promised: "The doors of learning and culture shall be opened"[5], but they forced the children to boycott classes. They promised: "There shall be work and security"[6], but forced the workers to strike. They promised: "There shall be houses, security and comfort"[7], but enforced rent boycotts. They promised: "There shall be

[4] McCuen, *op. cit.*, pp. 72-73.

[5] Freedom Charter.

[6] *Ibid.*

[7] *Ibid.*

peace and friendship"[8], but intimidated and attacked those who did not join their "movement". They promised much, but took away education, jobs, houses and peace—proving they wanted chaos, not peace and stability and that the "people" meant nothing to them, except as stepping stones for their own selfish quest for power.

After more study and analysis of the unrest, the JMC laid out their counter-revolutionary strategy, defining both short-term and long-term goals.

First of all, establish short-term stability in the country by neutralizing revolutionary activity that could not be classified as actions of a democratic nature.

Those steps were:

First, limit intimidation by isolating those responsible for acts of intimidation. This meant that suspects were often jailed without trial.

Second, limit the SACP/ANC's ability to conduct armed propaganda by restricting the media from airing visual images of violence and destruction.

Third, restrict the political activities of organizations furthering the aims of the SACP/ANC alliance. As a result, thirty-three organizations had various restrictions placed on them.

The long-term goal was to eliminate the causes of unrest.

The counter-revolutionary campaign was launched in earnest with the declaration of a national State of Emergency by South African State President P.W. Botha on June 12, 1986. Botha indicated the emergency regulations had three objectives: 1) stability, meaning the restoration of law and order; 2) returning the country to normality; and, 3) creating circumstances conducive for constitutional, social and economic development.

The emergency regulations brought the usual howls of indignation from the media, the United Nations and the left-wing liberal network throughout the world. From their comfortable salons in London, chic cafes in Paris, and brie and chablis parties in Georgetown, they heaped condemnation on the actions of the South African government, conveniently overlooking the fact that their own governments had also detained people for so-called political crimes in periods of crisis. The French did it during the Algerian War and the Generals Revolt in the late 1950s; the British did it during the Second World War when they detained, under the 1940 Defense Regulation 18B as amended, some 747 members of Sir Oswald Moseley's British Union of Fascists[9]—they also made widespread use of detention in the Mau Mau

[8] *Ibid.*

[9] Trythall, A.J., *"Boney" Fuller, Soldier, Strategist, and Writer 1878-1966*, The Nautical & Aviation Publishing Co. of America, Baltimore, MD, 1977, p. 216.

uprising in Kenya, the Malay insurrection, and even use it today in the unrest in Northern Ireland; Abraham Lincoln suspended parts of the U.S. Constitution (the use of habeas corpus) during the Civil War and President Woodrow Wilson jailed the American socialist leader Eugene Debs for his opposition to U.S. policy during World War I. The U.S. also forcibly removed and placed tens of thousands of Japanese-American citizens in resettlement areas in the interior during World War II. It goes without saying that Marxist totalitarian governments, the black ruled dictatorships of Africa and the majority of member states of the United Nations today use indiscriminate detention without a peep of protest from those who pour abusive criticism on South Africa.

Be that as it may, the actions taken under the State of Emergency in South Africa had the desired effect.

Stability and a semblance of normality returned to South Africa to the point that it enabled the South African government to launch in earnest, as part of its long-term plan to eliminate the causes of unrest, new political initiatives designed to bring blacks into the political process in South Africa.

Stability is essential for any lasting democratic reform to take place in South Africa. This is so because there are some fundamental aspects of democratic societies that must be taken into account before democracy can take root in unfamiliar soil. Specifically there are three issues that are especially relevant to the situation in South Africa. First, for a democratic political system to survive there must be some degree of economic prosperity; second, for democratic reform to work it is necessary that there be adequate time and that political order be maintained; and third, democracy in a multi-racial, multi-religious and/or multi-ethnic society operates on different principles from democracy in homogeneous societies.[10]

As part of this initiative, the South African government lifted the ban on the SACP, ANC, UDF and other organizations. This action would not have been possible if the country were still mired in the violence and unrest that characterized the period between 1984 and 1986.

If any proof were needed as to the effectiveness of the JMC's success, one notes in passing that the SACP/ANC constantly demanded its dismantlement. They recognized it as the most formidable obstacle to the furtherance of their revolutionary goals. Until its recent dismantling, the JMC effectively coordinated South Africa's counterinsurgency efforts against the violence of the SACP/ANC alliance.

[10] Evans, E., "The American Catholic Church and the South Africa Issue", *Conflict Quarterly*, Vol. IX, No. 4, Fall 1989, University of New Brunswick, Fredericton, p. 38.

21

SOUTH AFRICAN COUNTER STRATEGY

Two factors greatly influenced the counterinsurgency efforts of the South African government: 1.) the history of revolutionary violence in southern Africa; and, 2.) their experience in South West Africa.

The South African government was well aware that revolutionaries in Angola, Mozambique and Zimbabwe were able to seize power only because they had secure bases in neighboring countries. Therefore, Pretoria sought to keep the ANC from establishing bases in the hostile countries that surrounded the Republic.

It also followed McCuen's advice on combatting revolutionary violence, ". . . the counter-revolutionary objectives should be to exploit any advantage gained by maintaining contact, retaining the initiative, and rolling back the revolutionary organization. That is, the counter-revolutionaries must follow the rebels from base to base and from phase to phase with operations designed to keep defeating them in their own media until the revolutionary organization has been destroyed and the counter-revolutionary organization has been firmly established."[1]

The South African aim was to keep the ANC off balance, to keep their terrorists as far away as possible, and to prevent them, via good police and intelligence work, from establishing a revolutionary organization inside South Africa.

They set out to accomplish this by using both military and economic

[1] McCuen, J., *Art of Counter-Revolutionary War, op. cit.* p. 78.

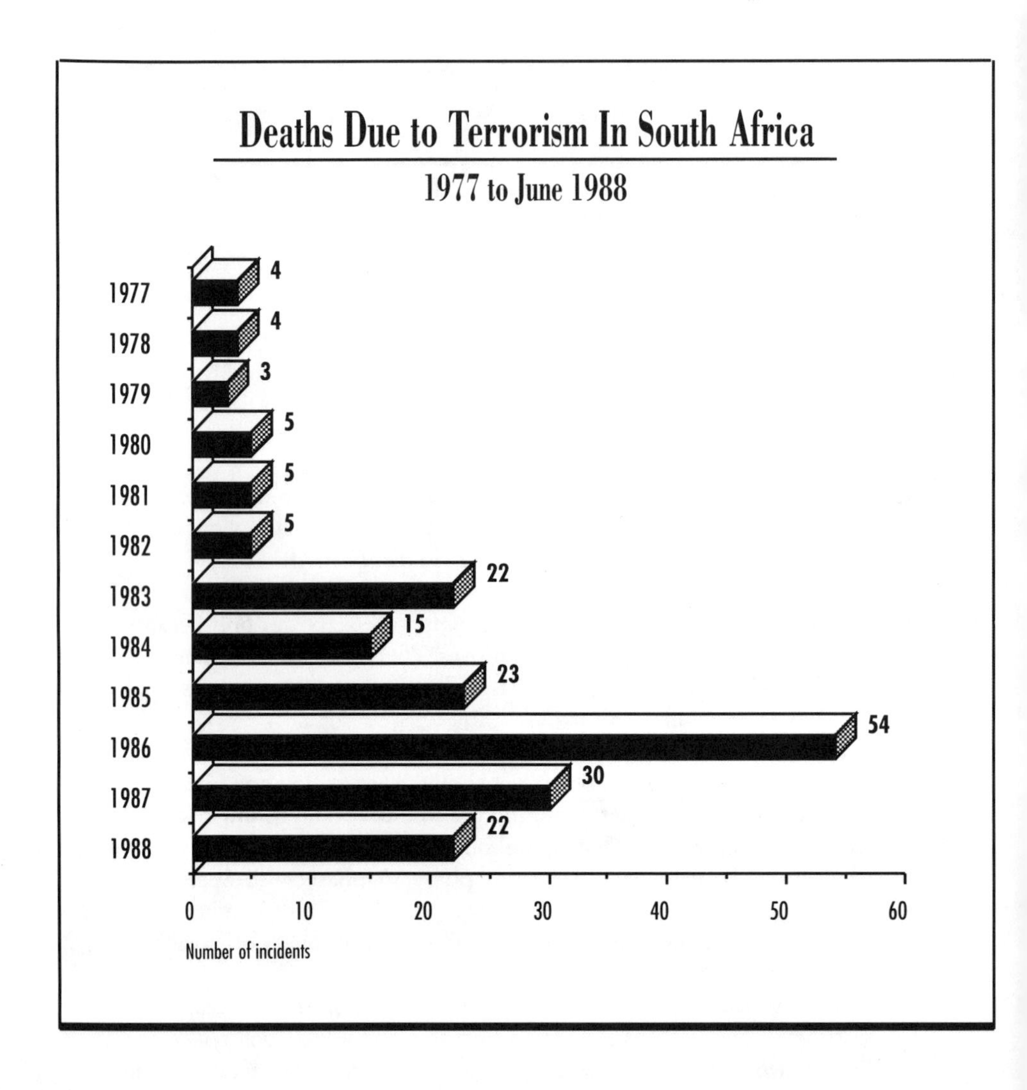
Deaths Due to Terrorism In South Africa
1977 to June 1988
1977
1978
1979
1980
1981
1982
1983
1984
1985
1986
1987
1988
4
4
3
5
5
5
22
15
23
54
30
22
0
10
20
30
40
50
60
Number of incidents

pressure. In spite of their hostility towards South Africa, the black African states in southern Africa are compelled to rely on it in varying degrees. South Africa provides commodities and manufactured goods they could not get as cheaply elsewhere. Since all of South Africa's neighbors' economies are in terrible shape due to their half-baked socialistic practices, they don't have the luxury of paying for higher costing non-South African-made goods.

They must get all or part of their electricity, medical and other services, markets for their products and jobs for large portions of their population from South Africa. This trade and these jobs provide much needed hard currency for South Africa's neighbors.

South Africa employs more than 300,000 blacks from neighboring states. About half of South Africa's black miners come from abroad and send their wages home. About 10 million people in a half-dozen countries are financially dependent on South Africa's mining industry.[2]

In addition, the South African rail and road transportation network moves its neighbors' goods to the sea for export throughout the world. Eight of the fourteen countries in southern Africa are landlocked and depend upon railroads to carry their goods to seaports for export overseas. South African railroads handle the bulk of Zaire's, Zambia's and Zimbabwe's foreign trade. Approximately seventy percent of Zambia's rail cargo moves through South Africa in spite of the TanZam railroad built by the Chinese to bypass railroads running through then white-ruled Rhodesia. At least sixty percent of Malawi's and Zimbabwe's exports, as well as imports, also go through South Africa.

This fact has grated on South Africa's neighbors. As their own economies have become more and more depressed from the fruits of socialism, they have become more dependent than ever on their white-ruled neighbor to the south. But, as L'Ange points out, ". . . The more the neighboring states have become dependent on South Africa the more they have resented it. For many years practical considerations dictated that they must accept the situation with the best grace possible; but as political dissatisfaction grew among black people inside South Africa, and particularly when it became organized and militarized . . . the neighboring states were forced to adopt increasingly political attitudes themselves. In the United Nations they had to stand up and be counted along with the vocal and voting opponents of apartheid."[3]

[2] Norval, M., *Red Star Over Southern Africa*, Selous Foundation Press, Washington, D.C., 1988, p. 141.

[3] L'Ange, G., "Countries In The Cross-Fire", *Challenge, op. cit.,* p. 326.

The increasingly political militancy of South Africa's neighbors was a boon to the ANC. If it were going to launch a successful revolutionary war inside South Africa it must have either secure bases in or safe transit routes through these states.

Although the ANC has constantly boasted about its bases inside South Africa, they exist only in the imagination of the ANC. The fact that any base needed to sustain military operations would be of such a size that it would quickly come to the attention of the police and security forces, puts to rest the ANC's claim.

The ANC, then, was forced to infiltrate its terrorists into South Africa from its bases in Angola and Zambia using transit facilities in Botswana, Mozambique, Swaziland, Lesotho and Zimbabwe.

Since South Africa's neighbors were dependent upon South Africa to keep their economies from collapsing, their attitude and assistance to the ANC was a risky business. South Africa put political pressure on the regimes by using a mixture of their economic and military clout.

The use of its military clout was important for two reasons: By attacking the ANC in their bases far from South Africa it demonstrated that the ANC terrorists were not safe in their so-called sanctuaries. It also demonstrated that South Africa was willing to use military force to back up its political threats. This second point is extremely important because nothing can unravel political and diplomatic threats as much as lacking the will to back them up with force.

By using its military to carry out retaliatory raids on ANC facilities in neighboring countries, Pretoria sent a signal that it was not a paper tiger and it was risky business to succor terrorists within one's borders.

Given the immense rail and road traffic that crosses the Beit Bridge over the Limpopo River separating Zimbabwe from South Africa, it is relatively easy for South Africa to put a serious crimp in Zimbabwe's economy. All it would require is for South Africa to prohibit Zimbabwean goods from entering the Republic.

Admittedly, this is action that in many eyes would be tantamount to a declaration of war by South Africa against Zimbabwe. Yet it is, if it ever came to pass, nothing more than what many nations are doing at present in their economic sanctions campaign against South Africa.

South Africa has not stopped Zimbabwean goods from passing through the Republic although it has, from time to time, tightened its customs and border checks on road and rail traffic between the two countries. This action has slowed down the flow of goods across the border, serving as a subtle demonstration that it could be much worse if Pretoria were to tighten the screws any further.

The major infiltration transit route for ANC terrorists is through Botswana into South Africa. In December 1987, South Africa caused a huge tie-up in traffic crossing from Botswana into South Africa. It did this by thoroughly checking every vehicle that tried to cross through the border checkpoint. The Botswana government accused South Africa of deliberate obstruction of its road traffic crossing the border. The South Africans denied the charge, claiming the police were looking for ANC weapons and explosives after the terrorist group threatened to carry out Christmas bombings in South Africa.

In any event, the incident did serve as a not-so-subtle warning to Botswana not to allow the ANC to bring its terrorism into South Africa from their country.

As L'Ange aptly put it, ". . . Botswana did not need to be reminded of what had happened to Lesotho in 1986 when a border blockade, also imposed to enforce total suppression of ANC activity, saw the country quickly running out of essential supplies. The fact that the blockade precipitated a military coup that overthrew the anti-Pretoria government of Leabua Jonathon was a bonus for South Africa."[4] The new government in Lesotho quickly tossed the ANC out of the country and the border is now completely open between the two countries.

There is a down side to South Africa's use of its threat to shut off the shipment of its neighbors' goods through South Africa. Pursuing such a policy would mean the loss of the considerable revenue derived from handling the shipment of its neighbors' goods. It would also cause the loss of South Africa's trade, which is considerable, with African countries as far to the north as Zaire. Loss of this trade would severely curtail a considerable portion of South Africa's foreign trade.

Even the minor incidents of traffic slowdown by South Africa have enabled its neighbors to blame their own problems on the white-ruled state to the south. South Africa has become a convenient scapegoat to blame for their own failed economic policies.

While South Africa holds the stick of threatened economic ruin over the heads of its neighbors, it also offers the carrot of economic assistance to those who clamp down on ANC activity. Mozambique, for example, accepted South Africa's economic and technical help in restoring and running Maputo harbor and upgrading the railroad linking it with the South African rail network.

Pretoria has used its military to raid ANC bases located in neighboring countries, which were being used as launching pads for terrorist acts inside South Africa. The South African government assured the people and the

[4] L'Ange, *op. cit.*, p. 349.

governments of those countries that the raids were not aimed at them, only at the ANC terrorists located in their midst. Raiding forces took extra precautions not to put the local police or military in harm's way.

These raids were not spur-of-the-moment affairs. They were done only after repeated attempts were made to get the governments of the affected countries to take action on their own to prevent the ANC from using their territory for spreading terror into South Africa. Only when these efforts had failed and after much deliberation at the highest levels did the government approve the raids.[5] After having exhausted its patience, the South African government sent specially trained military units in to destroy the ANC bases.

The first raid occurred on January 30, 1980, when South African forces struck three ANC safe-houses on the outskirts of Maputo in Mozambique, killing several ANC terrorists while losing one in the exchange of gunfire.

A year later they struck again in a different country. The targets this time were ANC safe-houses located in Maseru, the capital of Lesotho. Maseru was the location of an important ANC regional headquarters that directed ANC terrorist activities and infiltration into the Transvaal.

The ANC tried to blunt the raiding tactics of the South Africans by scattering their safe-houses throughout the cities in which they were located, reasoning it would make them harder to hit them all at once. It created a false sense of security, as they found out to their dismay in Botswana. On June 10, 1985 the raiders from South Africa struck ten ANC facilities scattered throughout Gaberone, the capital of Botswana. The raid was a carefully planned and coordinated operation that thwarted a planned ANC terrorist campaign inside South Africa.[6]

A year later South African forces again demonstrated their determination to strike at ANC facilities in neighboring states. In a most ambitious cross-border operation in May 1986, the South Africans simultaneously launched ground attacks against facilities not only once again in Gaberone, but also in Harare, the capital of Zimbabwe. While these ground attacks were in progress, the South African Air Force made an air strike on an ANC base outside Lusaka, Zambia. The Zambian strike must have raised the nervous stress factor of the ANC leadership as the raid struck close to home—their headquarters are located in downtown Lusaka.

Other raids and clandestine attacks were carried out in Swaziland, Zimbabwe and Lesotho. The raids bore fruit. *Africa Confidential* reported:

[5] Norval, M., "Guns of Gaberone", *Red Star, op. cit.,* pp. 119-130.

[6] *Ibid.*

"Pretoria's victories included the Nkomati Accord, neutralizing Mozambique; and the 20 January 1986 coup in Lesotho, putting in a pro-Pretoria government. This involved the expulsion of a formidable ANC regional intelligence unit which had cultivated good contacts in Lesotho's National Security Service. . . ."[7]

South Africa also supported two insurgencies in the former Portuguese colonies of Angola and Mozambique against Marxist regimes aiding the ANC. In both countries South Africa's action led eventually to the expulsion of the ANC.

The South Africans had taken over the task of supporting the anti-communist Mozambican resistance movement, RENAMO, from the Rhodesians after the Marxist Robert Mugabe took power in Rhodesia, now called Zimbabwe. So badly had the Marxist regime run the Mozambican state into the ground that, by 1984, it had lost control of three-quarters of the country to RENAMO.[8]

RENAMO's success caused the Mozambican Marxist regime of Samora Machel to turn to his hated neighbor for help. Machel told the South Africans that if they would stop aiding RENAMO, Machel would boot the ANC out of its sanctuary in Mozambique. Over some opposition within the South African Defense Force and South African intelligence community, the South African diplomats leaped at the offer. As usual, the diplomats prevailed and a non-aggression pact called the Nkomati Accord was signed on March 15, between the two countries. South Africa stopped supporting RENAMO and the ANC was kicked out of Mozambique.

On the other side of the continent the South Africans had been supporting the anti-communist Angolan resistance movement UNITA. Led by Dr. Jonas Savimbi, UNITA was, and still is, trying to liberate Angola from the Marxist government in Luanda. The Angolan regime was giving aid, support and bases to their Marxist soul-brothers of the ANC and the South West Africa People's Organization (SWAPO). SWAPO was trying to seize power in South West Africa/Namibia which, until April 1, 1989, was under the administrative control of South Africa.[9]

UNITA was valuable to South Africa's counterinsurgency efforts in

[7] *Africa Confidential*, Vol. 30, No. 2, January 20, 1989, p. 7.

[8] See: Norval, M., "Trouble in Marxist Paradise", *Red Star Over Southern Africa, op. cit.*, pp. 186-196; Wheeler, J., "From Rovuma to Maputo: Mozambique's Guerrilla War", *Reason*, December 1985.

[9] See: Norval, M., *Death in the Desert: The Namibian Tragedy*, Selous Foundation Press, Washington, D.C., 1989.

Namibia. By the end of 1985 at least half of SWAPO's terrorists were tied down helping the Marxist Angolan army fight UNITA. Some ANC terrorists from the ANC training camps in Angola were also forced to fight UNITA.[10] Those that were tied down fighting UNITA were not able to infiltrate and perpetrate terrorist deeds in South Africa.

Savimbi's guerrillas also provided a valuable intelligence function. They were operating throughout Angola in areas where South African reconnaissance units found it extremely difficult to penetrate and could better observe activity in the various ANC camps. This intelligence gathered by the guerrillas was often shared with the South Africans. From these camps ANC terrorists infiltrated through Botswana and Zimbabwe into the Republic of South Africa to launch their terror attacks. South Africa was interested in any information about them, their training and personnel movements. Often such information came from UNITA.

As part of the American-brokered Namibian peace settlement, South Africa ceased its support of UNITA in return for Angola's closing down the ANC terrorist training camps and booting the ANC terrorists out of Angola.[11] The bulk of the 6,000 ANC terrorists were transferred to Uganda near Kampala.[12]

Pretoria's use of the carrot and stick had a definite effect in throwing a monkey-wrench into the ANC's terrorist operations in South Africa.

A critically important aspect of a successful counterinsurgency program is having good intelligence. Since the ANC didn't have any bases inside South Africa, keeping tabs on the ANC was extremely difficult. South African counter strategy, however, mandated that, in spite of the harder task, they had to know what mischief the ANC were planning. As McCuen noted, ". . . They must ensure that security forces have time to react. They must know where, when, and how to attack. . . ."[13]

The surgical precision of the South African raids on ANC facilities in neighboring states attests to the success and efficiency of the South African intelligence network. They took to heart McCuen's advice that "the governing authorities must organize their intelligence network around a clandestine apparatus which spreads its roots deep into the population. . . ."[14] The ease with which ANC networks were eliminated in South

[10] See: Ottaway, D., "Dissidents Criticize ANC Leaders", *The Washington Post*, May 17, 1990.

[11] See: "Umkhonto packs its bags", *Africa Confidential*, Vol. 30, No. 2, January 20, 1989, p. 6.

[12] See: "ANC in Uganda", *Africa Confidential*, Vol. 30, No. 6, March 17, 1989, p. 8.

[13] McCuen, J., *Art of Counter-Revolutionary War, op. cit.*, p. 113.

[14] McCuen, J., *op. cit.*, p. 114.

Africa shortly after they were set up showed the extent of the security forces intelligence network.

The South African intelligence network was extensive. It had penetrated the ANC from top to bottom both in and out of the country. Pretoria had agents close to the National Executive Committee (NEC), inside the hierarchy of the SACP, in *Umkhonto we Sizwe*, in ANC cells inside South Africa and in numerous ANC front groups.

South African security force agents had infiltrated the SACP/ANC alliance before the banning of the ANC. These secret agents have not only kept the authorities informed on the ANC's illegal activities but have, on occasion, broken their cover and testified in open court about the activities of their erstwhile comrades. This was especially true of Gerard Ludi.

Ludi had infiltrated the SACP by means of involving himself as part of his police duties in radical leftist front organizations while attending Witswatersrand University. He took a giant step forward by joining the Congress of Democrats in 1961. In 1962, he traveled to the Soviet Union and the following year was invited to join the banned underground SACP.

After the Rivonia arrests and trials of the top ANC leadership in 1963, Ludi moved freely within the top echelons of the SACP. His secret life came to an end when he was the star witness for the prosecution in the trial of Bram Fischer, the head of the SACP organization still left within South Africa. Most of the top leadership of the SACP had fled the country after the Rivonia raid had decimated their ANC partners. Fischer, scion of one of South Africa's most distinguished families, had been a member of the SACP since the late 1930s, but Ludi's testimony was instrumental in sending him to prison.[15]

Another successful South African intelligence agent was Craig Williamson. For ten years, until 1980, he was a secret agent who worked closely with anti-South African front organizations rising to high positions in several of them. He was vice-president of the National Union of South African Students, deputy director of the Geneva, Switzerland-based International University Exchange Fund, and vice-chairman of the UN-approved International Non-Governmental Organizations Sub-Committee on Racism, Racial Discrimination, Apartheid and Decolonialization. As an apparent true comrade of the SACP/ANC cause, he addressed the United Nations committees in New York on anti-apartheid activities engaged in by the fronts he represented. So convincing was his activity that he traveled throughout the world, meeting and working with Marxist supported revolutionaries,

[15] See: Pike, H., *A History of Communism in South Africa, op. cit.*, pp. 368-428, for more details of Gerard Ludi's activities.

especially in Latin America and Africa, and attended conferences and seminars in both the West and the Soviet bloc.

As a result, he worked at one time or another for the ANC, the SACP and *Umkhonto we Sizwe*. The information he gathered was extremely valuable to the South African security forces in their counter-terror campaign against the ANC. A South African turncoat finally exposed Williamson's true identity in 1980, and, as a result, he returned to Pretoria and the Security Branch police until his retirement in 1985.[16]

Another celebrated South African intelligence agent was South African Police Lieutenant Olivia Forsyth. Her secret agent's career, like Williamson's and Ludi's, started with radical left-wing student groups. Forsyth penetrated first the National Union of South African Students, then similar groups of leftist ANC front organizations before ending up within the top echelons of the ANC in Angola.

The South Africans didn't have to rely solely on South African police and intelligence agents penetrating the ANC. They were quite successful in recruiting agents within the ANC itself. *Africa Confidential* reported, ". . . the ANC is conducting a major security sweep of suspected wrong-doers or agents of Pretoria within its ranks. The main effects of this so far have been felt within *Umkhonto we Sizwe*, in the treasury department, and in the South African Communist Party (SACP). . . .

"The most sensational development has been the detention of Thami Zulu, the powerful military commander of the Swaziland Mozambique front. His detention follows the exposure last year of the Natal Military Command operations chief, Comrade Cyril. The latter, who operated under Zulu's command for several years, committed suicide when he was exposed as a spy on behalf of Pretoria. . . ."[17]

The ANC wasn't the only target of Pretoria's agents. "The SACP is having to cope with the allegation that one of Comrade Cyril's closest associates was also a long-term agent of Pretoria. The suspect, now in detention outside the Front Line States, is said to have had the specific task of spying on the Party. The alleged spy served with the Party's rising stars 'Che' Ogara and Peter Mayibuye at the Lenin School, and attended the 1984 Moscow Congress. Security men believed that the suspected spy betrayed countless Party secrets to Pretoria including the sensitive work of the Regional Party Committee in Swaziland and was close to a number of Party leaders. If these allegations are true, the South African Security Police must

[16] Interviews with Craig Williamson, July 1983 and April 1984.

[17] *Africa Confidential*, Vol. 30, No. 18, September 8, 1989, p. 3.

have acquired volumes of information from the association."[18]

Another spy, according to *Africa Confidential*, was Jessica Monare. She had been working in London at the ultra-sensitive Party secretariat which was responsible for churning out ANC propaganda. "In 1984 Party barons were toasting this courageous daughter of the working class—she was the only black woman delegate to the Sixth Party Congress in Moscow that year. This year, after she had been accused of espionage, the same barons in Havana were grimly assessing the damage."[19]

Another spy, Gloria Sedibe, known as Comrade September, exposed virtually the entire ANC presence in Swaziland in 1986.[20]

These were some of the agents that were discovered by the SACP/ANC alliance. Unfortunately for the SACP/ANC, there are still many of their comrades who, while appearing to be fighting for the SACP/ANC alliance, are also on the payroll of Pretoria's intelligence services. Not only are they continuing to provide the South Africans with up-to-date information, but they have to be causing the ANC fits. This can't help but add to the climate of suspicion and distrust within the organization. Because of its nature as a conspiratorial Marxist revolutionary group, suspicion and back-stabbing are the normal daily climate. The thought that your organization is riddled with spies only increases the suspicion, heightens tensions, and has a detrimental effect on the group's efficiency—another added bonus for Pretoria.

Some of the most effective counterinsurgency actions by the South African government were its State of Emergency measures. These acts allowed the security forces to clamp down on the ANC agitators and their cohorts in the various front groups such as the United Democratic Front (UDF).

The government applied censorship to the media which had conducted its own media war against the government and was openly sympathetic to the ANC. This action, as expected, raised pious howls of indignation from the international media. But, as former *Newsweek* foreign correspondent Holger Jensen points out, ". . . South Africa is a country at war and no publication should be allowed to further the cause of revolution. Here, in all fairness, it must be pointed out that many of the country's press curbs would not have been imposed had it not been for some very irresponsible reporting by the media. . . ."[21]

[18] *Africa Confidential*, Vol. 30, No. 18, *op. cit.*, p. 4.

[19] "South Africa: The Party Faithful" *Africa Confidential*, Vol. 31, No. 1, January 12, 1990, pp. 3-4.

[20] See; *Africa Confidential*, Vol. 30, No. 2, January 20, 1989, p. 7.

[21] Jensen, H., "The Media War" *Challenge: Southern Africa Within the African Revolutionary Context*, p. 301.

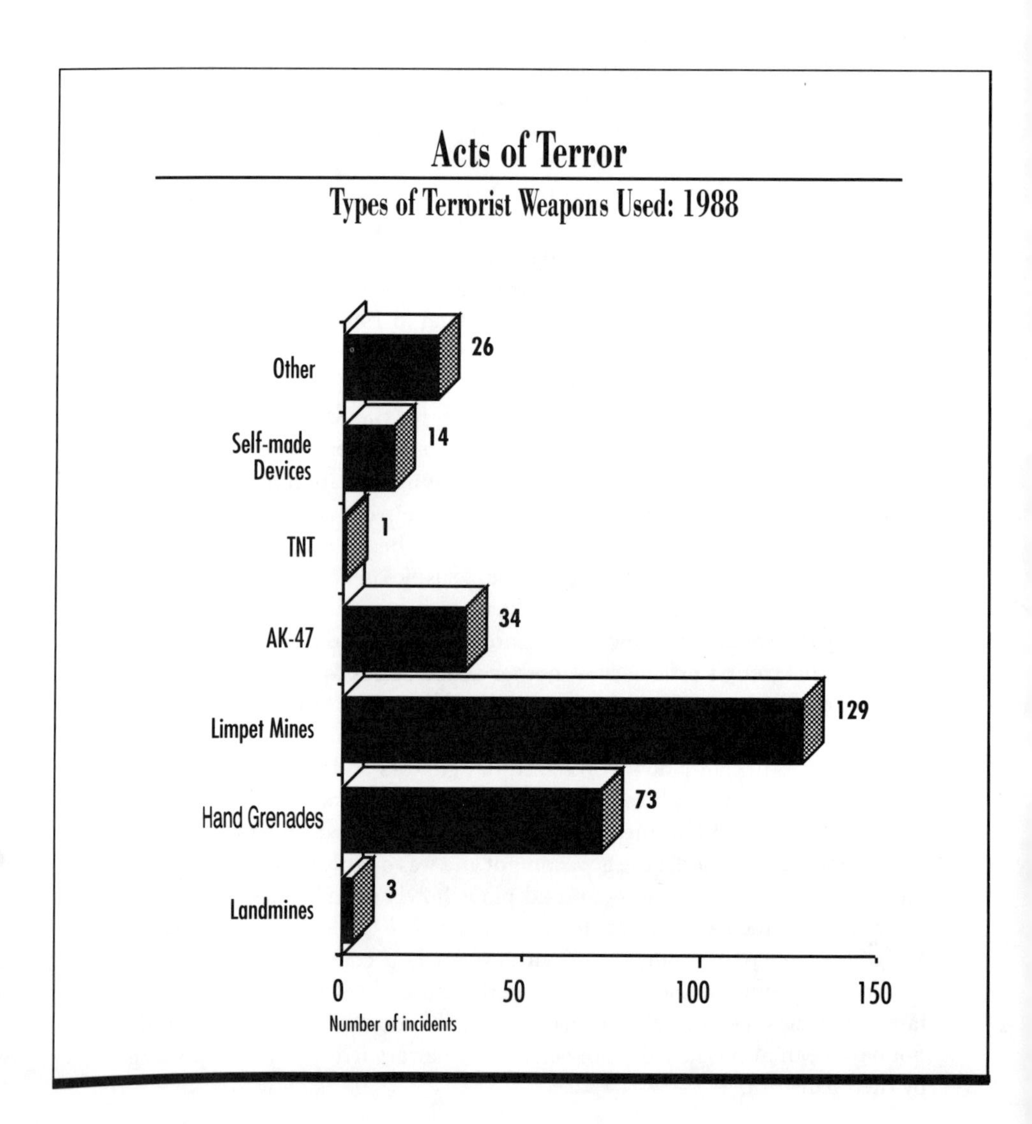
Acts of Terror
Types of Terrorist Weapons Used: 1988
Other
26
Self-made Devices
14
TNT
1
AK-47
34
Limpet Mines
129
Hand Grenades
73
Landmines
3
0
50
100
150
Number of incidents

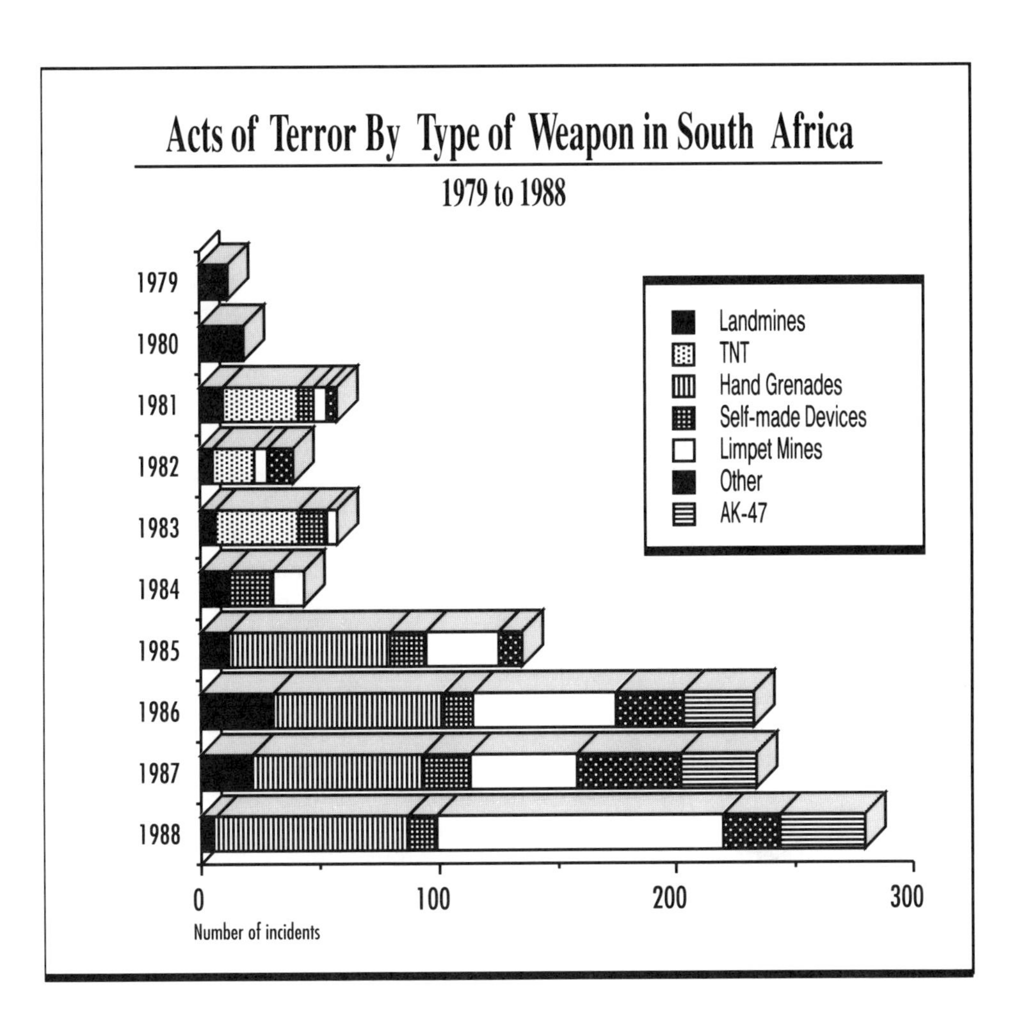
Acts of Terror By Type of Weapon in South Africa
1979 to 1988
1979
1980
1981
1982
1983
1984
1985
1986
1987
1988
Landmines
TNT
Hand Grenades
Self-made Devices
Limpet Mines
Other
AK-47
0
100
200
300
Number of incidents

Such restrictions hindered the ANC and its internal front allies because, as Ted Koppel of ABC TV Nightline explained it, "... The media, particularly television and terrorists need one another. . . . They have what is fundamentally a symbiotic relationship. Without television, international terrorism becomes rather like the philosopher's hypothetical tree falling in the forrest—no one hears it fall and therefore it doesn't exist."[22]

The unrest in South Africa in 1985 brought on the emergency regulations. Full scale rioting broke out in South Africa, especially in the Johannesburg, Pretoria, Veereninging area—the so-called Vaal Triangle. From there it spread over the country under the leadership of the Congress of South African Students (COSAS) and other youth groups affiliated with the United Democratic Front (UDF) with most of the violence occurring in the Vaal Triangle and the Eastern Cape.

As the violence increased it became better organized. It continued escalating in 1985 and the government declared a partial State of Emergency in the areas where the violence was most prevalent. The emergency regulations were issued to restrict gatherings, stone-throwings, arson, attacks on the property and persons of the police, and local government officials. All had been targets of attack by terrorists armed with grenades, Molotov cocktails, acid-bombs or firearms.

The regulations had their positive effects and the ANC found it harder to carry out its terrorist activities. It became exceedingly difficult for its cadres to conduct crash courses in grenade-throwing or to carry out limpet and land-mine operations and other terrorist acts in the restricted areas.

Slowly a sense of normalcy was returning to the strife-torn areas affected by the emergency regulations. Electrical power, interrupted by terrorist attacks on electrical transmission lines, was restored, refuse collection, postal and other services were restored and law and order returned.

Early in 1986 the situation had stabilized to the extent that the government lifted the partial State of Emergency.

The peace and calm didn't last long as the ANC greeted the lifting of the emergency by resuming its terror campaign. "Necklace" murders once again became common inside the black townships as the ANC tried to re-establish its disrupted terrorist networks and intimidate the people into supporting its activities. The UDF began organizing a national work stoppage, nationwide mass meetings and planned a mass march on Pollsmoor Prison, outside of Cape Town, where Nelson Mandela was being held.

[22] *Challenge, op. cit.*, p. 287.

The Congress of South African Trade Unions (COSATU) was in cahoots with the UDF and was busy planning a nationwide strike to coincide with the work stoppage in an attempt to bring the economy of South Africa to a halt. All this was supposed to take place on June 16, 1986.

White farms in some areas were being subjected to arson attacks. On other farms laborers were intimidated not to show up for work by beatings and killings. In the Eastern Cape, herds of cattle and sheep were mutilated in gruesome ways reminiscent of the Mau Mau uprising in Kenya during the 1950s.

Radio stations in neighboring black states beamed broadcasts into South Africa calling for revolution. Most featured ANC president Oliver Tambo's call for the total disruption of every factory, farm and white household; the destruction of the new Tricameral parliament putting a stop to recently launched reform efforts; and, the elimination or repentance of so-called collaborators or else they would feel the "people's wrath"—murder by the necklace.

If these plans had come to fruition they would have escalated the unrest situation in South Africa. That would have helped the SACP/ANC alliance's violent revolutionary war program. It would have resulted in considerable loss of life, countless injuries, destruction of property and a real possibility of a loss of national confidence so crucial to a successful counterinsurgency effort.

It was against this ominous background that, on June 12, 1986, at a joint session of the three Houses of Parliament, State President P.W. Botha declared a national State of Emergency. Botha said that the increase of violence was of such a nature and extent that it seriously endangered the safety of the public and the maintenance of law and order. Claiming that the ordinary laws were not sufficient to cope with the situation to enable the government to ensure public safety and maintain public order, the State of Emergency became a necessity.

This was done to create a situation of relative normalcy so that every citizen, no matter his color, could earn his or her livelihood in peace, schools could reopen, businesses could resume and the reform program launched by the South African government could continue.

Did the nationwide proclamation help or hinder South Africa's counterinsurgency efforts?

It helped immeasurably as noted by Williamson: ". . . the imposition of the state of emergency caused a marked decline in insurrectionary actions. From May 1986 to May 1987 the number of such actions fell by 79 percent. By May 1987 the black death rate attributable to insurrection had fallen by 94.9

percent. The state of emergency also permitted the resumption of schooling and essential administrative work such as refuse removal, water supply, electricity, street maintenance, sewage, public transport, fire fighting and postal services. Clinics and other medical services were able to resume work in black areas formerly out of bounds to them because of violence. Social workers returned to the townships, and recreation facilities were no longer called 'freedom parks' "[23].

Although the South African government was getting kicked in the teeth by the international media, the UN , and the world-wide left-wing network for promulgating and continuing its State of Emergency, South Africa's actions were not unprecedented. Great Britain had resorted to similar measures at one time or another in Malaya, Kenya, Cyprus and Northern Ireland. Canada had used similar measures to counter the violence of the Quebec separatist movement. Even Abraham Lincoln, who has achieved near sainthood in the eyes of Americans, suspended the writ of habeas corpus and sent federal troops to quell draft riots with loss of life during the American Civil War. Woodrow Wilson was not above jailing opponents, such as Eugene Debs, who opposed his policy of leading America into World War I.

The point is that all states use extraordinary measures to insure their survival, democracies as well as dictatorships, as recent events in the Soviet Union vis-a-vis Lithuania have demonstrated.

This should come as no surprise to anyone, for those running any state feel particularly exposed and vulnerable and will defend, in the name of the people of the state, that nation's existence. Franz Oppenheimer, in his sociological study of the state said: "What then, is the State as a sociological concept? The State, completely during the first stage of its existence, is a social institution, forced by a victorious group of men on a defeated group, with the sole purpose of regulating the dominion of the victorious group over the vanquished, and securing itself against revolt from within and attacks from abroad. . . ."[24]

While many may quarrel with Oppenheimer's Darwinian view of the state, none should dispute the fact that all States will defend themselves against revolt from within (see for example: U.S. Constitution, Article I, Section 8) and against foreign invasion.

This is especially true for Oppenheimer's "revolt from within". O'Neill points out that ". . . effective counterinsurgency invariably involves a number

[23] Williamson, C., *Challenge, op. cit.*, p. 287.

[24] Oppenheimer, F., *The State: Its History and Development Viewed Sociologically*, Arno Press & The New York Times, N.Y., 1972, p. 15.

of security measures—detention without trial, resettlement of sections of the population, control of the distribution of food, curfews, restrictions on movement, the issuance and checking of identification cards, and the imposition of severe penalties for the carrying of unauthorized weapons—in order to separate the population from the insurgents. While such sanctions may be undesirable from an ideal or moral standpoint, they have proved effective, especially when applied consistently, fairly, and judiciously."[25]

Even the ANC admitted that their recent terrorist efforts had been thwarted. They blamed it on restrictions on organizations and the arrest of regional and national leaderships.[26]

The counterinsurgency measures implemented by the South Africans were, with the exception of those trying to break its international isolation, successful. The country, as the decade of the 1980s ended, was in virtually no danger of falling to an SACP/ANC-led armed revolt.

[25] O'Neill, B.E., Keaton, W.R., & Alberts, D.J., *Insurgency in the Modern World*, Westview Press, Boulder, CO, 1980, p. 22.

[26] See: ANC, "Message to the People of South Africa from the National Executive Committee, January 8, 1988".

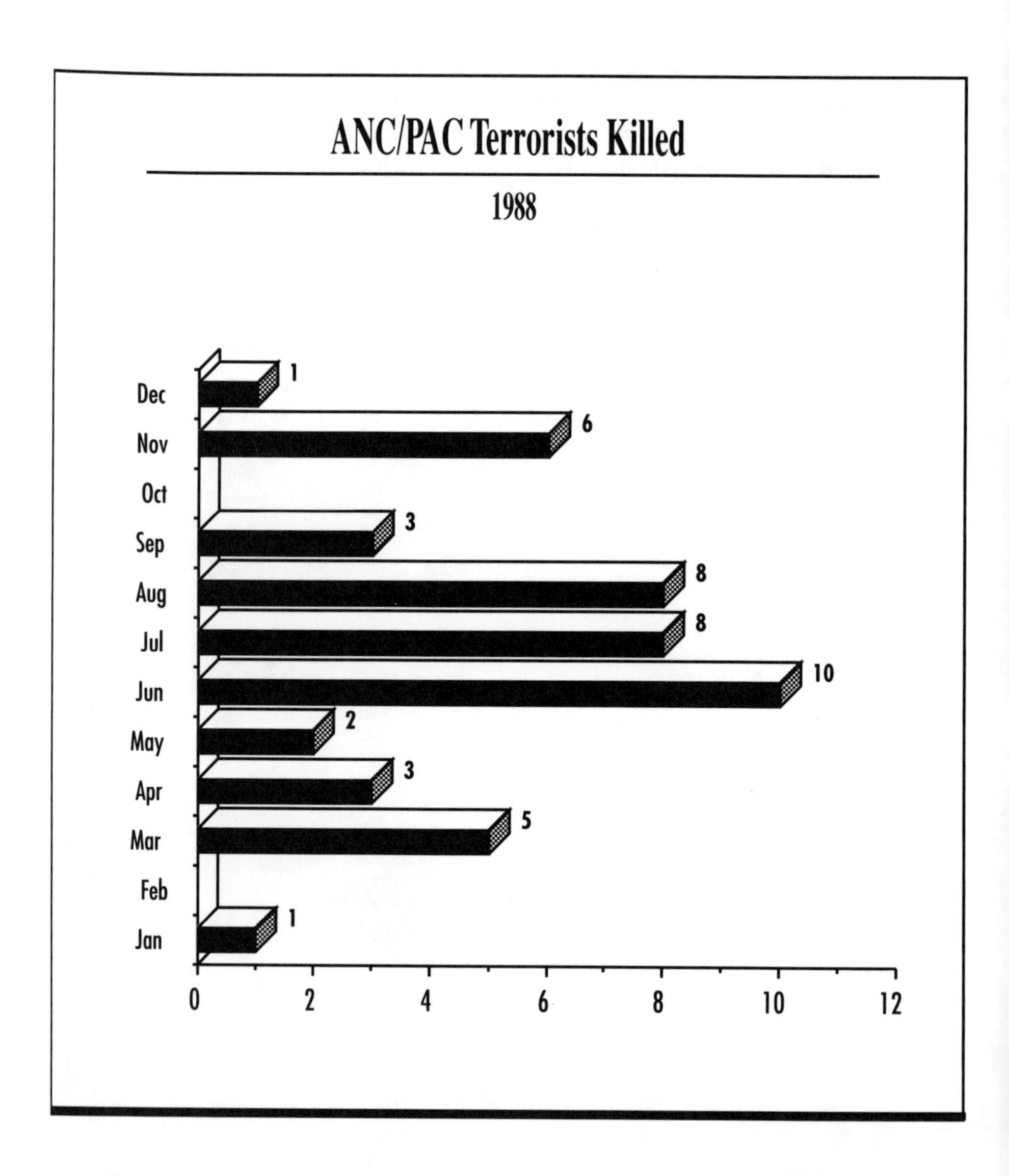
ANC/PAC Terrorists Killed
1988
Dec
Nov
Oct
Sep
Aug
Jul
Jun
May
Apr
Mar
Feb
Jan
1
6
3
8
8
10
2
3
5
1
0
2
4
6
8
10
12

22

NEGOTIATIONS— THE ROUGH ROAD AHEAD

Virtually all revolutionary wars in the post-World War II era have ended at the negotiating table. This was the case in Algeria, Angola, Mozambique, Vietnam and, more recently, in South West Africa/Namibia.

When one or both parties realize that their goals are unlikely to be achieved through violence, they tend to move away from settling differences by force to resolving them at the conference table.

In South Africa this tendency has been reinforced by the political initiatives taken by the new South African State President F. W. de Klerk. These measures are designed to dismantle apartheid and bring into the political process all of South Africa's diverse cultural and ethnic groups.

The freeing of Nelson Mandela and the unbanning of organizations such as the ANC , PAC and the SACP contributed to creating a new attitude. Thus, all the players in the game are in a position to sit down and discuss the future of South Africa.

A word of caution is needed because negotiations per se are not the end-all and be-all to the problems in South Africa. Codevilla and Seabury, in their insightful book *War Ends and Means*, point out: "The whole point of negotiations at the end of a war, just like negotiations prior to or during a war, is for each side to determine what the other side is and is not willing to kill and die for, to relate that to what one's own side is willing to kill and die for, and then to make a deal with the other side to advance one's own interests as best one can. . . ."[1]

[1] Seabury, P. & Codevilla, A., *War Ends & Means*, Basic Books, Inc., New York, 1989, p. 248.

Hanf cautions us that, as a result of his study of communal conflicts, in some thirty-two cases world-wide, one-fourth of the negotiations resulted in further lengthy and bitter fighting; negotiations have resolved conflicts in only half of the cases, with the important proviso that in half of these, there was mutual recognition that they couldn't live together, thus partition was the only solution.[2] Hanf also warns that most cases of co-existence through compromise were preceded by bloody struggles.

There may be some who question whether the low level of terrorist activity generated by the SACP/ANC alliance inside South Africa would be considered a "bloody struggle". Since 1900, fewer than 9,000 blacks have died in all civil conflicts with the government.[3] While the loss of life in civil strife is always a tragedy, South Africa's suffering pales in comparison with the untold millions who have lost their lives in civil conflicts in Angola, Uganda, Ethiopia, Mozambique, Nigeria, the Soviet Union, China, and Cambodia. But the inescapable fact remains that blood has been shed in the revolutionary struggle in South Africa.

But what does this have to do with the prospects of a negotiated settlement in South Africa? The answer is a warning that the current evolving negotiations may be nothing more than another tactic in the SACP/ANC's revolutionary assault on South Africa and that peace is still somewhere in the future. In the view of Codevilla and Seabury, "Indeed, it seems that 'peace' negotiations by antagonists who are not in clear and present danger of rout, starvation, or some other catastrophe tend to be themselves acts of war aimed at changing the balance of power. . . ."[4]

The ANC clearly considers negotiations as part-and-parcel of its revolutionary strategy "aimed at changing the balance of power". As the Mass Democratic Movement, an ANC front, has said, "We see negotiations as one of the many terrains of struggle. . . . A national movement may be forced to negotiate, in some situations, in order to achieve a more limited goal, e.g. a breathing space or a tactical retreat before resuming the struggle on a more intense basis. . . . In other words, victory is never achieved at the negotiating table alone. . . . Another reason why we stress that the struggle is not won or lost at the negotiating table alone, is that negotiations are a mode

[2] See: Breytenbach, W., "The ANC: Future Prognosis", Institute For Futures Research, University of Stellenbosch, p. 18; see also: Hanf, T., "The prospects of accommodation in communal conflicts", in Giliomore, H, & Schlemmer, L. (eds), *Negotiating South Africa's Future*, Southern Books, Johannesburg, 1989, p. 113.

[3] Duignan, P. "South Africa: What's to Be Done?", Hoover Institution Reprint Series, No. 111, Stanford, CA., n.d.

[4] Seabury & Codevilla, *op. cit.,* p. 251.

of struggle where neither party is able to dictate the terms of a settlement. . . . Our objectives do not get changed merely because we are negotiating, just as the presence or absence of armed struggle does not affect our commitment to the type of SA enshrined in the Freedom Charter."[5]

The SACP publication *Umsebenzi* stresses: "The process must involve the masses to ensure that power is indeed transferred to the People"[6], and: "Our sights must be clearly set on the perspective of a seizure of power."[7]

The Marxists are quite adept at using the negotiations process for their own ends as their efforts in the Korean and Vietnam Wars have demonstrated. Buying time until conditions are better for one's own position is a skill the Marxists have honed to a fine art. Lenin, one of Marxism's prime revolutionary prophets, advocated using negotiations when necessary as a delaying tactic to ultimately advance the cause of world socialism. "By now only an utter idiot can fail to see that we were not only right in overthrowing our bourgeoisie (and their lackeys, the Mensheviks and Socialist-Revolutionaries), but also in concluding the Brest-Litovsk Peace Treaty. . . . In the first place, if we had not concluded the Brest-Litovsk Peace Treaty we would at once have surrendered power to the Russian bourgeoisie and thus have done untold damage to the world socialist revolution. . . ."[8]

Lenin and the Bolsheviks signed the peace treaty taking Russia out of World War I. In so doing, they gave up almost forty percent of pre-World War I Russian territory, including the Ukraine, in order to buy time for them to consolidate their revolution in Russia. Lenin rationalized the treaty in terms of the future gain for his world revolutionary scheme. "We, however, say that while the loss of the Ukraine was a grave national sacrifice, it helped to steel and *strengthen* the workers and poor peasants of the Ukraine as revolutionary fighters for the world worker's revolution. The Ukraine's suffering was the world revolution's gain. . . ."[9]

The ANC fully subscribes to such chicanery and the more unstable and chaotic they can keep the internal situation in South Africa by using negotiations, the more they'll negotiate in a manner that the ghost of Lenin would applaud.

[5] " Negotiations As a Terrain and Method of Struggle", *Discussion Papers for the Conference for a Democratic Future*, Issued by Mass Democratic Movement (MDM), n.d., pp. 3-8.

[6] *Umsebenzi*, Nov. 1989.

[7] *Ibid.*

[8] Lenin, V.I., "The Proletarian Revolution and Renegade Kautsky", in: *Lenin's Selected Works In One Volume*, International Publishers, New York, 1971, p. 474.

[9] *Ibid.*

The ANC will need the negotiation process in order to gain time to build up their organization inside South Africa, and to eliminate their opposition as they are trying to do in Natal with the UDF-Inkatha faction fights.

There is a great potential, however, for a rift to develop within the ANC. Nelson Mandela is an old man, who would like to achieve something more than being South Africa's most famous criminal. For this reason he will push for a settlement, but the militant "young turks" will likely object and delay the whole negotiating process and push the ANC to continue on its revolutionary path. In short, the ANC will attempt to build and entrench each of the four pillars of their revolutionary strategy within South Africa.

The SACP/ANC sees unbanning of the SACP, ANC, UDF and other sympathetic organizations as a golden opportunity to achieve what they have failed to for years—build a revolutionary organization inside South Africa. The SACP/ANC alliance are confident that the de Klerk measures will enable them to set up a nationwide organizational structure and mobilize such massive support among blacks that they will be able to keep ever mounting pressure on the government during the negotiating process. Therefore, they will use the demonstrations and marches to mobilize and intimidate the people in the classic Marxist revolutionary sense. They will try to use these events to enable them to create "revolutionary bases."[10]

They are fully prepared to take advantage of the presumption that such negotiations may be long and difficult. One can look at the years involved in the negotiations leading to the independence of South West Africa/Namibia to get an idea of what may lie ahead.

"What you forget," Thabo Mbeki, head of the ANC's international department and a member of the SACP politburo, told *The Washington Post*, "is that time won't be on Pretoria's side. Once we get back there and can start organizing and mobilizing mass support, our position will grow stronger every day, while the government's grows weaker. We will be able to put more and more pressure on them as time goes by."[11]

The South African government may not be as harmed by lengthy negotiations as Mbeki thinks. *Africa Confidential* notes, "De Klerk has created for himself acres of political space. . . . De Klerk's main concern now is to consolidate in preparation for a long period of negotiations and to try by all possible means to persuade the white electorate to catch up with him. . . . In effect the government has until the next scheduled general election, in 1994, to agree with other political forces on a new constitution. . . . While the

[10] "Radio Freedom", Radio Ethiopia, March 2, 1990.

[11] Sparks, A., "S. African Tide Seen Turning", *The Washington Post*, February 6, 1990.

government will want the transition to be as lengthy as possible, it will be under severe—perhaps intolerable—pressure to move faster. . . ."[12]

Mbeki may be whistling in the dark for there are factors that cast doubt on the SACP/ANC's ability to claim to be negotiating on behalf of the majority of South African blacks. It is also well to remember that the South African government is no stranger to the negotiation process. It learned a lot as a result of the prolonged negotiations leading to the independence of South West Africa/Namibia.

One critical lesson of the Namibian negotiations, overlooked by the international press, is that the longer the public can see a liberation movement at first hand the quicker it loses its mystique. As it loses its almost mythical aura it brings to the surface for public scrutiny some of its many less appealing characteristics. The SACP/ANC alliance has many skeletons in its closet that it would prefer to keep there. If exposed to the harsh glare of publicity they could cost support inside South Africa as well as externally with the moderate and liberal international establishment. The SACP/ANC will not, for example, like to have its human rights violations in its training camps in Angola and Zambia brought under the scrutiny of the human rights proponents of the world.[13]

Like its former partner in terror, the South West Africa People's Organization (SWAPO), the ANC treated dissidents within its ranks horribly. They were executed after sham trials or sent to prison camps where living conditions were squalid and harsh at best. Even in the regular training camps conditions were miserable and discipline was strict. For example, marriage by ANC cadres required the permission of the secretary general. In the ANC it was not a right as it is in civilized countries, but a privilege. There were numerous instances where couples seeking to get married were forcibly kept apart by the ANC because it looked with disfavor on the proposed union.[14]

The ANC not only has warts that disfigure its contrived shiny image, but it has serious schisms within its own ranks.

The clash between the militants and the negotiators has already been discussed. It is not the only squabble that plagues the ANC. There are others that create their own stresses and tugs that exert a centrifugal effect upon the

[12] "South Africa I: Two Kings, one crown", *Africa Confidential*, Vol. 31, No. 4, February 23, 1990.

[13] See: *Africa Confidential,* Vol. 30, No. 1, January 12, 1990, and Vol. 31, No. 4, February 23, 1990.

[14] See: *Africa Confidential*, Vol. 31, No. 1, *op. cit.,* p. 3.

ANC. Although at present these differences have not had the effect of fragmenting the ANC, that danger is real. When it occurs it will diminish the current stature of the ANC and make it just another political entity that must share the stage with others in the negotiations over the course of future events in South Africa. The ANC would have to act as a normal political party and political parties do not have their own armies or diplomatic representatives. The ANC would have to adapt. No longer would it be the dominating presence negotiating with the South African government. That is the potential danger posed by these factions made bolder by the unbanning of the ANC.

There is a group within the ANC, commonly called either the Africanist or black nationalists, whose basic philosophy puts it at odds with the ANC's professed vision of a non-racial South Africa. This faction represents the view that only the blacks can solve the problems of the blacks and that the whites are the problem. This is obviously a reflection of the Black Consciousness Movement's ideology of the 1970s. Yet it still has supporters and advocates within the ANC and its fronts. Not only that, but the ANC's rival of long standing, the Pan African Congress (PAC), continues to be a militant spear carrier of the "black power, whites must go" doctrine in South Africa. The PAC is not prepared to negotiate. It wants to carry on with an armed struggle. If the ANC were to renounce the armed struggle, it would lose the support of the militants in its ranks.

Since the ANC accepts whites, includes them in its leadership both in the parent (ANC) and its fronts (UDF, MDM, etc.), cultivates support among them (church groups and liberal academics, for example), such activity is anathema to the Africanists within the ANC. A resurgence of racial pride is not in line with the ANC philosophy and would cause serious friction within the organization. It would encourage challenges within black South Africa to the ANC's claim as the sole spokesmen and leader for blacks in the country.

As more and more blacks take part in the political dialogue the tendency will be that skin color will increase in importance. It has nothing to do with any alleged resurgence of apartheid either de facto or de jure. Blacks will look to blacks, instead of whites or Indians or Coloureds to serve as their elected leaders. That shouldn't surprise anyone as it has happened here in the United States as well. Nevertheless, it is a tendency that will present challenges to all the major political forces in South Africa, including the ANC.[15]

There is also friction within the ANC between the so-called Chartists and those supporting a different post-apartheid society in South Africa as

[15] See: Breytenbach, W., "The ANC: Future Prognosis", *op. cit.*, p. 21.

contained in the ANC's "Constitutional Guidelines for a Democratic South Africa". The Chartists advocate a new order in South Africa based solely on the concepts of the Freedom Charter with its latent appeal to socialism, as noted elsewhere. In an international climate unsympathetic to the notion of centralized state planning, the ANC Chartists are still pushing full speed ahead for the comprehensive nationalization of the South African economy. Some heavy hitters in the ANC leadership are Chartists. *The Wall Street Journal* reported that Joe Slovo still insists on ". . . a redistribution of the country's land. . . ."[16] He said he wanted to remind whites that they do not own the mines, factories and land, but that they own only their skills and talents.[17]

The non-Chartists may be termed opportunists who tend to come from the so-called moderate wing of the ANC led by Thabo Mbeki. Their brain child is the 1988 constitutional guidelines which focus on a future South Africa and contain ideas and proposals that are a deliberate attempt at winning over white support. This is done by playing down socialist economics and stressing a multi-party democracy. Such a policy obviously doesn't sit too well with either the Chartists or the Africanists.

There is also friction between the internal and external leadership of the ANC. This has become more obvious since the unbanning of the ANC. The lifting of restrictions hasn't improved the efficiency of decision making in the ANC. With part of its leadership still in Zambia and part in South Africa decision making is still proving "slow and cumbersome."[18]

The external leadership has suffered a setback due to the abject failure of its armed struggle strategy, the incapacitating illness of ANC President Oliver Tambo and the worsening relations between the ANC and the government of Zambia.[19]

Meanwhile, it has been the internal leaders, the ones in the front organizations, that have been on the frontline of the struggle, so to speak. They have created their own constituencies and, having acquired a taste for running their own show, are less than happy to step aside for the external leaders returning from exile.

This is especially prevalent in the labor movement. Labor is emerging as

[16] Thurow, R., "Slovo Cheered on Return to South Africa", *The Wall Street Journal*, April 30, 1990.

[17] Younghusband, P., "ANC military leader returns", *The Washington Times*, April 30, 1990.

[18] See: Ottaway, D., "Mandela Finds His Mission Impeded", *The Washington Post*, April, 7, 1990.

[19] See: *Africa Confidential*, Vol. 30, No. 17, August 25, 1989, p. 1.

one of the significant political power blocs in South Africa. Their leaders are building themselves a potential political power base and personal ambition may well take precedence over dicta from the SACP/ANC alliance.

There is little unity within the existing labor movement. Many unions within the Congress of South African Trade Unions (COSATU), for example, look with horror on the Freedom Charter as being too moderate. They want a more socialist society.[20]

Other unions in COSATU do not trust the Africanist wing of the ANC and still others view the thought of negotiations with capitalists as selling out the cause.

It is interesting to note that there were no representatives of the labor unions in the ANC's delegation that met with the South African government during the first week in May 1990.

At present most of these rumblings have been kept in the background and are taking a back seat, for the time being, to the unity of purpose of opposing apartheid. They will, however, move to the forefront more and more as apartheid continues to crumble.

Looming over all is the question of ethnic diversity. As shown earlier, South Africa is far from a homogeneous society. As *The Washington Times* points out: "In the first place, South Africa is a land full of tribal conflicts—between the Dutch-descended Afrikaners who form the base of the National Party and the English-descended whites who historically have dominated the economy, and between the several black tribal groups that make up the majority of the population: Zulus, Xhosas, Tswana, etc. Within these groupings there are profound ideological as well as social and cultural differences."[21] The fact that the leadership of the ANC is predominately Xhosa will tend to exacerbate rather than smooth ethnic tensions as the various ethnic groups seek their piece of the political pie in a post-apartheid South Africa. Breytenbach notes: "The global shifts away from confrontational to cooperative politics . . . will undoubtedly have an effect on ANC politics, patterns of leadership and personalities.

"The tendency towards increased ethnicity—particularly in the event of the possibilities for power sharing increasing—will probably lead to a pre-eminence of blacks, as opposed to people other than blacks in the ANC. . . . However, the tendencies towards increased ethnicity with the passage of time and their anticipated increasing inclusiveness in the body politic, are fundamentally contradictory forces that will present challenges to all major

[20] See: *Africa Confidential*, Vol. 30, No. 19, for example.

[21] "South African Ambiguities", *The Washington Times*, May 4, 1990.

political actors in South Africa, including the ANC. It is uncertain how it will react to this."[22]

Each side in the negotiation process will press for items that reflect its interests. de Klerk, on behalf of the South African government, will seek a proportional representative-type democracy in which one-man, one-vote will not be the ruling formula. He will also seek to protect the rights and property of the whites as much as possible.

The ANC, on the other hand, will push for African-style democracy through which blacks in general and the ANC in particular will control the country. They will also give only paper guarantees for civil liberties, property rights and democratic processes. The ANC and Nelson Mandela, as demonstrated throughout this work, have a long history of cozying up to mankind's dreaded disease of Marxism and state socialism. They have long advocated setting up a political system in which they could use force and intimidation to gain unrestricted power and, perhaps, proving again the saying about democracy in Africa: one man, one vote, one time.

Another major problem facing the ANC is the question of money—or more precisely the lack of it.

It takes an enormous amount of money to build and sustain a political organization as it attempts to sell its message to the people. We in the United States are used to costly election campaigns from the local to national level. This costly process is conducted within the American political system involving the two major political parties. Both parties have been around a long time and have local and national organizational structures that allow both to reach out into virtually every nook and cranny of the country.

Imagine what it would cost if one or both of the political parties had to start from scratch, build up their organization, raise funds and, at the same time, run an election contest. This is precisely what the ANC faces in South Africa.

The ANC has organized itself with the aim of conducting a revolutionary campaign of violence inside South Africa. It was not structured to be a fund raising group to mount a political campaign and win support by persuasion. But that is precisely what the ANC must do. It must transition successfully from a revolutionary terrorist group seeking to get its way by coercion to, in essence, a political party that must sell its message to a diverse society. It will be a difficult task.

Given Nelson Mandela's visits to Qadaffi and Arafat and his support of Castro, all violent revolutionaries, one can legitimately question whether,

[22] Breytenbach, W., "The ANC: Future Prognosis", *op. cit.*, p. 21.

under his leadership, the ANC can evolve into a political party committed to peaceful change in South Africa. For one who publicly preaches peace, he certainly hangs out with some of the world's worst jackals.

Finally, one must question the role of the Soviet Union in the continuing saga unfolding in South Africa. *Glasnost* and *perestroika* notwithstanding, Mikhail Gorbachev has no intention of presiding over the dissolution of the Soviet Empire. Neither has he abandoned the idea of using the Soviet Union as a base for the expansion of world communism: "The CPSU (Communist Party of the Soviet Union) is an internationalist party by its nature. People abroad who hold the same views as us may rest assured: In the struggle for peace and social progress the party of Lenin will champion the unity and active cooperation of all revolutionary forces."[23]

As Rubinstein has pointed out, ". . . it takes a giant leap in faith to contemplate a major change in Soviet policy or outlook. This would require a revision of the cardinal assumptions on which Soviet policy in the Third World has been based; to wit, that regional conflicts are the main source of opportunity for Soviet intrusiveness; that these regional conflicts are extremely useful in weakening U.S. power and enhancing the USSR's advantages vis-a-vis the United States. . . ."[24]

There is no question that the Soviet Union is facing major problems and has seen its clients in Eastern Europe rejecting communism and deserting the Soviet camp. One, however, should be cautious before assuming that troubling times will cause the Soviets to end its support for groups like the ANC even at the risk of disrupting potential trade ties with the U.S. Granted, it is highly unlikely that trade concessions to the Soviets will hinge on their dropping support of the ANC, but even if they did, Rubenstein says the Soviets would probably not comply if their past history is any guide: "Yet in the past, in situations of promise or peril, when a fundamental choice was required between commitment to a regional client and cooperation or accommodation with the United States, what was so striking about Moscow's policy was its readiness to jeopardize the prospects for obtaining the coveted Western technology, credits, and trade that would undoubtedly have been forthcoming had Soviet moves been less tension-generating and confrontational."[25]

Given such past behavior it is not difficult to imagine that the Soviets

[23] Gorbachev, M., "Social and Economic Development", *Vital Speeches*, L.I. No. 13, April 15, 1985, p. 387.

[24] Rubinstein, *Moscow's Third World Strategy*, pp. 290-291.

[25] Rubinstein, *op. cit.*, pp. 291-292.

will look upon the situation in South Africa as offering them opportunities hard to resist. They will no doubt continue to be a meddling influence via the SACP/ANC alliance in South Africa.

What this indicates is that the road to a new political arrangement in South Africa will be long and difficult, full of pit-falls and obstacles. The only prediction one can make with any assurance at this stage is that the South Africa of tomorrow will be quite different from the one of today.

As the various political forces jockey with each other over control of South Africa's future they would all do well to have in mind the important admonition given to new physicians: *Primum non nocere*. First, do no harm. Given Africa's post-colonial experience, all South Africans should be wary of substituting the oppression of socialism as advocated by the SACP/ANC alliance for that of apartheid.

Index